THE VICEROYS OF INDIA

Mark Bence-Jones

THE VICEROYS OF INDIA

Constable · London

First published in Great Britain 1982
by Constable and Company Ltd
10 Orange Street London WC2H 7EG
Copyright © 1982 by Mark Bence-Jones
Reprinted 1984
ISBN 0 09 463810 1 (hardback)
ISBN 0 09 465780 7 (paperback)
Set in Monophoto Ehrhardt 11pt
by Servis Filmsetting Ltd, Manchester
Printed in Great Britain
by BAS Printers Ltd, Over Wallop

Contents

Illustrations

Acknowledgements

I would like to begin by expressing my gratitude for the help given me by the last of the Viceroys, the late Admiral of the Fleet Earl Mountbatten of Burma, KG, PC, GCB, OM, GCSI, GCIE, GCVO, DSO, FRS. To the many other people who have helped me, notably by allowing me to quote from unpublished sources, providing me with illustrations and giving me personal reminiscences, I am no less grateful; and would mention the following, not a few of whom have given me hospitality as well as help: the Marquess of Dufferin and Ava; the Earl of Minto, MBE, JP; the Countess Mountbatten of Burma, CD, DL, JP, and Lord Brabourne; the late Doreen, Lady Brabourne, CI; the late Vera, Lady Cranworth, CBE; Lord Holderness, PC, DL; Lord Northbrook, DL, JP; Lady Katharine Dawnay; Lady Joan Gore-Langton; Lady Elizabeth Matheson, RRC; Sir Gilbert Laithwaite, GCMG, KCB, KCIE, CSI; Mrs Mildred Archer; Mr Henry Babington Smith; Mr John Lewin Bowring; Mrs M. Chalk of the Broadlands Archives; Miss Elizabeth Fitzroy, MBE; Mr J.C. Lyall; Mr Philip Mason, CIE, OBE; Dr Adrian Mathias; Captain Peter Montgomery, VL, JP; Mr Hugh Montgomery-Massingberd; Mr John Montgomery-Massingberd; Mr Malcolm Muggeridge; Mrs Gervas Portal; Mr Richard Price; the late Mrs L.W. Smith and Mrs Peter Swan; Mr John Strachey; Dr David Watkin; Mr Michael Wright, Editor of *Country Life*, and Miss Elisabeth Hunt, the *Country Life* Photographic Librarian.

A special word of thanks is due to the Hon. David Lytton Cobbold for his great generosity in allowing me to use photographs from his collection, many of them from the fascinating Indian exhibition at his home, Knebworth House, Hertfordshire.

Unpublished Crown copyright material in the India Office Library or India Office Records transcribed or reproduced in this book appears by permission of the Controller of Her Majesty's Stationery Office; other unpublished material in the India Office Library by permission of the Director of the India Office Library and Records. While speaking of the India Office Library, I would like to thank the staff of that invaluable institution; particularly the

Director, Mr B.C. Bloomfield, the Deputy Librarian, Mr Ray Desmond, and Dr Richard Bingle; and Mrs Pauline Rohatgi and Miss Jill Spanner of the Prints and Drawings Department.

The office and the men before it

'The greatest office in the world' was how Lord Mountbatten described the Viceroyalty of India to the present writer. Speaking in terms of power, this was a hyperbole, as the last holder of that office was himself fully aware; for although the Viceroy was the most powerful personage in Britain's Indian Empire – a ruler and not a figurehead like, say, the Governor-General of Canada – he was held on a rein which stretched all the way back to London where the Secretary of State and the Prime Minister kept it as tight or as loose as they saw fit, naturally tending to tighten it as communications improved. But judged in the light of his Empire, the Viceroy was certainly in the running for the title of world's greatest ruler. 'The Emperor of China and I govern half the human race and yet we find time to breakfast' the ruler of British India used to say as far back as the eighteen-twenties, when his territory was considerably smaller than that of the Viceroys whose history does not start until thirty years later.

The Emperor of China, when there was one, certainly beat the Viceroy in both the area and population of his dominions; but the Viceroy – who towards the end of the British Raj ruled over some four hundred million souls – came a close second as regards population. And while Russia, the United States and Brazil all exceeded the Indian Empire in area, as China did – though the Indian Empire was itself larger than the entire continent of Europe without Russia – in population none of them approached it. And if in theory the Emperor of China beat the Viceroy on both counts, the Viceroy, with his efficient system of government and his large and well-equipped army was the effective ruler of many more square miles and human beings than the Celestial Emperor.

Only the Autocrat of All the Russias and the President of the United States can really be compared with the Viceroy as rulers; and while they both ruled over larger territories than he did and enjoyed considerably more power, they fell far behind him in the number of their subjects. In the days when the Russian autocrat was an Emperor, he might be said to have beaten the Viceroy; for his superiority in power and territory made up for his deficiency in population. But when compared with the Soviet dictator of later years or the American President, the Viceroy had the advantage over these two more powerful rulers of being Viceregal. In his capacity as Viceroy, as the representative of the British Sovereign in the Indian subcontinent, he possessed a far greater measure of the 'divinity that doth hedge a King' than any other proconsul or Head of State of his time not actually born to the purple. On State occasions he sat on a throne behind which stood attendants bearing the traditional Indian emblems of Royalty: the gold and silver sticks and maces, the peacock fans, the *chowri* or whisk made of a yak's tail. He had his own Bodyguard of scarlet lancers, smart and glittering as the Household Cavalry. His palaces and his retinue of servants running into thousands provided a setting for him that might be described as the Court of the Great Mogul run with the quiet precision of the Court of St James's. To the majority of Indians, the Viceroy was in a more real and immediate sense the heir of the Moguls than the Sovereign six thousand miles away in Britain.

As well as performing the functions of Royalty, the Viceroy, in his capacity as Governor-General, was the chief executive of British India; wherein lay the main burden of his office. In this respect he was an autocrat, subject to the control of Whitehall; the only check on his power in India being the fact that he governed as the head of a small Executive Council and in normal circumstances abided by the decision of its majority. He could, however, if he wished, overrule his Council; but by one of those typically British unwritten laws he avoided doing so unless he felt it was absolutely necessary. And since his colleagues in Council were appointed by the Government at home, he was obliged to work with them even though he disagreed with their views; unlike the British Prime Minister who can get rid of dissentient Cabinet colleagues at will. This was one notable respect in which the Viceroy's Council differed from the British Cabinet, to which it bore a certain resemblance. Another difference was that it was not responsible to a Legislature. There was in fact a Legislature in British India throughout the period of the Viceroys; and during the course of that period it became increasingly democratic. But it could always be overruled by the Viceroy and his Executive Council or by the Viceroy on his own.

In addition to his two roles as Viceroy and Governor-General, the Viceroy acted as his own foreign minister. And towards the end of the Raj he took on yet another identity as sole representative of the paramountcy of the British Crown over the Rulers of the Princely States; which he had hitherto represented as Governor-General in conjunction with his Council. The States numbered nearly six hundred and together comprised something like forty per cent of the area of the Indian subcontinent; ranging from Hyderabad and Kashmir, each of them the size of Britain, down to petty principalities no larger than the landed property of an English squire. The difference between the States and the territory of British India proper with which they were interspersed – giving the map of India, in the days when the States were coloured yellow and the rest red, a speckled effect – was that whereas British India was administered directly by the Viceroy and his Council through the hierarchy of provincial Governors and lesser officials, the States were still ruled by their Chiefs; in whose affairs the Viceroy only interfered if circumstances required him to do so; such as when a Chief was considered guilty of misrule.

The ruler of India was first given the title of Viceroy in 1858; when as a result of the Mutiny, Britain's Indian Empire was transferred from the East India Company to the Crown. Up till then, the Company had governed British India and exercised a paramountcy over the States, while maintaining the fiction of Mogul sovereignty by keeping the Great Mogul as an honoured pensioner in his palace at Delhi. The Company was in theory an independent trading corporation, although successive Acts of Parliament had brought it increasingly under the control of the British Government; so that the ultimate responsibility for Indian affairs was eventually shared between the Company's Chairman and a Cabinet Minister known as the President of the Board of Control.

That the British East India Company should have turned from trading to ruling an Empire is one of the most remarkable accidents of history. Up to the middle of the eighteenth century, the Company's Indian possessions were limited to the three settlements of Madras, Calcutta and Bombay, each of which had a few minor settlements dependent on it, and each of which was in charge of a Governor or President – hence the term Presidency, which continued to be applied to the provinces of Madras and Bombay until the end of the Raj. From 1746 onwards, the rivalry of the French and the unsettled state of India owing to the break-up of the Mogul Empire made it necessary for the Company to engage in military operations to protect its settlements and trade. Thanks to the leadership of the young Company servant Robert Clive, who combined great daring in war with a talent for intrigue, the French and their Indian allies were not only defeated, but the British in Calcutta became masters of the whole rich province of Bengal. This, however, gave the Company a frontier to defend against troublesome neighbours. It was owing to repeated attempts to solve the frontier problem, rather than through any deliberate policy of conquest, that during the eighty years following Clive's final departure in 1767 the British flag continued to advance; so that by 1849, apart from a few little French and

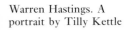

Warren Hastings. A portrait by Tilly Kettle

Portuguese territories, the whole of India had come under the Company's sway. Only part of it, however, was actually ruled by the Company; the rest consisted of the Indian States. Some of these had arisen out of the ruins of the Mogul Empire and been brought under British protection by treaty; others had been set up by the British themselves, for the benefit of Indian notables helpful to their cause.

Originally, the three Presidencies of Madras, Calcutta and Bombay were independent of each other. The acquisition of Bengal made the Calcutta Presidency far more important than the other two; so that in 1774 its Governor, Warren Hastings, became the first Governor-General. Where Clive established British power in India, Warren Hastings extended and consolidated it by his successful wars against the fierce Marathas and also against the French, who were once again giving trouble. At the same time he laid the foundations of the administrative, financial and judicial systems of the Raj; he encouraged Indian learning and he looked after the welfare of the *ryot* or peasant. His achievement is all the more remarkable in view of the constant and bitter hostility to which he was subjected by certain members of his Council, particularly by the notorious Philip Francis, with whom he was obliged to fight a duel. Francis subsequently managed to convince Edmund Burke and other influential figures in Parliament of the Governor-General's alleged misdeeds; with a result that in 1787, two years after his return home, Hastings was impeached. He was eventually acquitted; but the trial dragged on for seven years and cost him the greater part of his fortune.

Hastings was succeeded by the senior Member of his Council, John Macpherson, a charming scoundrel who was the worst sort of Nabob. There was a controversy as to whether he was properly appointed or only officiating; whatever the rights of the matter, he was removed after a year and a half and replaced by the first peer to be sent out from home to govern British India: Lord Cornwallis, a soldier of moderate ability but sterling worth. Such was his reputation for sound commonsense and tireless devotion to duty that his surrender at Yorktown, which marked the collapse of the British cause in the American War of Independence, did not in any way affect his career. In India he was an immediate success; setting his face against jobbery and carrying out many reforms. He also commanded the army in person in the first war against Tipu Sultan, the 'Tiger of Mysore', who had set his heart on driving the British out of India. Tipu was defeated and obliged to pay a heavy indemnity and also to hand over his two sons as hostages; Cornwallis, who was wounded in the campaign, gave up his own share of the prize money which amounted to £50,000 for the benefit of the troops; with whom he was always very popular.

To assist Cornwallis in his reforms there was 'Honest John' Shore, a Company servant of great rectitude and dullness, a revenue expert, a Classical scholar, a student of Eastern languages and a poet of sorts. He was described by one of Hastings's ADCs as 'A good man, but as cold as a greyhound's nose'.[1] In 1793, having been made a baronet, he succeeded Cornwallis as Governor-General; but he was much too nervous and irresolute to be any use as a ruler. On leaving India in 1798 he was raised to the Irish Peerage as Lord Teignmouth; in his later years he became well known for his Evangelical piety, being associated with William Wilberforce and Zachary Macaulay as a leader of the so-called Clapham Sect.

The next Governor-General, Richard Wellesley, Earl of Mornington – who, early in his reign, was made Marquess Wellesley, the name by which he is best remembered – could not have been more of a contrast to his predecessor. This diminutive thirty-eight-year-old Irish nobleman, with a haughty mien and the looks of a beautiful boy, was anything but irresolute; and where Shore's chief object had been economy, his was aggrandisement, regardless of expense. Where

Shore's private life was one of Nonconformist respectability,
Wellesley's was raffish; though it might have been better had his wife
been willing to come to India. Verdicts on Wellesley are contradictory. Some rank him with Clive and Warren Hastings as one of
the founding fathers of the Raj. Others have depicted him as vain,
arrogant, narcissistic, a 'brilliant incapacity' and a 'Sultanised
Englishman', bent principally on exalting his office and himself. But
as one of the best-known of the Viceroys – Curzon – who was not
unlike him in some respects, has written: 'The truth does not lie
midway between these extremes, it is to be found in both of them.
Wellesley was at the same time both great and small, a man of noble
conceptions and petty conceits, a prescient builder of Empire and a
rather laughable person'.[2]

The Directors of the Company had sent Wellesley to India with

A Levée held in Calcutta by Cornwallis, who can be seen standing in the right-hand doorway

strict injunctions to keep the peace; but on his arrival he found a perilous situation, the result of Shore's weak policy. There was the threat of an Afghan invasion; the Maratha Confederacy had gathered a large force in the Deccan; and in the far South Tipu had recovered sufficiently from his defeat at the hands of Cornwallis to be intriguing once again with the French. Wellesley was fortunate in having a brilliant military adviser in the person of his younger brother Arthur, the future Duke of Wellington; together they lost no time in ridding Southern India of Tipu, who was killed in the final assault on his stronghold of Seringapatam. With a shamelessness wholly characteristic of him, the Governor-General proceeded to ask for a Marquessate or the Garter as a reward for this success, hinting that a Dukedom would be even more in order; and he did not conceal his disappointment when he was fobbed off with a Marquessate only in the Peerage of Ireland – 'this double gilt potato' as he called it. Having defeated Tipu, the Wellesley brothers turned their attention to the Maratha powers and reduced them for the time being to obedience; Arthur made his name as a soldier by his decisive victory at Assaye, which in later life he would maintain had been the closest-fought battle of his whole career. The Afghan threat receded and the

Company's dominions were advanced as far north as Delhi, bringing the Great Mogul under British protection.

However necessary and successful Wellesley's wars may have been, their cost did not commend them much to the Directors; who were even less pleased when the 'Magnificent Marquess' spent lavishly on such projects as his College of Fort William for training young civilians. To make matters worse, he considered that the existing Governor-General's residence in Calcutta – a house no grander than the mansions of the leading citizens – was unworthy of his station; and proceeded to clear a splendid site between the main part of the city and the open space of the Maidan, where he built a palace to the design of Lieutenant Charles Wyatt of the Bengal Engineers, a lesser-known but highly-talented member of the great family of architects.

Marquess Wellesley as Governor-General, 1800. A painting by R. Home

The new Government House was completed in 1803 at a cost of £63,291; a sum which, even though the Directors may have regarded it as excessive, was remarkably little for what was – and continued to be until upstaged by Lutyens's New Delhi masterpiece in the present century – the finest governor's palace in the world; a symbol of the growth of British power. The splendour of its Ionic façades is matched only by the admirable simplicity of its great rooms. It is a house ideally suited to the climate, catching the breeze from all four quarters thanks to its plan, which is, as is well known, an adaptation of the plan of Kedleston Hall in Derbyshire, a central block containing the State apartments joined to four wings by curving corridors. The corridors and wings are the same height as the central block and treated continuously with it, creating a far more palatial effect than at Kedleston, where they are subordinate. Before the trees grew up in its grounds, Government House dominated the Calcutta scene in a way that no other building did. It made an impressive showing from all four sides; gleaming white or ochre, depending on what colour it had been painted after the previous monsoon. From the main square of the town, the portico and the immense flight of steps up which each new ruler would ascend in state could be seen through the northern entrance. From the opposite direction, the south front with its dome could be seen at a great distance, facing across the Maidan towards Clive's citadel of Fort William. The ceremonial steps on the north front led up to a room more than a hundred feet long, which was balanced by a room of similar dimensions in the south front; the two being joined by the much broader Marble Hall, running from north to south, with its two rows of Doric columns. There were three similar rooms on the floor above, that over the Marble Hall being the Ballroom, with Ionic columns instead of Doric. The two southern wings contained the private apartments of the Governor-General and his family; one of the two northern wings was for Council meetings and the other for guests.

Having barely finished his first palace, Wellesley started on another one at Barrackpore, fifteen miles up the Hughli from Calcutta. Here, close to the military cantonment which gave the place its hybrid name, there was a green and shady park beside the river which he had appropriated as a country retreat for himself and his successors; building a temporary house to serve until his second palace was completed. As well as building palaces, Wellesley invested his office with a Viceregal pomp unknown to his predecessors; the ball he gave to inaugurate the new Calcutta Government House and to celebrate the Peace of Amiens cost over £3,000 in illuminations alone. By 1805 the Directors had tired of his extravagances and decided to recall him; their relations with him having already reached breaking-point. They also ordered that all work on the palace at Barrackpore should cease. To usher in a regime of economy, they persuaded the ageing Cornwallis to return to India. He had barely set foot on the Calcutta waterfront when he made it clear that he intended to go back to the old simple ways. Seeing the splendid cavalcade of carriages, Staff officers and servants that Wellesley had sent to meet him, he said: 'Too many people. I don't want them, don't want one of them. I have not yet lost the use of my legs, hey?

Government House, Calcutta, at the beginning of the nineteenth century

Gilbert Elliot, 1st Earl of Minto. A portrait by J. Atkinson

Thank God I can walk, walk very well, hey!' And walk he did.[3] The Indian climate, however, proved too much for the sixty-six-year-old veteran, who died after a reign of only two months; during which time he went as far as he could to economise, even to dismissing most of the Government House servants.

There followed the interlude of Sir George Barlow, an upright but cold and narrow-minded Member of Council, who having taken over as acting Governor-General on Cornwallis's death, so pleased the Directors by his retrenchment that they wished to keep him on for a full term. The approval of the Home Government was, however, necessary for this and it was not forthcoming. After nearly two years of haggling, while Barlow held the fort, the Company gave way and settled for Lord Minto; who as Sir Gilbert Elliot had represented British interests in the Mediterranean during the war with Re-

Earl of Moira, afterwards
Marquess of Hastings

volutionary France and in this capacity gave orders to Nelson. He
was known to be 'a quiet, sensible man'[4] of simple tastes; as
Governor-General he tried to strike a balance between Wellesley's
extravagance and Cornwallis's parsimony. Being kind and cultured
and possessing a good sense of humour, he was popular in India; but
he left little or no mark on history. He obeyed the Directors in
maintaining a policy of peaceful isolation as far as the Indian
subcontinent was concerned; but the Eastern repercussions of the
Napoleonic Wars obliged him to send two expeditions by sea to
capture Mauritius from the French and Java from the Dutch; he
accompanied the second of these expeditions himself.

Under pressure from the Prince Regent, who wanted the
Governor-Generalship for his old crony Lord Moira, Minto was
abruptly recalled in 1813; but he left in high spirits at the prospect of

seeing his wife again after seven years; family cares having prevented her from going with him to India. She awaited his arrival at Minto, their home in the Scottish Borders, looking forward as eagerly as he to the reunion. The day came when he was expected; the tenants had assembled and bonfires were ready to be lit. At last there was the sound of horses' hooves; Lady Minto's excitement became intense; but it was only one of their sons with the news that Minto had caught a chill and died on the journey north from London.

The Regent's friend Moira was a monkey-faced Irish Earl aged nearly sixty who, like Cornwallis, had fought in the American War of Independence. Having come to India simply because his finances were in a bad way, he started with the intention of following Minto's unadventurous policy; but his subordinates, who were disciples of Wellesley, made him think differently, so that his nine-year reign turned out to be another great period of expansion. His war to stop the Gurkhas of Nepal from encroaching into Northern India won him a tract of the Himalayan foothills where in 1819 a certain Lieutenant Ross founded a settlement which grew into Simla, the future summer capital of the Raj. His campaign against the freebooting Pindari tribes of Central India and their Maratha allies – in which he himself commanded part of the army – broke the Maratha power once and for all and added territory to the Bombay Presidency that included the former Maratha stronghold of Poona.

In recognition of his success against the Gurkhas, Moira was made Marquess of Hastings; so that some Indians believed him to be a reincarnation of the more famous Hastings of a generation earlier, with whom he had no connection; and who happened to be still alive when he was given his new title. To add to the confusion caused by his change of name, his wife, until he received his Marquessate, was known as the Countess of Loudoun; since she held this Scottish title in her own right. She was the first Lady Sahib to reign at Government House, where she and her husband outdid Wellesley in pomp and circumstance. As yet another sign of a return to Wellesley grandeur, they thought of completing the unfinished palace at Barrackpore, only in a more modest way. Instead they pulled it down and enlarged Wellesley's temporary house into an imposing mansion with a portico and colonnaded verandas.

The next Governor-General, Lord Amherst, is probably the most forgotten of all the rulers of British India. It was he who made the remark about half the human race being governed by himself and the Emperor of China – to whom he had in fact been sent in 1815 on a diplomatic mission which proved unsuccessful. He was no more successful in India, where he seems to have been rather out of his depth; though he was also unlucky. He was involved against his will in a long and costly war against the King of Burma, which caused a serious mutiny of sepoys in the Barrackpore cantonment in 1824. Amherst and his wife were in residence at Barrackpore when the mutiny took place and for twenty-four hours they were at the mercy of the mutineers.

An earlier sepoy mutiny had been the undoing of Amherst's successor, Lord William Bentinck, when he was Governor of Madras at the beginning of the century; but as Governor-General this somewhat radical scion of the great Whig House of Portland enjoyed a tranquil reign, and was therefore able to devote himself to a policy of reform. More than any of his predecessors, he believed that India should be governed for the good of the Indians; many of his measures had this object in view, notably his abolition of the barbarous custom of *suttee* and his efforts to put down the thugs or paid assassins. He admitted Indians to posts in the public service and took steps to

Lord William Bentinck. A portrait by Sir Thomas Lawrence

educate them; at the instigation of Thomas Babington Macaulay, who came to India in 1834 as the Law Member of his Council, he established the principle that they should be taught through the medium of English. This, while it was to have an unfortunate effect on Indian learning, laid the foundations of Indian nationalism; for not only did it give the educated classes of the future a common language, something they had not hitherto possessed; but it enabled them to absorb Western ideas of democracy and human rights.

In his campaign of economy to restore the finances of British India after the depredations of the Burmese War, Bentinck cut down on the trappings of his office and affected a subfusc simplicity in accordance with his radical tastes. 'Lord William Bentinck on the throne of the Great Mogul thinks and acts like a Pennsylvanian Quaker' wrote the French naturalist, Victor Jacquemont, who toured India during his reign. 'You may easily imagine that there are people who talk loudly of the dissolution of the Empire and of the world's end, when they behold their ruler riding on horseback, plainly dressed and without escort, or on his way into the country with his umbrella under his arm'.[5] Calcutta society was also affronted by the way in which Bentinck and his amiable scatter-brained Irish wife – whose advice he always sought before taking any important decision – threw open the doors of Government House to all and sundry, even to ships' stewards and 'less elevated' Indians; though they tended to draw the line at Eurasians.

When Bentinck resigned in 1835 on account of ill-health, his right-hand man, Sir Charles Metcalfe, an able and liberal-minded

Lord Auckland receiving the Raja of Nahun in Durbar. A drawing by Emily Eden

civilian, took over as acting Governor-General; and as in the case of Barlow, the Directors endeavoured to persuade the Government to confirm him in the office. But after he had granted freedom to the Indian Press – a measure which Bentinck had favoured – they would have nothing more to do with him and allowed the Government to send out Lord Auckland, a well-intentioned nonentity who is generally regarded as the worst of all the rulers of British India apart from the dubious Macpherson. As well as being weak and hesitant, he was responsible for the disaster of the First Afghan War; but it is from the letters and journals of his two adoring sisters, Emily and Fanny Eden – who since he was a bachelor accompanied him to India – that we learn of his worst sin, which was that he was always bored.

Unfortunately for the Directors, the next Governor-General, Lord Ellenborough, found India anything but boring; in fact his time there was one continuous adventure. Not content with having inherited Auckland's Afghan War, he embarked on another war in Western India which ended with Sir Charles Napier's celebrated dispatch *'Peccavi'* – I have Sind. Although he had never been a soldier, he went in person on a campaign against Gwalior and narrowly escaped being shot. Apart from the expense of his bellicose policy, he alienated the civilians by showing undue favouritism to the military; and he made himself a laughing-stock with his bombast. He declared that he would 'come Aurangzeb' over everybody and 'turn the old Royal Family out of the palace at Delhi and convert it into a residence for himself'.[6] He issued a grandiloquent proclamation about some gates brought back by his troops from Afghanistan, which were alleged to have been removed from a famous Indian shrine eight centuries before, but turned out to be fakes. When the Duke of Wellington was told of how Ellenborough was planning a monster parade in which the Indian Army was to be arranged in the form of a star with a throne for himself in the centre, the old warrior burst out: 'And he ought to sit upon it in a strait-waistcoat'.[7] The fact that Ellenborough had been deserted by his wife, the beautiful but wayward Jane Digby, might well have had something to do with his vagaries; she had since had a succession of husbands and lovers, including the King of Bavaria, and was to end happily and respectably married to a Bedouin Sheikh.

After two years of the swashbuckling synthetic soldier Ellenborough, the Directors and Government decided to replace him with a quiet and unassuming but none the less genuine Peninsula veteran who had lost a hand at Ligny, Sir Henry Hardinge. The situation in India called for a Governor-General with military experience; for a trial of strength was imminent between the British and the Sikhs of the Punjab, whose army was out of control following the death of the great Sikh ruler, Ranjit Singh. In 1845, a year after Hardinge arrived,

the Sikhs invaded British territory; and the Governor-General took the field against them, in the somewhat anomalous position of second-in-command to Sir Hugh Gough, his own Commander-in-Chief. He was present at the battle of Ferozeshah, which he believed to have been the most perilous day for British India since the beginning of the century; for the Sikh army, which was trained on Western lines, put up a far stouter resistance than any Indian troops the British had ever encountered.

After the defeat of the Sikhs, Hardinge – who was rewarded for his success with a Viscountcy – decided not to annex the Punjab; but set up the young son of Ranjit Singh as Maharaja under the eye of a British Resident supported by a garrison. Two years later, in 1848, the remnant of the Sikh army rebelled and Gough had to fight another Sikh War. This time, although the youthful Maharaja had not been implicated in the rebellion, the Punjab was annexed; and a team of dedicated young civilians, headed by the brothers Henry and John Lawrence, took over its government. The reason for the change of policy was that Hardinge had by now been succeeded as Governor-General by a dynamic little Scotsman with piercing eyes and aquiline features who came to India at the age of thirty-five with the reputation for being a genius. He was, of course, the Earl of Dalhousie – soon to be made a Marquess for his success in dealing with the Sikhs – who as Governor-General was to acquire a reputation second only to that of Warren Hastings; but whose career, like that of his great predecessor, was also to be the subject of violent controversy. Annexation was the keynote of Dalhousie's policy; where his predecessors had preferred to leave as much territory as possible in the hands of friendly Indian rulers, his idea was a centralised India governed directly by British administrators. It was a policy that sowed a whirlwind which his successor was to reap; not so much in respect of the Punjab, or the province in Lower Burma annexed after the Burmese War of 1852, as through his annexation of an important group of states in Central India and of the Kingdom of Oudh. These states were at peace with the British and bound to them by treaty; the rulers of Oudh, the largest Muslim state in the North, had been the faithful allies of the Company since the time of Clive. The fact that Dalhousie had the excuse of dynastic disputes in the case of the Central Indian states and in the case of Oudh, misgovernment, did not prevent his high-handed methods from arousing the fears and suspicions of other Indian rulers; who fully expected it to be their turn next.

As though the work of setting up new administrations in the countries he annexed were not enough, Dalhousie's reforming and improving hand was felt all over the subcontinent. He made education available to all classes; he developed irrigation; he gave India a postal and telegraph service and a Public Works Department; he constructed the first Indian railways. And yet, for all his great achievements, he was not liked. He was too autocratic, too arrogant, too hard on his subordinates; he 'instilled a great dread of himself into the official mind'.[8] And if he was terrifying to his inferiors, his quick temper and his proud and sensitive nature did not make for smooth relations with his colleagues; he quarrelled with Gough and engaged in mortal conflict with Napier, who was his next Commander-in-Chief. He became increasingly lonely, particularly so after 1853 when he lost his wife, who died of seasickness aboard the ship in which she was travelling home to recover her health. He later had the company of his daughter, who came out to join him; but until then he used to say that his only confidant in India was a mouse

Marquess of Dalhousie. A portrait by J. Watson-Gordon

which frequented his room at Government House and to which he would throw crumbs.

And still he worked on; sparing himself even less than he spared his officials. His health was not good even when he first came to India; by the time he left in 1856, though he was only forty-three, he was an invalid on crutches, hardly able to venture out of doors. As he stood by a window of Government House, awaiting the arrival of

Lord Canning, his successor, somebody asked him what his feelings were. 'He drew himself up and with great fire replied: "I wish that I were Canning and Canning I, and then wouldn't I govern India!" Then of a sudden the fire died away; and with a sorrowful look he said: "No, I don't. I would not wish my greatest enemy, much less my friend Canning, to be the poor miserable broken-down dying man that I am".'[9]

Clemency Canning

On the face of it, when he became Governor-General, Charles, Viscount Canning was a man favoured by fortune. As the son of George Canning, the great Foreign Secretary who was Prime Minister for three months, he had an inherited political advantage; while his mother, who was a considerable heiress, had left him very comfortably off. At Eton and Christ Church he won academic laurels and made friends; he began his career as one of a set of high-minded young future statesmen that included Dalhousie and James Bruce, destined as Earl of Elgin to succeed him in India; as well as Gladstone and Sidney Herbert. Before he was thirty, he was a member of the Government; at forty-three, he was ruling an Empire.

Charles Canning was tall and, as a young man, handsome; with features in the antique mould, like his father's: a lofty and noble brow, eyes full of expression, a finely chiselled nose, well-shaped if slightly sensuous lips. It is not surprising that he should have won in marriage a girl as fascinating as she was beautiful: the eighteen-year-old Charlotte Stuart, daughter of the diplomatist Lord Stuart de Rothesay. When one reads of how Charlotte Canning was 'perfectly lovely from infancy',[1] of how her husband's cynical and misanthrophic nephew would in his old age speak of her as the only really virtuous woman he had known, and of how her conversation was always 'so chaste and high-minded',[2] she seems almost too good to be true; but her diaries and letters are full of humour and down-to-earth common sense. Winterhalter has succeeded in capturing her quizzical smile and the intelligence in her dark, heavily-lidded eyes; while making her slender neck far longer than it can possibly have been. But if the length of her neck has been exaggerated, we know on good authority that her hair was so long that her maid, while combing it for her, would constantly tread on it.

This picture of the tall, handsome, well-endowed young statesman and his charming wife is not, however, all the truth. For one thing, the marriage was childless. And more serious, it had, after ten blissful years, gone wrong. The fault was not with Charlotte, who for the rest of her life remained constant in her devotion to her 'Carlo'; but it

Charles, Viscount Canning. A portrait by George Richmond

seems that Canning fell in love with another woman. There appears to be no record as to the identity of the woman in question; and indeed, our knowledge of the whole unhappy affair is scant, so that some writers have been inclined to dismiss it as idle gossip. But such evidence of it as exists seems authentic enough; though there is no truth in the legend that Canning was appointed to India in order to get him away from the other woman's influence.

That he should have allowed his affections to be alienated from a wife like Charlotte, whom he had hitherto loved so passionately that he could hardly bear to let her out of his sight, would denote a certain weakness in Canning's character. It may have been due to some latent moral defect that his career, until his Indian appointment, was not quite as successful as might have been expected; given his position as his father's son, his early promise and his many good qualities such as ability, soundness of judgement, integrity and a capacity for hard work. For when Palmerston – under whom, as a Peelite, he was then serving – appointed him to India, he had achieved no higher office than that of Postmaster-General. He was also handicapped as a politician by being a poor speaker, though he had a sonorous voice; and by having the sort of mind which sees all sides of a question but cannot so easily see which side should be taken. Then, to all but his closest friends – who found him a delightful companion with a strong sense of fun – his manner was cold and reserved; so that while being widely respected, he did not inspire much affection.

When he heard of Canning's appointment, Dalhousie wrote: 'His manners will please here and he will do the externals of his office exceedingly well . . . if times are quiet, I believe he will do very well indeed. If he falls on troubled times, it remains to be seen of what metal he is made.'[3] The general feeling in Calcutta when Canning took over was that he would not be a strong ruler; but that after so many years of Dalhousie's autocratic regime this was no bad thing. People who had been so much in awe of Dalhousie that even after he had left they did not mention his name without lowering their voices found Canning a relief and were prepared to like him, for all his austere and forbidding manner; though at least one of the civilians who watched him being sworn-in at Government House on that February day in 1856 did not think much of his looks.[4] Indeed, opinion seems to have been divided as to Canning's appearance when he was in India; many were highly impressed by the tall, clean-shaven Governor-General, 'stately in bearing, with a cold, pale, handsome face';[5] others thought him lacking in dignity and found something unattractive about his mouth and upper lip – possibly because of his habit of not wearing his false teeth. But everyone who met him found him courteous and kind, though abrupt and

Lady Canning with her
watercolours

increasingly abstracted as the cares of office grew heavier. To those
fortunate enough to get him on to a subject that interested him, he
could converse agreeably. He was also surprisingly accessible, being
glad to hear the opinions of people in all walks of life, particularly of
influential Indians.

Canning's social deficiencies were amply made up for by Charlotte, who quickly won all hearts by her beauty, her graceful bearing,
her charm and her intelligent and highly informed conversation.
India had never known so glamorous a Lady Sahib. Having spent
much time at Court, as a lady-in-waiting and a close friend of the
Queen, with whom she had visited several of the Courts of Europe,
she was able to bring a little of the elegance and style of Windsor,
Buckingham Palace and the Tuileries to the entertainments of
Government House. She insisted that she and Canning should enter
the Ballroom and the Marble Hall in state together, instead of as had
previously been the custom, the Governor-General making his State
entry by himself, leaving his wife to come in afterwards through a

side door. She endeavoured to put an end to the aberration of women remaining glued to their chairs when she came up to talk to them. But while teaching her guests how to comport themselves, she did her best to draw them out; always willing to be amused. She frequently found this difficult, and realised that both men and women were desperately shy in her presence. She realised too that most of the wives were absurdly young and that she herself, in her late thirties, was one of the oldest women in Calcutta society.

'It is quite a mistake to suppose that the society here is *bad*' Charlotte wrote to her mother at the end of 1856. 'Even flirting is very rare and of the mildest description, and I really believe hardly any woman but *me* goes out riding without her husband.'[6] This dullness was one of the things to which she had to get used, like the heat and the prevalence of cholera – of which the Cannings had a stark reminder a couple of months after their arrival when their French chef died of the dread disease. She had also to get used to Government House, which, like almost every other Lady Sahib, she found inconvenient. Having her sitting room on the second floor of the south-west wing above Canning's workroom made her feel as though she were 'recovering from a long illness';[7] so she took possession of a room on the floor below in the south-east wing which, with the help of chintz, blue Sèvres, miniatures and prints of the Royal children she was able to make 'pretty and cool and English'. She resigned herself to being followed by a procession of servants in scarlet and gold wherever she went; and to the certainty that if at any time she felt like a song at the piano, she would be 'singing to the sentry, the *jemadars*, six bearers, two *bheesties*, three *punkah-wallahs*, etc, and a great many more people than that'.[8] She regretfully hardened her heart towards the *punkah-wallahs* as the weather grew hotter, having at first felt guilty that they should have had to pull at their ropes day and night to keep her cool. She learnt to put up with lizards, bats and cockroaches in her bedroom.

While Charlotte was settling into the house, Canning threw himself into his work. His chief concern in these early months was the state of the Indian finances, which owing to Dalhousie's expansionist policy were showing an annual deficit of more than two million sterling. He was soon lamenting that a new Governor-General was 'little better than a galley-slave'.[9] For this, to a certain extent, he was himself to blame; for while agreeing with Macaulay's dictum that the fault of doing too much was one very easy for a Governor-General to fall into, he failed to abide by it. And while persistently doing too much, heedless of the dangers of overwork in the Indian climate, he suffered through being unmethodical and slow; his literary fastidiousness causing him to waste precious time in polishing the prose of official documents. The mahogany dispatch-boxes from the various Departments would pile up unopened in his room; though he rose at five each morning and wrestled with papers from then until dusk, so that his meetings with colleagues and subordinates had generally to take place at night. It became increasingly difficult for him to find time for exercise; he rode little and walked less. For his Private Secretary and the rest of his Staff, it was a hard life. In other respects, they found him kind and easy-going; he never asked how they spent their time off duty. But when he heard that his amiable but raffish nephew Lord Dunkellin, who was his Military Secretary, had given tickets for a public festivity to three ladies of easy virtue, he promptly dismissed him; though he reinstated him after a few months.

Possibly Canning immured himself in his work-room for even longer hours than necessary on account of his marital troubles; though his Private Secretary, Lewin Bentham Bowring, who was with him throughout his time in India, did not notice any estrangement between him and Charlotte. Yet even someone as close to the Cannings as Bowring might not have noticed how things stood between them seeing that circumstances kept them so much apart. Left to her own devices in the hot weather, Charlotte felt 'utterly useless';[10] but like a true Victorian lady, she did not allow herself to be bored. She began a series of drawings of Indian trees and flowers; having a knowledge of botany such as enabled her to produce a plan for rearranging the Calcutta Botanic Gardens and an artistic talent comparable to that of her sister, Louisa Lady Waterford. She wrote long letters to her family and to the Queen, containing vivid descriptions of the people, the scenery, the flora and the fauna of India, all of which she observed with an artist's eye. She went for rides in the lanes behind Alipore, sometimes with Canning but more often by herself; continuing after dark by the light of the fireflies, going at a hand gallop until she was too hot to bear it any longer.

To vary the monotony of Calcutta, there were visits to Barrackpore. Though she found the park 'too English' and the house 'ill monté', she quickly fell in love with the place; and set about improving things with '450 yards of rose-chintz, a great many armchairs, small round tables, framed drawings, etc, and flower-pots in numbers'.[11] She also made an Italian garden, as well as a walk bordered with poinsettias, leading down from the house to the river; she planted exotic shrubs and opened out the great banyan tree. While at Barrackpore she entertained a succession of guests, including many quite humble civilians, officers and clergy, who together with their wives and children were invited to come here for a rest-cure; lodging in the bungalows in the park, but having their meals in the main house with their exalted host and hostess. Charlotte noted how 'a ride upon the elephants has a wonderfully reassuring effect upon people who arrive very much alarmed at us'.[12] She herself would often go out on an elephant to sketch.

'I am certainly getting to like India' Charlotte wrote in November.[13] Canning may then have felt rather less enthusiastic, having just been obliged to declare war on Persia, which was attacking Herat in the west of Afghanistan. The quiet times, for which Dalhousie had believed him to be particularly suited, were already over. The Persian war was brought to a satisfactory close after a few months in April 1857; but by then there had already been a mutinous outbreak among the sepoys of the Barrackpore garrison over the introduction of a form of cartridge which was believed to be greased with beef or pork fat. Through his leniency in dealing with this outbreak, Canning was afterwards accused of having not been fully aware of its seriousness; but in fact he took a graver view of it than most of the people under him; as can be seen from what he wrote at the time to a friend in England: 'It has been a much more anxious matter than Persia, ten times over; for a false step might have set the Indian Army in a blaze'.[14] Even before he became Governor-General, he had spoken of the possibility of a rising; something of which the vast majority of the British in India never dreamt until it actually happened. He did, however, allow himself to be lulled into a false sense of security early in May, when the sepoy mutiny appeared to have died down. Before the middle of the month, it had broken out again with far greater violence at Meerut, an important garrison near Delhi.

Among the likely causes of the Indian Mutiny, there was the resentment arising from Dalhousie's annexations, particularly from the annexation of Oudh, which was the chief recruiting-ground of the Bengal Army. Then there was a widespread fear that the British were planning a forcible conversion of the Indians to Christianity. A recent law permitting Hindu widows to re-marry, modern inventions like the telegraph, reforms in education, advances in medical science, all seemed part of a concerted attack on the Indian religions; as did the alleged greasing of cartridges with animal fats, which would have flouted Muslim tenets just as it would have defiled the caste of the Hindus. These and other things assumed a sinister religious significance in Indian eyes not only on account of an increase in Christian missionary activity, but because of the advent of a new generation of sternly evangelical civilians and soldiers; men like Herbert Edwardes in the Punjab who believed that Britain's mission was to convert the Indians as well as to rule them and who did not scruple to proselytise.

In the spring of 1857, it was widely believed by Indians that Canning was himself of this school. One of them told an acquaintance of Charlotte's that 'every Lord Sahib came to do something –

Barrackpore

Lord Ellenborough to re-conquer Afghanistan, Lord Dalhousie to annex countries . . . this Lord Sahib had come to convert them all'.[15] To act as a kind of super-missionary was far from Canning's intention, though he and Charlotte were both very devout Christians; he had no sympathy for the proselytisers, declaring that a certain colonel who had attempted to convert sepoys was 'not fit to be trusted with a regiment'.[16] But some of Canning's earlier measures encouraged this belief; notably an Act enabling troops of the Bengal Army to be sent if necessary overseas, which was already possible with those of the Madras and Bombay Armies. To cross the 'dark water' in a ship was another defilement of caste; though the fact that they might have been ordered to do so did not appear to worry the Madras and Bombay troops, who were just as likely to be high-caste Hindus as the troops of Bengal. A few days after hearing of the outbreak at Meerut, Canning issued a proclamation to the effect that the Government had no designs on Indian religions; but this was now probably too late to be of any good. He himself regretted that he had not issued such a proclamation sooner.

The day after they rose at Meerut, the mutineers entered Delhi, massacred the Europeans and persuaded the octogenarian Great

Mogul, Bahadur Shah, to throw in his lot with them; that he agreed to do so can to a certain extent be blamed on Canning's decision that he should be the last of his line to be treated with Royal honours. By the end of June, the British had lost control of large areas of the North-Western Provinces, most of Oudh and parts of Central India; the line of communication from Calcutta to the Punjab was cut. The insurgent sepoys had been joined not only by Bahadur Shah and his family but by many Chiefs and nobles; while in Oudh the revolt had grown into a rising of the inhabitants at large.

In those terrible weeks, Canning showed remarkable powers of leadership. Normally slow to decide and act, he now, in the words of one of the most dynamic of the men who served under him, 'cast away his over-caution'.[17] From the very start, he was fully aware of the gravity of the situation; on 19 May, barely a week after Delhi fell, he predicted that if there was a further outbreak, 'the flame would spread without a check straight on end for 700 or 800 miles, over the richest tracts in India.[18] He was desperately short of European troops, through no fault of his own, having more than once informed the British Government of this fact before the crisis, to no avail. There were only four European regiments along the entire Ganges valley. There was only one, outnumbered ten times over by sepoys, in Bengal; which though now quiet, was where the trouble began; everything there still depended, in Canning's own phrase, 'upon the turn of a word – a look'.[19] The situation was highly critical until reinforcements arrived from home, which in the nature of things would not be for some considerable time. By good fortune, however, a contingent was then on its way from England to China, to settle a dispute over an alleged insult to the British flag. Canning, on his own responsibility, sent an urgent message to his old Oxford friend, Lord Elgin, who was accompanying the expedition as Plenipotentiary, asking for the troops to be diverted to India. To this, Elgin, who received Canning's letter at Singapore, readily agreed.

Like all great leaders, Canning placed full confidence in his subordinates. To John Lawrence, Chief Commissioner of the Punjab, who by managing against all odds to hold that province was to play a decisive role in saving British India, he telegraphed: 'You will be supported in every measure that you think necessary'.[20] He sent a similar promise of support to Sir Henry Lawrence, who had been his own inspired choice for the post of Chief Commissioner of Oudh, and who was to lead the heroic defence of the Lucknow Residency until fatally wounded by a shell in July.

But however much he was prepared to give his subordinates a free hand, he never hesitated to direct them on major issues. When, at a particularly desperate moment, the usually so resolute John Lawrence proposed abandoning Peshawar or even the whole of the

Punjab in order to concentrate his forces on Delhi, Canning enjoined him to 'hold on to Peshawar to the last'. Giving his reasons, he went on to say: 'If we were now to abandon territory, no matter how distant, it would be impossible that faith in the permanency of our Rule should not be shaken'.[21] In the event, Lawrence was able to recapture Delhi without having to abandon Peshawar or anywhere else in the Punjab. At the end of the year, when reinforcements had arrived from England and the tide had turned, Canning twice overruled his Commander-in-Chief, the tough old veteran Sir Colin Campbell; insisting that a force should be left in Lucknow, from which Campbell, having evacuated the Residency garrison, intended withdrawing altogether; and that the reconquest of Oudh should take place without delay, instead of being postponed until after the reduction of Rohilkhand, which was Campbell's plan. Campbell's considerations were purely military; Canning knew that the recovery of Oudh would have a far greater propaganda value than that of Rohilkhand. 'Every eye in India is upon Oudh, as it was upon Delhi' he declared. 'Oudh, and our dealings with it, have been in every native's mind for the last two years'.[22]

The Mutiny caused Canning's work to grow to such proportions that visitors often found him completely hidden from view by a wall of mahogany dispatch-boxes; which, two or three deep, enclosed him on all sides. He wrote day and night until his eyesight failed and he sank from exhaustion. He seldom found time to venture out of doors; though occasionally he allowed himself a walk in the grounds of Government House by way of exercise; when passers-by would see, through the railings, his solitary figure pacing quickly round and round. Walking may also have been his way of working off his feelings; for we are told that after hearing the news of the massacre of women and children at Cawnpore, he spent the whole night pacing up and down the Marble Hall, overwhelmed with remorse at having been unable to prevent the tragedy. This is perhaps the only recorded instance, throughout the alarms and frustrations of the Mutiny months, of his feelings getting the better of him; usually he maintained an appearance of stoical calm. So did Charlotte, who was as determined as he was to set an example in the prevailing atmosphere of panic. To keep up the morale of Calcutta society, they continued to entertain. 'Many people wish us to put off the ball on the Queen's Birthday' wrote Charlotte towards the end of May. 'I would not for an instant suggest such a thing.' In the event the ball was, as she recorded, 'a very fair one . . . the respectable and serious made a point of coming, and a number of natives'.[23] The European guard of honour who, by custom, presented arms at the entry of the Governor-General, offered to remain in the basement until the ball was over; but to the Cannings this was 'not to be thought of'. So the guard of honour was dismissed as usual, leaving the house and the guests under the sole protection of the Indian troopers of the Bodyguard.

There were many rumours to support the popular belief that the Cannings were careless over security. According to one newspaper, the venerable Indian major-domo of Government House had plotted and then absconded; Charlotte was amused to read this story just as the functionary in question was handing her a cup of tea. The fact that Government House was still guarded by Indian troopers aroused much criticism, until in August Canning agreed very reluctantly to the Bodyguard being disarmed. They continued to be posted on the stairs and in the corridors, only without their weapons; and they were replaced by English pickets at night.

Charlotte no longer regaled her family and friends at home with descriptions of the beauties and curiosities of India, but kept them informed of every new development of the crisis. She even wrote on Indian affairs to Canning's friend and political colleague, Lord Granville, who was so impressed by one of her letters that he read it to the Cabinet. 'Ah, ah, a capital letter' said Palmerston. 'Unlike a lady's letter; it is all to the point.'[24] Instead of drawing pictures of flowers, Charlotte now set to work making clothes for the refugees who were pouring into Calcutta, helped by her two English maids, her own three tailors and four extra tailors brought in specially. She also gave away most of her own 'large trousseau', while desiring that her things should go 'to officers' wives and others who are ladies'[25] – she was not being snobbish but sensibly assumed that women with a position to keep up needed to wear something better than the ordinary hand-out. These more favoured refugees were invited to dine at Government House, together with 'crowds of officers', some back from the fighting, others just off the troop-ships lying in the Hughli. The resources of Government House were stretched to the utmost in August, when the Cannings had to put up Elgin, Sir Colin Campbell and the other great military commander, Sir James Outram, who all three of them arrived, together with their respective staffs, almost at the same time. Campbell was still the Cannings' guest when, towards the end of September, news came that Delhi had been recaptured. They were then at Barrackpore, and through sheer joy, Charlotte and the gallant old Sir Colin went for a ride together on an elephant.

Another memorable picture of Charlotte during the Mutiny is of her riding forth, flanked by generals and staff in full uniform, to present the newly-raised Calcutta Volunteers with their colours. Canning had at first been reluctant to accept the British community's offer to organise itself into this force; feeling that a regiment of trigger-happy Calcutta merchants and lawyers might well have done more harm than good. His hesitation in this respect and in the matter of disarming the Bodyguard, together with his reticence and lack of emotion, all gave the impression to the thoroughly alarmist European inhabitants of Calcutta that he did not appreciate the full gravity of the crisis; whereas he probably viewed it with even greater pessimism than they did. They accused him of indecision and inefficiency; attacking him with increasing violence in their newspapers. He made himself still more unpopular with them by steadfastly refusing to discriminate between Europeans and Indians; his Arms Bill applied to Europeans and Indians alike; newspapers in English as well as in the Indian languages could be prosecuted under his emergency measure to restrict the Press.

The popular outcry against Canning reached its height after he issued, at the end of July, a Resolution ordering officials to refrain from punishing captured sepoys who had not come from mutinous regiments, deserted or committed crimes; and to avoid unnecessary acts of harshness, such as the burning of villages. It was a praiseworthy attempt to ensure that the reprisals which were an inevitable consequence of the Mutiny would be carried out in a spirit of justice – to put a stop to indiscriminate hangings of men merely because they were sepoys and other atrocities shameful to the name of Britain. But British public opinion, at home as well as in India, was clamouring for vengeance; enraged by the Cawnpore massacre and by reports, which were wholly untrue, of sepoys raping British women. Canning's Resolution was seen as an unwarrantable piece of leniency, calculated to hinder his countrymen in their righteous task of punishing the Indians. It was attacked hysterically by the Calcutta Press, and the newspapers in England took up the cry; Canning was subjected to all manner of slander and abuse. *The Times* called him 'a prim philanthrophist from Calcutta' and spoke sneeringly of the 'Clemency of Canning'. Thus originated Canning's sobriquet of 'Clemency' which, from being used derisively, was to become a proud ornament to his name.

Canning, in his own words, did not 'care two straws for the abuse of the papers';[26] nor did he worry overmuch when in October his Calcutta critics petitioned the Queen for his recall. To him, it was of far greater consequence that he should have received addresses in support of his policy signed by several thousand of the richest and most influential Indians of Bengal, Bihar and Orissa. Writing to Lord Granville, his most loyal friend in the Cabinet, he expressed his firm belief that the permanency of British rule in India depended largely on the goodwill of men such as these. He went on to defend his policy in what has been called 'one of the noblest apologies in English history':[27] 'As long as I have any breath in my body, I will pursue no other policy than that which I have been following; not only for the reason of expediency and policy above stated, but because it is just. I will not govern in anger'.[28] Granville rallied to Canning's support; the Queen and Prince Albert were no less staunchly on his side. To the Queen, Canning had already written of 'the violent rancour of a very large proportion of the English Community against every native Indian of every class' which he feared boded ill for the future.[29] To this the Queen replied: 'Lord Canning will easily believe how entirely the Queen shares *his* feelings of sorrow and indignation at the un-Christian spirit shown – alas! to a great extent here – by the public towards Indians in general and towards *sepoys without discrimination!*[30]

At the height of the outcry, the Lieutenant-Governor of Bengal urged Canning to make public certain documents showing how scandalously some of the British officials had behaved when carrying out reprisals. But this Canning would not do. 'I had rather submit to any obloquy' he said, 'than publish to the world what would so terribly disgrace my countrymen. It is sufficient that I have prevented them for the future.'[31] This last remark was over-optimistic, in that the black chapter of British atrocities certainly did not end with his Resolution; the value of which lay not so much in curbing the British as in reassuring the Indians.

In November, the tide of English public opinion turned in Canning's favour. To a certain extent the change of heart was brought about by the arrival of a memorandum sent by him to the Directors, which satisfactorily refuted most of the lies that had preceded it from Calcutta and won him even the guarded approval of *The Times*. There was also the good effect of the news of the recapture of Delhi and other British successes. By the end of 1857, the insurgents had to all intents and purposes been defeated; though the campaign of reconquest was to drag on for another eighteen months.

The most important territory still to be recovered was Oudh. Early in the New Year, Canning drew up a proclamation – to which Charlotte incidentally suggested an amendment – promising mercy to the rebellious Talukdars or nobles of Oudh and their followers if they submitted to the British authorities; but declaring the land of the whole province forfeit, except for the estates of half a dozen named individuals known to have been loyal. Surprisingly, given the prevailing mood of unforgiveness, Canning's Oudh Proclamation aroused a storm of criticism as being too severe. It was denounced in Parliament; and the bombastic Ellenborough, now President of the Board of Control, rebuked Canning for it in a long and 'studiously offensive' dispatch.[32] Ellenborough's effusion, however, rebounded on its author; because it was somehow leaked to *The Times* so that he had to resign. Canning, who had himself come near to resigning, heaved a sigh of relief at the exit of 'The Elephant', as he called him; and with the wry humour which appears so often in his letters to close friends, but which was never revealed to the world at large, told Granville of how, having offered a *lac* of rupees for the capture of the fugitive Nana Sahib, perpetrator of the Cawnpore massacre, he had been outbidden by Nana, who had offered two *lacs* for his head: 'There is something complimentary in his impudence and upon the whole, I prefer it to Ellenborough's'.[33] He bore the new outcry as philosophically as he had borne the previous one; declaring that the past twelve months had made him 'a moral rhinoceros'.[34] His sufferings at the hands of a fickle public won him a tribute from no less a personage than the aged Metternich; who observed that the sudden change from the cry of too much clemency to that of too much severity indicated that 'he had exactly seized the proper medium'.[35]

Canning's apparent severity in confiscating the entire land of Oudh was in fact a clever way of teaching the Talukdars a lesson and at the same time winning their gratitude and loyalty; for having kept them in suspense, uncertain as to what their fate would be, he announced after the ending of hostilities that their lands and villages would mostly be given back to them. His treatment of the Oudh Talukdars was part of his policy of conciliating the Princely, aristocratic and otherwise influential classes of India and strengthening them as a buttress to British rule. To this end he restored to the Princes their right to adopt heirs, according to Hindu and Muslim custom, if they had none of their own; a right which Dalhousie had taken away from them, providing them with a grievance that was certainly a cause of the Mutiny. Canning was able to show that he was in good faith by positively insisting that the Maharaja of Mysore, who had no natural heir, should adopt one; whereas it had been the Maharaja's intention to bequeath his vast territory to British India. At a lower level than that of the Princes, Canning actually went so far as to create a landowning class in regions where none had previously existed; and he gave powers roughly similar to those of an English Justice of the Peace to the Oudh Talukdars and to the Sirdars of the Punjab, as well as to some bankers and merchants in Lucknow. Those whom he entrusted with these powers on the whole exercised them well. Another way in which Canning brought influential Indians into the public life of British India was by nominating Princes and landowners to the Legislative Council after the constitutional reforms of 1861 had provided for Indian opinion to be represented in it.

In setting out to win the loyalty of the Princes and the aristocracy, Canning was eminently successful. The Mutiny can be seen as the last stirring of the old Mogul India; henceforth, that older India

would be strongly wedded to the British Raj. The future, however, lay not so much with the Maharajas and the Talukdars, as with the new educated and Westernised middle class, the product of the Universities which Canning had himself established in the Mutiny year. Though Canning can hardly be expected to have foreseen this, he could perhaps have made it easier for educated young Indians to join the official élite of the 'Covenanted' Civil Service; the subordinate 'Uncovenanted' Service being still the highest to which the great majority of them could aspire. Yet to have done more than he did in this respect would probably have been beyond his power, considering how far relations between the British and the Indians had deteriorated as a result of the Mutiny. That Canning should, in such unfavourable times, have succeeded in forging enduring links between the British rulers of India and a large and prosperous Indian aristocracy was achievement enough. His achievement would have been greater had he succeeded in making the British less liable to regard the Indians as inferior beings, which was his secondary object in enhancing the Indian aristocracy. But his policy could not change an attitude of which he was himself all too aware. 'The word "niggers" is now in daily use by every newspaper's correspondents' he observed sadly. 'It will be a bad day for us when that word becomes naturalized in India.'[36]

In theory, there was absolutely no racial or religious discrimination in British India; the Government service at all levels was open to Indians of any creed just as much as it was to British. This was upheld, together with the principle of religious toleration, in the Queen's Proclamation announcing the transfer of the government of

India from the East India Company to the Crown; which Canning read out to a great assembly outside the Fort at Allahabad on 1 November 1858. On that date, Company rule was finally brought to an end; it had been used by the British Government as a scapegoat for the Mutiny, for which the Government was itself just as much responsible. Nevertheless, 'John Company' was by the eighteen-fifties an anachronism; like the fiction of Mogul sovereignty which was finally disposed of by the banishment of the pathetic Bahadur Shah to Rangoon. The 1858 Act declared the sovereignty of India to be vested in Queen Victoria. It abolished the Directors and the Board of Control, replacing them with a Secretary of State advised by the India Council, a body made up of men who had served in India in a senior capacity. And it gave the Governor-General a new and more exalted identity as Queen's representative with the title of Viceroy. Charlotte wondered whether this would mean that they would have to introduce some of the customs of the Viceregal Court in Dublin; she recorded Canning's dismay at the prospect of 'Drawing Rooms and *kissing*';[37] but in the event the Viceroy of India never followed the Irish Viceroy's custom of kissing the ladies who were presented to him.

A sequel to the Queen's Proclamation was the founding by her of an Indian Order of Knighthood, the Star of India. This was yet another move in Canning's policy of bringing the Indian ruling class closer to the British; for the Order was to consist of Indian potentates as well as the Viceroy and leading British officials and soldiers. Charlotte is said to have been responsible for the Order's motto, 'Heaven's Light Our Guide', an English rendering of a motto in Latin suggested by Prince Albert.

Canning believed that the Queen's Proclamation, with her promise to respect the religions and also the ancient laws and customs of her Indian subjects, would give more confidence if 'ratified by the Viceroy's own lips'[38] in as many places as possible. Accordingly, from 1859 onwards, having hitherto been confined to Calcutta and Allahabad, he made long journeys through Upper and Central India which were in the nature of triumphal progresses; his vast and magnificent camps, his enormous retinue and the array of troops in attendance on him all being calculated to impress the people with the power and grandeur of Britain. He held Durbars at Lucknow, Cawnpore, Agra, Lahore and elsewhere, stating the Queen's intentions that were just as much his own to the greater and lesser Chiefs; confirming them in their rights, rewarding those of them who had shown conspicuous loyalty with titles and other special benefits.

Charlotte, though she disliked camp life, accompanied Canning on most of his travels; and in the early summer of 1860, when owing to

Lady Canning on an elephant in camp at Futtehghur, 1859

an unexpected crisis he was obliged to leave her at Simla and return to Calcutta at short notice, she explored the Himalayas on her own. She covered more miles of the Indian subcontinent than any Lady Sahib before her; her mode of conveyance varying from railway-train to *jampan* or sedan chair, from horse-drawn carriage to camel carriage, from pony to elephant; from the comparative luxury of *Sonamukhi*, the old green and gold Governor-General's house-boat, towed by a steamer on the Ganges, to a board tied to inflated buffalo skins on which she shot the rapids of less navigable rivers. She penetrated the jungles of Central India; she went to Coonoor in the far South and north to the Khyber and the borders of Tibet; she crossed and recrossed the gorges of the Sutlej by bridges made of logs and in baskets swinging from ropes. She climbed to over 15,000 feet and made what she called a 'honeypot descent', chaired in the linked arms of her attendants, which she assured her mother 'was not the least improper . . . I had put on all my warmest clothing, and had an old Balmoral cloth riding-habit, and a pair of strong dark cloth trousers'.[39] She once had a narrow escape and lost many of her personal belongings when her tent caught fire.

The crisis which brought Canning back to Calcutta from Simla in the May of 1860 – cutting short the only hot weather in the Hills which he was able to allow himself during his time in India – was the

Lord Canning in 1860

intemperate opposition of the Governor of Madras, Macaulay's brother-in-law Sir Charles Trevelyan, to the Government of India's scheme for new taxation. This was made necessary by the state of the Indian finances, which having not yet been put to rights when the Mutiny broke out, were reduced to utter chaos by the time it was over; for it cost India more than thirty-eight million sterling. And as a result of the Mutiny, there was an increase of something like ten million in the annual military expenditure. To help Canning in his task of saving Britain's Indian Empire from bankruptcy, James Wilson, founder of the *Economist* and a former Financial Secretary to the Treasury, was sent out from England to join his Council. Wilson introduced income tax; an innovation that was fair enough in that it affected only the better-off who had hitherto paid hardly any taxes at all. But since the classes affected were the most vocal ones, it aroused an opposition which alarmed even Canning; who declared that 'danger for danger, he would rather risk governing India with 40,000 European troops without new taxes, than 100,000 with them.[40] Nevertheless, thanks to the policy of Wilson, and of Samuel Laing – another English financial expert who took Wilson's place after his untimely death – the vast deficit left by the Mutiny had all but vanished by the time of Canning's departure.

The financial troubles and the formidable task of reconstruction

Lady Canning (right) with
Lady Campbell, Simla,
1860

Lord Canning's camp,
Mirzapore, 1860

and reorganisation which had to be tackled as soon as the Mutiny was
quelled meant that Canning's labours, towards the end of his reign,
increased rather than diminished. But he was now less able to stand
the long hours at his desk; he would complain that he was always so
exhausted by dinner time that he just could not speak. The

cumulative effect of overwork and the Calcutta climate must inevitably have impaired his faculties as a ruler; and it also seems that the powers of leadership which he developed under the stress of the Mutiny became atrophied with the return of more normal times. His natural indecision once again began to show itself; as it did in 1860 when there was trouble between the European planters and the peasants in the indigo-growing districts of Bengal. In this matter, while sympathising with the peasants and describing their condition as 'worse than slavery',[41] he appears to have been anxious to win the favour of the planters. The indigo affair is not the only instance, in these later years, of his trying to placate that very same non-official British community whose hostility to him during the Mutiny he so nobly disregarded. As well as becoming irresolute and over-sensitive to public opinion, he gradually lost his grip of affairs; so that one of his ablest assistants, writing soon after his departure, was to speak of these years as Canning's 'miserable period of no-government'.[42]

The period was longer than it need have been; for Canning, whose term was due to end in the spring of 1861, offered to stay on an extra year in the mistaken belief that he would thereby see some of his administrative and constitutional reforms accomplished. It was an offer very much to the liking of the Secretary of State, Sir Charles Wood, who fully shared Canning's ideals; though his masterful disposition – which together with his long association with Indian affairs won him the nickname of 'Maharaja' Wood – made for occasional friction between him and the Viceroy. In offering to stay on, Canning paid no heed to Granville's words of warning, 'How many of your friends are already gone, who can say what havoc another year may make among the remaining'[43] – words which gained portent with the news of Dalhousie's death. With a constitution already undermined by five consecutive hot seasons in Calcutta, he must have known what effect yet another would very likely have on him, not to mention Charlotte, who was by now longing for 'home'. But however disappointed she may have been at the prospect of further exile, she was now enjoying a happiness that had for so many years been denied her. The cloud which had hung over her married life had at last lifted. One would have imagined that her husband's eyes were opened to her true worth by her courage and by the loyal, affectionate and unselfish support which she gave him throughout the ordeal of the Mutiny; yet according to a young ADC of Canning's – who may have been prejudiced, having himself conceived a romantic passion for Charlotte – he was 'as sulky as possible' when she arrived to join him at Allahabad in the summer of 1858.[44] In the following year, however, they somehow drew close to one another once again and from then onwards they were the lovers they had been during the first ten years of their marriage.

Though India had made her thin and lined and robbed her of her youth, Charlotte, in these later years, acquired what those who saw her spoke of as a 'spiritual beauty'.[45] At a Government House ball in August 1861, when the Monsoon weather in Calcutta must have been at its most enervating, she was 'unusually radiant and lively';[46] dressed in white satin with a diamond coronet and a long spray of ivy in her hair. By now, home was well and truly in sight; her mind was full of pleasant plans for their retirement. To make the prospect ahead of her even sweeter for Charlotte was the knowledge that the attacks on Canning had long since ceased and that the homecoming Viceroy would be widely acclaimed by his countrymen for his part in saving British India. He had already been promoted to being Earl Canning; he would shortly be given the Garter. Though Canning himself was never anything but extremely modest about his achievement, it had always mattered very much to Charlotte that he should have received adequate recognition for all he had done.

About a month after that ball at Government House, while Canning went up country to Allahabad to hold the first Investiture of the Star of India, Charlotte set off on a trip to Darjeeling, to sketch and to get a sight of Mount Everest. She felt badly about not accompanying Canning, or as she herself put it in a letter to him, 'following like the faithful little dog'.[47] On her return journey to Calcutta, she contracted a severe form of malaria; Canning arrived back at Government House a couple of days after her to find her seriously ill. A week later she died in his arms. Next morning, as dawn broke, she was buried in the garden at Barrackpore by the side of the terrace walk above the river, which was at that moment just beginning to turn pink with the first rays of the rising sun.

We are told that Charlotte's death made Canning at once into 'an old, decrepit man'.[48] This is strikingly borne out by a photograph in which, though not yet fifty, he looks frail, aged and infinitely sad; his chin covered by a wispy beard grown in the previous year. He broke down altogether on reading Charlotte's diaries and realising for the first time what sufferings he had caused her and how great had been her devotion to him. From now until his departure from India in the following March, he stayed as much as he could at Barrackpore; every night when he was there he would slip silently from the house and visit her grave, on which a light was always kept burning. It was a dreadful moment when he had to tear himself away from her grave for the last time, before handing over the Viceroyalty to his friend Elgin, who was his successor. On his arrival back in England, he barely had time to visit Charlotte's mother and the recently-widowed Queen before he fell ill. Six weeks later, he died. He appears to have been suffering from a disease of the liver; but there is no doubt that his grief for Charlotte hastened his death.

Elgin and Plain John Lawrence

The officials who watched the arrival of the new Viceroy at Government House in March 1862 were struck by the contrast between him and his departing predecessor. In the words of one of them, 'Canning looked pale, wan, toilworn and grief-stricken . . . Elgin, on the other hand, came up gaily, ruddy in face, massive and square in forehead, buoyant in manner and stalwart in frame'.[1] Another of those present put it less reverently in a letter to his wife: 'Lord E. with his white head and bright red smiling face and spherical figure, and Lord C. pale, slim and grave. The first like a farmer got up in grand clothes, the other like a real nob'.[2]

In fact James Bruce, eighth Earl of Elgin, was even more of a 'nob' than Canning; his family claimed kinship with the ancient Scottish kings and had been high in the Peerage of Scotland since the seventeenth century. But he was a relatively poor man; his father having nearly bankrupted himself acquiring and bringing to England the great collection of Grecian antiquities known as the Elgin Marbles. Since succeeding to his titles and estates in 1841, he had spent most of his time abroad in the service of the Crown; governing Jamaica and Canada, acting as Plenipotentiary in China. He had healed some of the differences between the French and English Canadians; he had brought a lengthy and troublesome dispute between Britain and China to a satisfactory conclusion. He had acquired a reputation for tact and cool sense and for being tough when necessary; as he was when he ordered the burning of the Imperial Summer Palace at Peking to punish the Manchu Emperor for his breach of faith.

Elgin's appointment to succeed Canning was more or less a foregone conclusion; he had already been thought of as a likely successor to Dalhousie. To become the ruler of India had long been his ardent wish; it had continued to be so, even after he had seen at first hand what ruling India could entail when he stayed in Calcutta as Canning's guest at the height of the Mutiny. While there is nothing intrinsically wrong in a single-minded ambition of this sort, in Elgin's case it goes with other evidence to suggest that he was

The 8th Earl of Elgin. A portrait by George Richmond

something of a careerist. There is what a kinsman of his wrote of him, perhaps a little unkind: 'My namesake is very knowing and very shrewd and possessed of a perfect knowledge of the side upon which his bread is buttered. So much so that if he ever gets into a sinking ship every blessed thing will go overboard including crew, passengers and even perhaps little Elgins to boot!'[3] There is his portrait by Richmond: a hint of ruthlessness in that comfortable, balding, bucolic face, framed by silvery hair and side-whiskers. It would also seem – though this cannot be proved conclusively – that he altered the published copy of a letter in order to give the impression that the diversion to India of troops destined for China which helped to save the situation in the early months of the Mutiny was carried out on his initiative rather than, as was the case, on Canning's.

But while Elgin might not have been quite such a good fellow as he appeared – indeed, some of his associates at home thought him vain and a bore – he made an excellent impression on his arrival in Calcutta; to which he came without his wife, who did not join him until the following cold weather. After the austere Canning, he seemed so genial and sociable; 'very cheery and chatty with everybody'.[4] His manner was especially pleasing to the non-official Europeans – the fact that he, like so many of them, was Scottish, may also have helped. Like most of the British in India, they were grateful to him for having sent his troops to their aid in 1857; and he also deliberately set out to conciliate them during the year he spent in Calcutta after his arrival. When, at the beginning of 1863, he was about to go up country, the Calcutta Europeans showed their regard for him by giving him a public entertainment at the Town Hall as a send-off.

While making himself popular with the Europeans, Elgin was just as enlightened as Canning in his attitude to the Indians. 'It is a terrible business this living among inferior races' he had written when staying in Calcutta in 1857.[5] He was pained at finding himself walking about among the salaaming servants of Government House 'with perfect indifference, treating them, not as dogs, because in that case one would whistle to them and pat them; but as machines with which one can have no communion or sympathy'.[6] When an English soldier was sentenced to death for killing an Indian while attempting to rob him, Elgin sternly refused to yield to European public opinion and grant a reprieve; the murder, he declared, was carried out 'under an impulse which would have been resisted if the life of the native had been estimated at the value of that of a dog'.[7] He was determined to stand by the Queen's promise to respect the customs and religions of India; mistrusting the missionary zeal of Edwardes and others like him as much as Canning had done. He objected to Indians having to pull *punkahs* over ordinary private soldiers just because they happened to be white; and felt sure that the Americans would have invented something to make this unnecessary.

Elgin knew that much of the injustice and callousness shown by the British to the Indians stemmed from fear. India was now at peace, but it was an uneasy peace; there were constant rumours of plots, massacres and new insurrections. While being firmly resolved to put down any real disturbances which may have occurred, the Viceroy did his best to allay the panic; making light of the alarmist reports which he received. 'By the bye, last night was fixed upon by my anonymous correspondents for my own assassination' he told the Secretary of State drily, when recounting to him some of the wilder stories that were going around.[8]

Canning had expected Elgin to 'sail with the wind'[9] in carrying on his policy of trusting the Indian upper classes. Elgin, however, was doubtful about putting too much reliance on the landed aristocracy; fearing, as he said, 'the frightful corruption, both of mind and body' to which the inheritors of wealth and position were exposed in Oriental society − in fact he took a somewhat radical view of all aristocracies, European as well as Oriental.[10] This is an instance of how Elgin, though very much under the shadow of his great predecessor, quickly showed every sign of having a mind and a policy of his own.

In February 1863, Elgin, accompanied by his wife and his grown-up daughter, set off up country. The leisurely river passage in the old *Sonamukhi* was now a thing of the past, for the railway extended as far as Benares. Here, as well as at Cawnpore, Agra, Delhi and elsewhere, he held Durbars; that at Agra being an occasion of particular splendour; though he was himself inclined to question the popular belief 'that all Orientals are children, amused and gratified by external trappings and ceremonies and titles and ready to put up with the loss of real dignity and power if they are only permitted to enjoy the semblance of it'.[11]

For the hot weather, the Elgins established themselves at Simla; occupying a house high on the ridge which went by the unlikely name of Peterhof; it had a big, chalet-like roof with gables at each end and two tiers of wooden verandas, the upper ones overhanging the lower. Though possessing a large room for entertaining, it was of quite modest proportions and had many of the characteristics of the usual hill station house: the corrugated iron roof on to which monkeys jumped, the perpetual leaks, the falling plaster. Towards the end of September, the Viceregal party set out on an autumn tour through the Hills. Elgin's original intention was to go as far as Peshawar; but an outbreak of hostilities against the fanatical Sitana tribesmen on the North-West Frontier made him decide to go instead to Lahore, in order to confer with the Punjab Government. It was ironical that Elgin should have had a border war on his hands after less than two years as Viceroy, having been judiciously pacific in his dealings with India's neighbours. 'I am wholly opposed to that prurient intermeddling policy which finds so much favour with certain classes of Indian officials' he had told the Secretary of State, Sir Charles Wood, not long before.[12]

A month after starting on his journey, Elgin walked across a bridge made of plaited twigs that swung violently over the rocky gorge of the Chandra River. The effort gave him a heart attack; he was laid up at the nearby hill station of Dharmsala and after a week or so his doctors realised that he would not recover. The strenuous upland tour, coming on top of the hard work of the past eighteen months, had proved too much for a man who, though little more than fifty, looked considerably older and had been in poor health for some time.

Elgin faced death with calm fortitude; he was in a sense prepared for it, having left his home in Scotland with a presentiment that he would never return. He took leave of his Staff, saying 'It is well that I should die in harness';[13] he dictated a farewell note to his Council. His last days were cheered by the staggeringly beautiful scenery around him: forest-clad hillsides and snowy heights, fair prospects over rice-fields far below. He sent his wife to choose an idyllic spot where he could be buried; his last wish being that his monument should be very simple.

Forty years after Elgin's death, the monument over his grave was badly damaged by an earthquake; as though even the elements were trying to obliterate the name of this most forgotten of Viceroys; a Viceroy whose times were uneventful and who never had the chance of accomplishing any measures of his own; but who, had he lived, would probably have introduced far-reaching constitutional reforms. Elgin is forgotten, however, not so much because he died before he could achieve anything, but because he failed to inspire his contemporaries in India with any thoughts of what he might have achieved. 'This is very sad, of course,' one of them wrote on hearing of his death, 'but I cannot say on public grounds that I can bring myself to think it a calamity.'[14]

Peterhof, Simla

When Elgin died, India and England were not yet in full telegraphic communication. It was therefore still not known who was to succeed him when, about six weeks after his death, a steamer touched at Ceylon. The men in the first boat which put out to the ship from the shore called up to ask who was to be the new Viceroy. The answer came: 'John Lawrence, and he is on board'.[15]

The speed with which India's new ruler had made himself ready to leave England – having had no idea that he was going to be Viceroy until ten days before he set out – was typical of the man whose swiftness of action held the Punjab during the Mutiny. And in the Punjab before the Mutiny, when Lawrence, together with his brother Henry and the rest of that devoted band of resolute young Puritans such as Nicholson, Abbott and Edwardes, worked to bring law, order and prosperity to the newly-annexed province, an immense energy had been his outstanding quality. It was an energy which made him as good at putting down rebellions as finding facts; which enabled him to spend as many long hours at his desk as in the saddle. Along with his energy went complete honesty and a simple religious faith, the conviction that God was on his side. He spoke to the people of the Punjab in the language of the Old Testament; he could be fierce, but he could also be merciful. While advocating and supporting the sternest measures during the Mutiny, his clemency was as notable as Canning's once it was over. Lawrence's biographer may exaggerate when he claims that the exact opposite of the saying, 'Scratch the Russian and you will find the Tartar', might have been applied to him – 'Scratch him skin-deep and you will find him to be all tenderness'[16] – yet there was plenty of humanity and also humour beneath his rugged exterior.

There is a touch of humour – the dry humour of Ulster, where he had his roots – in Lawrence's eyes, which look searchingly at us from under thick, lowering brows in his portrait. Apart from this touch, all is duty and determination in the features of that leonine head, with the moustache, the longish untidy hair and the thick and furrowed neck. 'He was a rough, coarse man, in appearance more like a navvy than a gentleman' one of the younger generation of Civilians who served under Lawrence wrote of him;[17] but this Civilian and his friends found him an inconsiderate martinet and so were prejudiced against him, unlike his older disciples who loved him. 'Plain John' Lawrence, however rough and philistine he may have been, was certainly a gentleman by birth; his father, though of obscure County Antrim stock, was a colonel in the army; his mother, a clergyman's daughter, came of a branch of the well-known Northern Irish gentry family of Knox. Nevertheless, his background was very different from that of Canning and Elgin and of most of the previous rulers of British India; he was the first Indian Civilian since 'Honest John' Shore to be appointed to the highest office. His appointment, in

defiance of the established custom of more than half a century, was mainly for the reason that he was a national hero: acclaimed as the 'Saviour of the Punjab' when in 1859 he ended his career as an Indian Civilian and retired to England. It was also felt that he, more than anybody else, would be able to deal with the trouble on the North-West Frontier, which at the time of Elgin's death looked like growing into a dangerous tribal revolt. Then it would not have been so easy at that juncture to find a candidate of the more traditional sort for an office which had killed three British noblemen in succession and the wives of two of them. The spell would surely be broken by sending out a Viceroy who was acclimatised to India, as was his wife.

Harriette Lawrence, an Ulster clergyman's daughter like her mother-in-law, was a wife such as Mr. Philip Mason had in mind when he wrote: 'A woman who married into the Punjab Commission had taken a step as decisive as entering a convent. She and her children became camp equipment, jolted in bullock-carts and on the backs of camels, exposed to dust, sun, heat, cholera, malaria, moving always from tent to bungalow and back again, gypsies without a home beneath the stars.'[18] But although Government House was Western luxury compared with what she was used to, Harriette was

Lord and Lady Elgin with their daughter, Lady Louisa Bruce, at Simla in 1863 'miserable'[19] when Lawrence told her that he was to go back to India as Viceroy. She thought of the separation from her children, the youngest of whom was only two years old; she also faced the more immediate prospect of being separated from her husband, for she was pregnant and had to remain in England until the following autumn. It comes as a surprise that a man who had retired full of honours four years previously and who was known as 'Old John' Lawrence just as much as 'Plain John' Lawrence, should have been a father-to-be; but at the time of his appointment he was only fifty-two; he, Elgin, Canning and Dalhousie having all been born within a few months of each other. He looked much older than his age; not florid and overweight, like Elgin, but craggy and careworn. Nevertheless he felt quite young enough to take on the Viceroyalty, which he was extremely proud to have attained; and he was happy at the prospect of going back to India, having found his work in London, as a member of the India Council, too sedentary for his liking. But at the thought of leaving his two-year-old son he burst into tears. The stern Saviour of the Punjab was devoted to children; proof of that 'tenderness' of which his biographer speaks. On the ship going out to India, a neglected infant whose constant squallings infuriated the other passengers was befriended and placated by the Viceroy-designate. When asked why he took such notice of it, he replied: 'That child is the only being in the ship who I can feel quite sure does not want to get anything out of me'.[20]

Lawrence arrived in Calcutta on 12 January 1864 to a hero's welcome. He steamed up the Hughli past ships lined with cheering sailors; there were more cheers from the soldiers on parade and vast crowds of Indians and Europeans to greet him. 'It was a proud moment to me when I walked up the steps of Government House, feeling as I then did that without political interest or influence I had been chosen to fill the highest office under the Crown, the Viceroyalty of the Queen' he told his son-in-law. But he added: 'It will be a happier moment to me when I walk down the steps with the feeling that I have tried to do my duty'.[21] He found the great house and the pomp with which he was surrounded oppressive; and was soon shocking the Europeans of Calcutta by his informality. He would walk to St John's Church on Sunday mornings, instead of driving there in state; varying his religious allegiance by walking to the Scotch Kirk. He would mingle with the crowd in the bazaars, his knowledge of Indian languages enabling him to hear what people were saying about him. When a fire broke out in one of the Indian quarters of the city – which happened all too frequently – he would walk to the scene so as to judge for himself the extent of the disaster. He went for early morning walks on the Maidan and on one of these occasions was chased by a buffalo; and once, when returning to

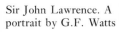

Government House after a walk at night, he was challenged and repulsed by the sentry at the private entrance who was new to the place and could not imagine that the Lord Sahib would arrive on his own two feet.

Eyebrows were also raised when the Viceroy was found working at his desk in shirt sleeves and without a collar, as had been his wont as Lieutenant-Governor of the Punjab. Once when he heard that he had given offence by receiving a Municipal Deputation in his slippers, he said to his Private Secretary in simple astonishment: 'Why, Hathaway, they were quite new and very good slippers!'[22] And when his frugal tastes and hatred of waste in any form made him introduce various economies in the running of Government House, he was accused of stinginess; though he gave the money which he thereby saved to the Sailors' Home and other deserving charities. His guests grumbled because he had got rid of the French chef – a functionary who, according to Canning, merely put on airs and left the dinner to be cooked by Indians – and they complained that the wine was poor compared with what Elgin had given them; not realising that Lawrence had bought up Elgin's cellar. It was also thought to be meanness on Lawrence's part when he refused to present the customary silver cup to be run for at the Calcutta Races; whereas he disapproved of racing on principle. As well as having a name for parsimony, the Lawrence regime was thought by many to be too democratic. 'Is it true that the Government House list has got so low that your name has been removed from it for fear you should meet your chemist at dinner?' an up-country friend asked the wife of a high official in 1865.[23]

Allowing for the prejudice of those who felt that the Lord Sahib ought to have been a real Lord and not a retired Civilian who was just Sir John, it would seem that Government House in the Lawrences' day was a little dull; more like a parsonage than a palace, with family prayers and croquet in the garden – the populace watching through the railings as the Viceroy wielded his mallet. Lawrence's uncouth manner and his loathing of banquets, balls and parties made him totally unsuited to the social side of his office; so that he was attacked in the newspapers for having 'let down' the Viceroyalty. But when it came to the great ceremonial occasions designed to impress the Indians, he left behind his ordinary self and assumed with ease the dignity and circumstance of an Eastern monarch. The Durbars which he held at Lahore, Agra and Lucknow were of unparalleled splendour; and all the more memorable in that he was able to address the assembled dignitaries in their own languages. The Durbar at Lahore was particularly moving, for he was back in his own country; with the Chiefs and Sirdars of the Punjab doing homage to the 'Jan Larens' they knew so well.

The holding of Durbars was unfortunately the only aspect of Lawrence's Viceroyalty in which he enjoyed an unqualified success. As a ruler he proved even more disappointing than as a Viceregal host; so that his five years as Viceroy turned out to be a sad anticlimax to his career. He knew India like no other Viceroy; he was a fanatic for work, as hard a taskmaster with himself as with others; and unlike the unfortunate Canning, he usually managed to get through the daily pile of dispatch-boxes. But experience and hard work alone do not make a ruler. Lawrence had a narrow and plodding mind, a painstaking concern for detail, more suited to administering a province than governing an Empire. It was the mind of a first-rate subordinate rather than that of a leader; he was much better at carrying out other people's orders than at formulating policies of his own. He was also too rigid and obstinate for an office in which he was dealing with powerful colleagues rather than with juniors, disciples

Sir John Lawrence

and friends; he had no genius for compromise. 'I find him like the Legitimist: he has learnt nothing and forgotten nothing' said Sir Robert Napier, who was Military Member of Lawrence's Council in the earlier part of his reign.[24]

Yet Lawrence was on more cordial terms with Napier than he was with either his subsequent Military Member, the formidable Sir Henry Durand, or with his first Commander-in-Chief, the foppish but valiant Sir Hugh Rose. Lawrence was constantly at odds with his colleagues in Council, who were on the whole a strong team; he was quite unable to persuade and influence them, in the way that a better Viceroy would have done; and seldom succeeded in carrying his own views except by exercising his right to overrule the majority. He found his Provincial Governors just as hard to manage as his Councillors; particularly the great Sir Bartle Frere at Bombay, who was unusual among Presidency Governors in being a Civilian rather than a minor politician sent out from England.

Lawrence was as weak in his dealings with the Secretary of State as he was in handling his colleagues in India – particularly up to 1866, when the Secretary of State was the redoubtable Maharaja Wood. Here again, it was a matter of temperament; though he was also

(*Above right*) John Lawrence with his Council and other senior members of his Government, about 1865. General Sir Hugh Rose (afterwards Field-Marshal Lord Strathnairn), Commander-in-Chief, sits on the Viceroy's right; and General Sir Robert Napier (afterwards Field-Marshal Lord Napier of Magdala), Military Member, on his left. Sir Charles Trevelyan, the turbulent Governor of Madras under Canning, who had returned to India as Finance Member, sits on Rose's right. The bearded figure standing behind Trevelyan is Colonel (afterwards Field-Marshal Sir) Henry Norman, Secretary to Government,

Military Department, who afterwards became Military Member and in 1893 was offered and declined the Viceroyalty. Standing in the middle between the Commander-in-Chief and the Viceroy is Sir Henry Durand, Foreign Secretary, afterwards Military Member and then Lieutenant-Governor of the Punjab, where he died as a result of being thrown from his elephant when the howdah was crushed passing through a narrow gateway. Standing at the extreme right of the group is Colonel (afterwards Sir) Richard Strachey

handicapped by not having the political influence of a Canning or an Elgin. His attitude towards the Home Government was that of a loyal civil servant; it was for him only to obey. In the words of a distinguished Indian historian, 'the Viceroy fainéant in India appeared to the Secretaries of State in London as a senior foreman awaiting orders'.[25]

The Secretary of State was to Lawrence rather what the Governor-General had been to him when he was governing the Punjab; just as he tended to regard the Provincial Governors as though they were so many Deputy-Commissioners with India as the 'Punjab writ large'.[26] In the Punjab, he had been able to give his subordinates a very free hand, because he knew them and trusted them implicitly; he and they were a band of brothers. Moreover, he knew the problems of their various districts as well as they did, so that he could always if necessary put them right. But when as Viceroy he applied the easy-going Punjab system to men whom he did not know so well and who were in many cases separated from him by a thousand miles or more, it just did not work. Thus, the fearful loss of life in the Orissa famine of 1866 might have been averted had he not been so ready to accept the assurances of the Lieutenant-Governor of

Bengal that everything was under control. This calamity caused Lawrence – the friend and protector of the Indian peasant – more grief than any other event of his reign. It is pathetic to see him standing by while his colleagues delayed and bungled; not the John Lawrence of Punjab days, going hell for leather to the scene of the trouble; but an old man wringing his hands. His letters on this matter are a sad confession of helplessness.

> The local officers would not admit that there was not ample grain stored in the province . . . I could not induce the Lieutenant-Governor to call a meeting . . . I cannot understand how he could have gone to Orissa and not have discovered the miserable condition of the people . . . I urged the Lieutenant-Governor to active measures, such as the importation of grain. But he, resting on local information, objected to act, and the views of the Council generally were with him. I might, and perhaps ought to have overruled them and insisted on prompt action; and I blame myself for not so doing . . . my Council was against me.[27]

'My Council was against me.' It is the *cri-de-coeur* of a man whose intellectual faculties are not what they used to be. 'I feel quite bewildered sometimes what to do' he lamented, when speaking of the eternal troubles between the peasants and the British planters.[28] Having found it impossible to ride his Empire on a loose Punjab rein, he went to the other extreme and fell back on the methods of rigid bureaucracy; he also tried without success to persuade the Home Government to allow him to choose his own Council, in the hope of making himself into more of a despot.

As it was, the only way Lawrence could get the better of his Council was by enlisting the support of the Secretary of State. Wood helped him to win a major battle over the question of tenant right. Having always been a friend of the poor, anxious to improve the lot of the ordinary cultivators of the soil, it was natural that Lawrence should have felt that Canning's land settlement in Oudh did not give the peasants adequate protection against the Talukdars. Canning himself, knowing Lawrence's reputation for 'levelling', had actually expressed the fear that if ever he became Viceroy, he would 'go far towards upsetting' his policy of exalting the Indian aristocracy.[29] In fact Lawrence's measures to protect the peasants in Oudh merely put into effect a proviso of Canning's that 'all subordinate rights' in the land should be respected;[30] but they were opposed by his Council on the grounds that they would alienate the upper classes and also attacked by the non-official community of Calcutta as a threat to private property. For almost the first time in his career, Lawrence felt 'the cold blast of unpopularity';[31] but he held his ground and threatened to resign if he were not supported by the Home Government on this issue. Wood duly backed him up, and his measures were adopted. He also improved the position of peasants in the Punjab and in Bengal, where there was the added problem of oppression by the European planters.

Although the peasants remained Lawrence's principal concern, he was now not quite the 'leveller' he had been in his younger days; and could lend a more sympathetic ear to the problems of landlords and Chiefs. To refresh his knowledge of their problems and points of view, he made it his business to talk to as many Indians as he could; though like Canning, he had little or no contact with the educated middle classes; he and his Council were as one in disagreeing with a proposal to make it easier for Indians to join the Covenanted Civil Service. They were, however, willing to allow Indians to hold more posts. And Lawrence was shocked, though he could not help being also amused, when Sir William Denison – the Governor of Madras who had acted as Viceroy before his arrival – speaking to him about a new batch of Civilians, 'drew himself up sharp, threw his head back and exclaimed: 'Gad, Sir, they have sent me out a Hottentot among them'.[32]

The strengthening of tenant right was the most important but not the only achievement of Lawrence's reign. There was much progress in the work of overhauling the machinery of government, which Canning had begun. There was a mass of new legislation and a codification of the laws by the eminent Anglo-Irish jurist, Whitley Stokes. There was the building of barracks, the making of railways and canals. There were great advances in public health, in which Lawrence – who had consulted Florence Nightingale on the matter before coming out – took a particular interest; so that Sir Richard Temple, one of his ablest disciples who cheered the closing weeks of his Viceroyalty by becoming his Finance Member, has conferred on him the worthy if unromantic title of 'Father of Indian Sanitation'.[33]

Though no Viceroy can have been less expansionist than Lawrence, his reign actually saw a small accession of territory in the North-East, the prize of a brief war soon after his arrival against the Himalayan state of Bhutan, which had insulted a British mission sent there in Elgin's time. The war at the other end of India's frontier, against the Sitana tribesmen, which had been a reason for Lawrence's appointment as Viceroy, was virtually over before he arrived; but across the border in Afghanistan a fratricidal conflict was raging between the two sons of the late Amir, Dost Mohammad, whose friendly demeanour throughout the Mutiny had been of great help to Lawrence in holding the Punjab. Lawrence remained strictly aloof from this conflict, being in no way tempted to take advantage of it in order to extend British influence into Afghanistan as a counter to

Russian expansion in Central Asia. He preferred that India's existing North-West Frontier should be well defended, that Afghanistan should remain independent and that there should be a clear understanding with Russia as to how far in the direction of India the British would allow her to go. Lawrence's attitude to the Afghan question came to be known as his policy of 'masterly inactivity'; its adherents in the years that followed were to be as powerful and as numerous as its opponents.

If Lawrence's Viceroyalty tended to be forgotten by subsequent generations of the British in India, it produced one measure for which they – or at any rate those of them in the higher reaches of Government – had cause to be grateful. This was the institution of the annual hot-weather migration of the Government of India to Simla, as a way of getting more work done and to be in closer touch with the Governments of the Punjab and the North-Western Provinces. Instead of spending only one or perhaps two hot seasons in the Hills and leaving his Council and Secretariat behind in Calcutta, as had been the custom of his predecessors, Lawrence insisted on going to Simla every year and taking his Council and other officials with him; and he felt so strongly on the matter that he threatened to resign if he could not have his way. The annual migration was duly agreed to, though not without opposition; and so, from 1864 onwards, Simla was the hot weather capital of British India. Henceforth, for six months of every year, an Empire was administered from a crazy cluster of timber and corrugated iron

The south front of Government House, Calcutta, in about the time of Lawrence

houses perched precariously on ledges among the deodars and rhododendrons eight thousand feet above sea level.

Peterhof, the house occupied by Elgin during his stay at Simla, became for the time being the official Viceregal summer residence. Lawrence was far happier here than in Wellesley's great palace; he always felt something of a stranger in Calcutta, whereas here he was in the part of India he knew so well. Here, too, it was very much easier for him to escape from the Viceregal formality which he found irksome; nobody minded if he went on foot up and down the steep zig-zag paths rather than taking advantage of his right – which he shared only with the Commander-in-Chief and the Lieutenant-Governor of the Punjab – of driving in a carriage. When Durand's daughter became engaged, Lawrence forgot his differences with her father and trudged up the hill to the house where she and her family were living to wish her happiness; accompanied only by a single red-coated *chaprassi* carrying a wedding present – a vast presentation inkstand which had clearly been a presentation to the Viceroy himself.

'It seemed strange to us to be once more together at Simla,' Harriette Lawrence afterwards wrote, 'for it recalled many happy memories of our early life when we were very small people indeed'.[34] She, no less than her husband, preferred Simla to Calcutta; her sitting room at Peterhof was close to his, so that she saw much more of him; she was able to join him when, tired out with his work, he would refresh himself by walking up and down the wooden veranda, enjoying the view. In the evening, they would go for an outing, she carried in a *jampan*, he riding or walking at her side. At Simla, he and she hardly ever missed their daily reading of the Bible together, even when he was at his busiest.

The godliness of the Lawrences prompted them to invite an unusual guest to stay with them at Peterhof: one of a small brotherhood of Moravian missionaries who lived and worked in extreme poverty on the borders of Tibet. This simple and saintly German duly arrived, having walked the hundred miles from his mission-station to Simla; he wore a rough garment of hair cloth with rope sandals on his feet; his only luggage being a coffee pot in one pocket and a Bible in the other. The Viceroy's Staff did their best to make him look presentable, and he came into dinner rigged out in a dress suit belonging to one of them, a tie belonging to another and a pair of shoes belonging to the Viceroy himself. Lawrence's attitude to missionaries differed from that of some of the more bigoted of his old Punjab comrades in that he approved of them only if they confined their proselytising activities to tribes which did not belong to any of the major Indian religions.

Lawrence was sad when, in the autumn of 1868, he left Simla for the last time. One afternoon, not long before he left, he went for a walk with his devoted disciple Richard Temple. As they stood beneath the setting sun on Prospect Point, gazing over a sea of hills and wooded valleys to the far-off peaks of everlasting snow, the Viceroy said to his companion: 'Think what a blessing it is that, although we are not very far from a mountainous frontier held by fierce and murderous tribes, yet in these hills the people are mild and harmless, so that here the sick, the holiday-makers after their hard work, the women and children and the helpless of all sorts, are safe from bloodthirsty marauders.'[35] As well as regretting Simla, he felt the parting with so many old friends; yet on the whole he was glad to be leaving India. He was now very tired and suffered much from severe headaches; he was also lonely, for Harriette and his daughters had gone home ahead of him.

He returned to England early in 1869 and was immediately made a peer. Those who saw him on his arrival declared that he looked 'much broken';[36] but in fact he had another ten years of active public life before him; he certainly had not come home to die like Dalhousie and Canning. As for Harriette Lawrence, she was to survive until 1917. The choice of a seasoned Indian Civilian as Elgin's successor certainly appeared to have disposed of the legend that India was a graveyard for Viceroys and their wives; but in other respects Lawrence's reign only served to convince people that a Civilian ought never again to occupy the Viceregal throne.

Mayo

If Lawrence was an obvious choice for the Viceroyalty, his successor was comparatively unknown; a forty-six-year-old Irish peer on whom Disraeli picked, allowing himself, as he so frequently did, to be guided by intuition. The new Viceroy was Richard Bourke, sixth Earl of Mayo, head of a branch of an ancient Norman-Irish house; a landowner of moderate means, a minor politician who had held the Irish Chief-Secretaryship on and off since 1852, a sportsman who had been an outstandingly successful Master of the Kildare Hunt. Disraeli's appointment to India of someone whose experience was limited almost entirely to Ireland seemed to many at the time eccentric; but it was a stroke of genius. For this dark horse from the hunting field of County Kildare proved every inch a winner.

To those who knew him well, Mayo may not have seemed so unlikely a choice as he did to the public at large. While he may have lacked intellectual brilliance and knowledge of Eastern affairs, his qualities and past career made him unusually well suited to be Viceroy – not least his success as a Master of Foxhounds which, as one of his colleagues in India afterwards pointed out, required tact, strength and management just as did the ruling of the Indian Empire. A splendid figure of a man, tall, broad-shouldered and powerfully built, with both determination and humour in his clean-shaven face, Mayo's presence alone made it easy for him to command. But he seldom had to command in order to get his way; he understood people and was able to carry them along with him. His enthusiasm, his cheerful gaiety, his genuine kindness of heart all contributed to a personal magnetism few could resist. And though India, when he was appointed to rule over it, was such a closed book to him that he felt obliged to devote most of the time that remained before his departure to intensive study at the India Office, yet in many respects his life had, up to then, been an ideal training for his Viceroyalty. Being the eldest of a large family of brothers made him a leader from an early age. Having reached manhood before his father succeeded his great-uncle as Earl of Mayo, he had been toughened by the spartan, outdoor upbringing of a son of the less affluent Anglo-

Irish gentry. The atmosphere in which he grew up was strongly Evangelical; which gave him a sense of duty and a bond with the Puritan giants of British India. But his Evangelical upbringing did not prevent him from being tolerant in matters of religion – as Viceroy he was never to forget that Queen Victoria now had more Muslim subjects than the Sultan – or from cutting a dash among the great patrician families of England, into one of which he married.

As a young man, Mayo had farmed on his own account and in a comparatively small way; gaining a practical knowledge of husbandry such as was possessed by few political peers of his time; which stood him in good stead as the ruler of an Empire where agriculture was all-important. And having lived through the 'Hungry Forties' in Ireland, he took with him to the famine-ridden land of India a first-hand experience of famine in its most horrifying aspect. During the Irish famine, he had thrown himself heart and soul into the work of relief; spending long hours in the saddle riding from one stricken area to another. In fact, the life he led in those days was not unlike that of a young District Officer in India; it might be said that Mayo came to the Viceroyalty with many of the virtues but none of the prejudices of the Indian Civilian.

If, during the Famine years, Mayo learnt what it was like to be a District Officer, his years as Irish Chief Secretary taught him the art of governing; for it was the Chief Secretary who ruled Ireland rather than the Irish Viceroy, who was little more than a figurehead. As the ruler of Ireland, he governed a country which had certain similarities to India. Not only were Ireland and India both predominantly agricultural and haunted by the spectre of famine; but both had, during the past few years, suffered disturbances. The abortive Fenian outbreak of 1867 can hardly be compared to the Indian Mutiny; yet the calm, firm and magnanimous way in which Mayo, as Chief Secretary, dealt with it showed him to be well capable of dealing with a similar crisis in India.

Mayo's apprenticeship as Irish Secretary taught him to economise his time, so that he was able to get through a vast amount of work without sacrificing either his exercise or his night's sleep. He was fortunate in having a mind that could quickly grasp any problem and as quickly hit upon the most sensible solution to it. The Irish Secretaryship also gave Mayo his reforming zeal as a ruler. He had what would now be called a social conscience, being regarded by many, Conservative though he was, as half a Liberal. Having been thwarted by British party politics in his ambition to improve the lot of the people of Ireland, he saw in the Indian Viceroyalty, with its much greater independence, a heaven-sent opportunity to do what he himself thought was right. In his joy at this prospect of broad horizons and freedom of action, the only expression he could utter

Lord Mayo in Star of India Robes

was: 'At last'.[1]

So energetic was Mayo, so keen to get to know every part of his Empire as quickly as possible, that before proceeding to Calcutta to assume office in January 1869 he made prolonged stays at Bombay and Madras in order to see as much as he could of the two chief provincial centres; starting early on the very morning after he landed at Bombay by going to inspect the city's sewage outflow. When, on reaching Calcutta, he arrived at Government House, he fairly jumped out of his carriage and 'beaming with the brightness of health'[2] strode buoyantly up the great steps to where Lawrence, looking old and shrunken, awaited him. The assembled officials were most impressed by the splendid, athletic figure of the new Viceroy; and as they walked away from Government House after Mayo's installation they remarked to one another that at last the spell would be broken and a statesman from home would get through the Viceroyalty without dying of it.

Lawrence stayed on in Calcutta for a week after the arrival of Mayo, who during that time formed the highest possible opinion of him; while not agreeing with him on every point. A new Viceroy who was less generous-minded might have been tempted to damn his famous predecessor with faint praise; but Mayo wrote of Lawrence to the Secretary of State with a touching, boyish enthusiasm. 'Nothing could equal the frankness and confidence with which he has treated me. He is one of the finest characters I ever met with – to a most generous and high minded disposition he joins an unrivalled knowledge of India and her people with great courage and clearness of purpose'.[3] Mayo wrote these words on the eve of Lawrence's departure; one suspects before and not after an episode which occurred on that same day. When the two Viceroys arrived back at Government House after a drive together, during which Lawrence had, with great earnestness, impressed on his successor the importance of treating the Indians kindly, the *syce* was slow and awkward in opening the carriage door; whereupon Lawrence leapt out in a rage and tugged the man's ear. Though he laughed at the time, Mayo did not forget this early lesson in how even the greatest of the British in India sometimes failed to practise what they preached; and throughout his Viceroyalty he was to be constantly stressing the need for kind and courteous behaviour towards the Indians. He would speak of what he called 'the abominable practice' of striking Indians as 'a cowardly and detestable crime'.[4]

It did not take long for Mayo to win for himself a popularity such as no previous ruler of British India had ever enjoyed. He had, to use an expression fashionable at the present time, charisma. There was his commanding presence, his smile and the joyous twinkle in his eye; his air of youthful vigour and tolerant strength; his quiet and deliberate way of speaking, with just a hint of a brogue. There was his reputation as a sportsman, the knowledge that he was one of the best riders and shots in India as well as being Viceroy. There was the magnificence of his entertainments. After the austerities of the Lawrence regime, he and Lady Mayo really brought back the glamour and gaiety to Government House; helped by a young and high-spirited Staff that included Major Owen Burne, a Private Secretary as popular as his Chief. The snobs of Calcutta society were quick to notice a spectacular improvement in the quality of the Government House wine; not realising that Mayo had bought up Lawrence's cellar, just as Lawrence had bought up Elgin's.

Those who met Mayo found him friendly, easy-going and informal; though such was the innate dignity of his manner that nobody would have presumed to be unduly familiar with him in return. There was, however, much more to him than dignity and charm; those who worked with him came to love him for his kindness and unselfishness, his efficiency and his sound good sense; they found him intelligent and well-educated, ready to interest himself in any subject, without being so clever as to rub people up the wrong way.

Two of Mayo's Council, the Home Member John Strachey and the Law Member FitzJames Stephen, both brilliant men with very much their own opinions – not for nothing were they the uncles, respectively, of Lytton Strachey and Virginia Woolf – were afterwards to declare that they had felt a greater regard and affection for him than for almost anybody else they had ever known. A more junior member of his Government described him as 'one of the noblest characters ever known in India'.[5] Burne, his Private Secretary, maintained that 'to work with Lord Mayo was really a recreation'.[6] One might find this hard to believe, since Mayo worked for twelve hours every day; though it really seems that he was able to endow those who worked with him with some of his own enthusiasm and tireless energy. He was also a most considerate Chief; and his remarkable talent for saving time meant that the work seldom got out of hand. Then, the health of those who worked with him benefited from the fact that he planned his day with a view to keeping as fit as possible. He found time for exercise, whether it was a hard gallop pig-sticking or a stiff walk through the marshes outside Calcutta after snipe. By starting work at daybreak, he avoided having to burn the midnight oil; though he sometimes did business with his colleagues in his dressing room, while changing for dinner. On these occasions, his little son Terence, who was always allowed to help him put on his Star, would be perched on his dressing table. 'Why, Terry-boy, you are my confidant, are you not?' Mayo used to say to him. 'You are *quite* discreet too, ain't you?'[7]

It might be argued that Mayo's success depended to a large extent on the exceptional brilliance of his Council; which also included Strachey's no less able brother Richard, and the dynamic Sir Richard Temple. But even one of the by no means unduly modest Stracheys, when writing privately to the other, gave Mayo the credit for the success of his Government.[8] Mayo's policies were very much his own; he had the last word in all major decisions of the Government of India during his reign; revising and often rewriting every dispatch himself. And the very brilliance of his colleagues might have been a liability rather than a help, producing a clash of wills such as there had been under Lawrence. It was a sign of Mayo's greatness that he was able to control his thoroughbred team and drive it at a spanking pace in the direction he wished to go. He and his Council were all, he said, 'exceedingly good friends';[9] and indeed, his Council never once outvoted him.

If Mayo was very much in control of his colleagues and subordinates, he was himself allowed a remarkably free hand by the Government of Gladstone, which came to power when he was actually on his way to India. Having as a Conservative to work under a Liberal Government from the very beginning of his reign turned out to be not an embarrassment as it might have been but a blessing in disguise, for the Liberals at that time were not much inclined to interfere in Indian affairs. It also kept India clear of British party politics; Mayo's Conservative friends supported the Government's Indian policy knowing that it was really his. With a Conservative Viceroy who was half a Liberal, assisted by the Stracheys and FitzJames Stephen who were Liberals made half Conservative by the Indian situation, nobody could say that India was governed along party lines.

Indeed, Mayo governed India not according to any political theories but according to what he saw as the needs of her people. Realising the need for strong and good government, he set out to make the administration more efficient. Though he was very much of his time in believing in Britain's Imperial destiny – 'Teach your subordinates' he told the Lieutenant-Governor of the Punjab, 'that we are all British gentlemen engaged in the magnificent work of governing an inferior race'[10] – he held enlightened views on the importance of educating the Indians, particularly the poor, and enabling them to play a part in the administration of their own affairs. It was he who was responsible for the Act passed by his successor appointing municipal committees by election, which gave the Indians a share in local government.

With his Irish experience and his sympathy for the peasants, Mayo was particularly concerned about famine. The very first letter he wrote as Viceroy to the Secretary of State, the Duke of Argyll, was about the steps he had already taken to deal with a severe scarcity of food in the North-Western Provinces and elsewhere; he had even ordered enquiries to be made as to the possibility of importing grain from abroad as a last resort: 'I am sure that Your Grace will feel that life must be saved at any cost'.[11] Fortunately rain came to the affected areas and the threat of famine receded; but Mayo continued his crusade against hunger. He put all his energy and drive into improving irrigation and speeding up the construction of railways and roads so that grain could be quickly transported to famine areas from regions where it was plentiful. Such was the importance attached by him to all branches of Public Works – he wanted India to have more schools and hospitals as well as more roads, railways and canals – that he took charge of the Public Works Department himself. This meant that he was, so to speak, his own Minister of Public Works as well as his own Foreign Minister; since the Foreign Department was the special responsibility of the Viceroy.

Mayo also sought to combat famine by improvements in agriculture; proposing the setting up of a separate Agricultural Department, something which in the event the India Office did not see fit to sanction for another thirty years. With his knowledge of farming, he usually had practical suggestions to make when papers to do with agriculture were sent up to him. He became increasingly familiar with conditions in rural India since he toured his Empire to a much greater extent than any of his predecessors; covering, during the course of three years, more than twenty thousand miles of the Indian subcontinent. This enabled him, in that time, to see more of India than the majority of officials, who were tied to particular regions, saw during their whole career. No other Viceroy ever acquired as much first-hand knowledge as he did of the problems of the 'man on the spot'.

Much of Mayo's journeying was done on horseback; sometimes he rode as much as eighty miles a day. He also travelled by river steamer and rail and by all the other modes of transport to which nineteenth-century rulers of British India and their womenfolk were obliged to resort – elephant, yak, camel, inflated buffalo skin on the Indus and Sutlej. Once in the Central Provinces, having decided at the last minute to visit a place which had been left out of his itinerary, he found that the only way he could get there was by going overnight by bullock-cart. And so, after dinner, sentries crashing to attention, he emerged wearing his uniform coat over his pyjamas; lay down in the cart amidst cushions and straw, lit a cigar – surely a hazardous proceeding in the circumstances – and pronounced himself to be most comfortable. 'Excellent conveyance, a bullock-coach' he observed next morning on arrival at his destination. 'Slept splendid.' He then put on the rest of his uniform and his Star for the State entry and cantered up looking resplendent; except that there was still a piece of straw attached to his coat.[12]

While on tour, Mayo got to know the District Officers and other quite junior officials by going out shooting with them at the beginning of a long day's work or on his way from one camp to another. Some of these officials were afterwards subjected by him to severe strictures for their shortcomings; others received generous praise. Many became his friends, though never his favourites or confidants. He wrote of one elderly but invaluable officer, whom he wished to be kept on in the Service after the retirement age: 'I walked and rode with him for many miles last year, and I believe that at present there are very few men in India who could keep up with him either on foot or on horseback'.[13] On the whole, he had a very high opinion of his subordinates and gave them as much credit as he could. 'I believe' he once said in a speech, 'that in the history of the world no sovereign was ever served by a body of men who were engaged in more arduous, more useful and more important duties than are the servants of our Queen in India'.[14]

The quality he looked for most in his subordinates was, as he put it, 'an enthusiasm which makes a man believe in the possibility of improvement and strive to attain it'[15] – that same enthusiasm which he himself possessed in such abundance. He would take notice of enthusiasts whose schemes had failed to arouse the interest of officialdom. 'His earnestness impresses me' he said of an officer in the Central Provinces[16] who was convinced that his district possessed valuable deposits of coal – though the Geological Department had told him that the stuff wouldn't burn and the Provincial Government had condemned it as being too dangerously inflammable. With the support of Mayo, who wanted India to achieve a greater measure of self-sufficiency by the development of her mineral resources, the gentleman's coal was at last taken seriously and a pit was opened; the district subsequently became an important coal-mining centre.

If enthusiasm was the virtue Mayo looked for most in his subordinates, the fault he most detested was obstructionism. The Strachey brothers never saw him so angry as when he heard that the Political Agent in Jodhpur was taking up an obstructive attitude to a scheme for the Government to manufacture salt there: 'Damn him, what does he mean by it?' he burst out. In a sense, Mayo was a man in a hurry; but he was not one of those egoists who strive after a greater personal achievement than is possible in the time allotted to them. He was far too sensible to think that he could achieve everything he wished to achieve in the brief period of his Viceroyalty; but he felt that all the administrators of British India needed to be men in a hurry because there was in general so little time. 'We are trying' he said, 'to do in half a century in India a work that in other countries has occupied the life of a nation'.[17]

However impatient he may have been to get things done, Mayo never omitted to count the cost; for someone who gave the impression of being very much an aristocrat in the grand manner, with an Irish open-handedness, he was surprisingly cautious in his attitude to money; tending, if anything, to over-rate financial difficulties. He had an abiding horror of deficits – and when he took over the Viceroyalty, the Indian finances had shown a deficit for the past three years. 'I don't care' he used to say, 'if I stop every public work and suspend every improvement in India, but I *will* have the public expenditure brought within the public income.'[18] By a strict avoidance of waste, Mayo was able to carry on with his improvements and public works while actually reducing expenditure; and he hoped for further savings by implementing a measure originally proposed under Lawrence, whereby the Provincial Governments would in future have to find the money for local expenditure out of their own revenues. Hitherto, the Imperial exchequer had received all the revenues and paid for everything; which had inevitably made for reckless spending on the part of the provincial authorities, who not only counted on getting all the money they wanted out of the Government of India, but generally took a malign pleasure in getting as much as they possibly could. Mayo was determined to fight such provincialism, of which he complained with some asperity to the Governor of Madras:

> In the struggle between the Bureaux, most people seem to forget that there is such a thing as an Empire and a People of India . . . and that we hold the purse strings not in the interest one day of the Madras Army, at another of the education of the Bengalee Baboos, and on a third to build palaces in Bombay; but that our sole object is to work for the good of all.[19]

Sir Richard Temple, the Finance Member, a talented and energetic administrator but given to self-advertisement, seems to have been inclined to represent the finances as being in a better state than they actually were; an expedient not at all to the liking of Mayo, who was afterwards praised by Temple himself for being as punctilious with regard to accounts as a 'trained auditor'.[20] Mayo's cordiality towards his Council was thus temporarily diminished so far as Temple was concerned; and as well as contending with him, he joined with the Strachey brothers in making fun of his pomposity behind his back. At one Council meeting, when Temple, in a particularly long-winded speech, was explaining how the export duty had been taken off shawls but not off rice, Mayo passed the Stracheys a scrap of paper on which he had scribbled a jingle such as might have been heard at a dinner of the Kildare Hunt:

Sir Richard's the white-headed laddie
Who always takes care of the gurls:
He keeps on the burden on paddy;
But takes off the duty on shawls.[21]

Though he aimed at increasing the revenues as well as reducing expenditure, Mayo was anxious for all export duties to be removed as soon as possible. With his concern for the peasants and the underprivileged in general, he disliked any taxation which affected the poor; and while agreeing to an increase in the tax on salt, he carried out various reforms in order to make its collection more equitable. He preferred to tax the rich, who were benefiting from India's growing prosperity; and so in 1869 he revived the income tax, which by 1871 had converted the deficit into a surplus. Before this happened, however, the rate of income tax had to be raised to three per cent, which brought Mayo a fleeting unpopularity with the wealthy *zemindars* of Bengal and the non-official Europeans of Calcutta.

While insisting that they should pay their taxes, Mayo was tactful and conciliatory towards the Indian landowning aristocracy, just as he was towards the Ruling Chiefs; who for their part admired him for his looks, his debonair but dignified manner, his courtesy and his love of sport. No other Viceroy could have convinced the Princes better than did Mayo that the policy initiated by Canning would endure and that annexation was definitely a thing of the past. It was he who laid down the pattern of Britain's future relations with them; those who ruled badly had their powers transferred to a Council of Management, or were possibly even deposed in favour of an heir approved by the British; those who governed well were subjected to the least possible control. Mayo can also be said to have started the custom, followed by all future Viceroys, of taking a friendly interest in the personal well-being of the Chiefs and their families. He founded the college for the education of sons of the Princely Order at Ajmer, which bears his name.

Mayo's ability to handle Oriental potentates was particularly valuable when in March 1869 he was paid a visit by Shere Ali, who in the previous autumn had finally defeated his brother and rival and made himself the undoubted Amir of Afghanistan. The Amir had wanted to meet the Viceroy at Peshawar, close to the Frontier; but Mayo preferred the meeting to take place further south at Ambala, which was on his way from Calcutta to Simla, so that he would not appear to be going any distance to meet the Afghan ruler; moreover Ambala had a second psychological advantage in that to get there the Amir had to travel through the Punjab, where there was much evidence of British power and achievement. Having won his point as

Mayo with the Amir of Afghanistan, Shere Ali, at Ambala, March 1869

to the venue, Mayo flattered Shere Ali by receiving him with Royal honours: 'I now begin to feel myself a King!' exclaimed the delighted Amir during the course of the visit.[22] The Amir had come to Ambala in a suspicious frame of mind, hoping for a formal treaty and a fixed subsidy, neither of which Mayo had any intention of granting. He returned to Afghanistan grateful and reassured, though he took with him little more than a promise of arms and money at the discretion of the Government of India and a jewelled presentation sword which he chivalrously vowed never to draw except in the service of Britain. Without risking the hazards of any form of embroilment in Afghanistan, Mayo was able to win the Amir's friendship and establish his influence over him. Two years later, Shere Ali showed his personal regard for Mayo by sending him the somewhat impractical present – in view of the distance from Kabul to Calcutta – of a hundred camel-loads of fruit.

Mayo's policy towards Afghanistan and India's other neighbours represented a middle course between on the one hand, the policy of active intervention, and on the other, Lawrence's policy of 'masterly inactivity' – called by its opponents 'meddling and muddling'. His aim was for India to be bordered by 'strong, friendly and independent states' more interested in keeping in with Britain than with Russia or any other power; which could best be achieved, in his opinion, by adopting towards these states a policy of 'watchfulness and friendly intercourse'.[23] After the successful meeting with the Amir, Mayo felt confident that he could come to an agreement with Russia over spheres of influence; and actually sent his own envoy to St Pétersburg, as though he were an independent sovereign. The Tsar Alexander assured Mayo's envoy that his government had no intention of expanding any further in the direction of India, and ordered a party of his troops to be withdrawn across the Oxus.

Unlike so many of his contemporaries in India and at home, Mayo had little fear of Russia, which he had visited as a young man. On that journey – about which he had afterwards written quite a successful book – he had taken note of Russia's weaknesses; now, as the ruler of many millions of Muslims, he reckoned that he could, if he so wished, stir up a *jihad* in Russia's Central Asian provinces. 'I could make of Central Asia a hot plate for our friend the Bear to dance on' he declared in 1870.[24]

Not long before he wrote these words, Mayo had entertained the Tsar's future son-in-law; though at the time when the young Prince Alfred, Duke of Edinburgh, second son of Queen Victoria, was the Viceroy's guest, his marriage to the Grand Duchess Marie was not yet in the offing. Prince Alfred was the first member of the British Royal Family to visit India, and he was received in Calcutta by the Mayos with suitable magnificence. Government House was adorned with gilt Louis furniture brought specially from Paris and – since it was Christmas time – – mistletoe thoughtfully procured by Lady Mayo from Simla. There was a State Banquet in the Marble Hall, a fancy dress ball and a great assemblage of dignitaries at which the Prince was invested with the Star of India.

The Royal visit was the social high-water mark of Mayo's reign; but at all other times when the Mayos were in residence at Government House in Calcutta or at Peterhof in Simla there was splendid Viceregal hospitality. As well as the formal entertainments, there were festivities of a more light-hearted sort; once, at Peterhof, the Staff got up a spoof Durbar, with Burne impersonating the Viceroy; which made Mayo 'roll off his chair with laughter'.[25] Mayo had a great liking for simple fun; and when he heard that a certain quite junior official and his wife were giving a party which sounded promising, he asked the official in question why he had not been invited. On being reminded that it was not etiquette to invite the Viceroy, he said: 'I suppose it is permitted by etiquette for the Viceroy to ask himself? . . . I come!' The official warned him that there would be 'no champagne or anything of the sort' as he and his wife were young and impecunious. 'Champagne,' said Mayo, 'they let me have as much of that as I want at Government House and, as a fact, I seldom touch it.'[26]

Group at Government House, Calcutta, on the occasion of the visit of

Prince Alfred, Duke of Edinburgh, January 1870. Lady Mayo and Lord Mayo sit in the middle, with their small son Terence on the floor between them. Prince Alfred stands on Lady Mayo's right, with one of his shipmates, Lord Charles Beresford, the future Admiral, looking over his right shoulder. Major Owen Burne, Private Secretary to the Viceroy, wearing a striped cravat, stands behind the lady on Mayo's left. Lewin Bentham Bowring, formerly Private Secretary to Canning and now Chief Commissioner of Mysore and Coorg, stands behind Mayo

Towards the end of 1871, when Mayo's popularity had reached its zenith, there were signs of unrest in various parts of India. Mayo, who was inclined to be over-pessimistic as to the weakness of the British Raj – 'we hold India by a thread' he once told Argyll[27] – did not make much of the disturbances. He spoke of them laconically as 'a slight Mussalman rustle';[28] it being generally supposed that they were incited by the Wahabis, a fanatical Islamic sect; though some of the worst of the troubles were caused by the Kukas, a fanatical sect of Sikhs in the Punjab. Even after the murder in September 1871 of the Chief Justice of the Calcutta High Court – a crime popularly attributed to a Wahabi conspiracy – he refused to allow himself to be unduly alarmed. And when in January 1872 a Deputy-Commissioner in the Punjab reverted to the worst Mutiny methods and summarily executed forty-nine Kuka raiders by blowing them from guns, Mayo's indignation knew no bounds. 'I cannot tell you how much I lament this occurrence' he wrote to Argyll. 'It must weaken authority and bring disgrace on our Government . . . the act was one of great and unnecessary cruelty and I must condemn it . . . I am quite prepared to face the outcry that will be made, for I know I am right'.[29]

The offending Deputy-Commissioner was eventually removed from the Service; but as it happened, Mayo did not have to face any outcry. A few days after he had written his indignant letter, he sailed from Calcutta to visit Burma and the Andaman Islands. The Andamans, used by the Government of India as a penal settlement, had been visited by no previous Viceroy or Governor-General; the authorities were none too happy about Mayo's visit, particularly in view of the Wahabi scare. But Mayo had been fascinated by the Andamans ever since he first came to India; he had plans for founding a hill station on Mount Harriet, north of the Chief Andaman settlement of Port Blair. He was also anxious to see the progress of reforms which he had initiated in the administration of the islands. He was not worried about any possible danger; taking the philosophical view that a really determined assassin could get him anywhere. Before leaving Calcutta, however, the news of fresh

Government House, Calcutta. The State Drawing Room. The French furniture was introduced by Lord and Lady Mayo

disturbances along the North-West Frontier produced in him a mood of unaccustomed gloom, as though he had a premonition of impending disaster; and at times during the voyage he seemed dreamy and listless. At other times his normal high spirits returned. The journey was in some respects a pleasure trip; the warship in which Mayo and his family and Staff travelled was followed by another steamer carrying a cheery party of the Viceroy's personal guests, including some neighbours from County Kildare.

Mayo's visit to the Andamans began with a tour of the convict settlement at Port Blair on the morning of 8 February. The most rigorous security measures had been taken, and all went well. In the afternoon, he visited another island in the group; then, the day's official engagements being over, he crossed back to the principal island and went up Mount Harriet. It was a stiff climb, to an altitude of more than a thousand feet; most of his party were exhausted after six hours of inspections in the blazing sun. But Mayo was perfectly fresh, refusing the one available pony so that someone else could have it. At the top, he sat down for ten minutes to admire the sunset; murmuring to himself: 'How beautiful!'[30]

It was dark by the time the party had descended to the waterfront, where the launch was waiting to take the Viceroy back to his ship. Torch-bearers led the way, lighting up the tall figure of Mayo, who walked between Burne and Major-General Donald Stewart, Chief Commissioner of the Andamans. Just as Mayo was stepping forward to board the launch, Stewart went to give an order and the guards who cordoned off the pier opened their ranks to let him through. Before they could close up again, a tall and muscular Pathan rushed

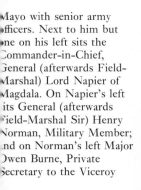

Mayo with senior army officers. Next to him but one on his left sits the Commander-in-Chief, General (afterwards Field-Marshal) Lord Napier of Magdala. On Napier's left sits General (afterwards Field-Marshal Sir) Henry Norman, Military Member; and on Norman's left Major Owen Burne, Private Secretary to the Viceroy

through the opening, 'fastened like a tiger' on Mayo's back and stabbed him twice between the shoulders.[31] Within a second or two, the man had been dragged away; and Mayo, who had staggered over the side of the pier, raised himself up out of the shallow water and said: 'Burne, they have done it!'[32] Then he said in a louder voice: 'I don't think I'm much hurt'.[33] A few minutes later he collapsed, the back of his grey *tussah* coat dark with blood. He was lifted into the launch, which immediately cast off; but by the time the ship was reached he was dead.

That Mayo, one of the best-loved of all the rulers of British India, should have been the only one to die by the hand of an assassin is irony such as is met with all too frequently in the history of mankind. His death seems to have been in no way related to any action of his as Viceroy, though many believed it to have been engineered by the Wahabis, in retaliation for certain firm if not unduly severe measures which he was obliged to take against them. There is no real evidence to suggest that it was anything but a private act of vengeance on the part of the assassin, a convict who, for good behaviour, was allowed some freedom. Mayo's death seems thus all the more tragic in its pointlessness; though it has a certain epic quality about it, in keeping with his life. It would have been a fitting end for any hero of story or legend: the darkness, the flickering torches by the water's edge, the springing figure with the knife, the stricken giant raising himself up out of the sea.

The obsequies of the murdered Viceroy were certainly on an heroic scale. The entire European population of Calcutta followed his coffin from Prinsep's Ghat to Government House, where it lay in state in the Council Chamber for two days while crowds of Indians

The Arrival of Mayo's coffin at Government House, Calcutta

and British came to pay their last respects. It was then taken in a warship back to Ireland and eventually laid to rest in the family burial-ground in County Kildare, where Mayo, before leaving for India, had himself chosen a place for his grave; as though for all his sense of buoyant anticipation at the prospect of his great office, something had told him that he would not return alive.

Of a Viceroy's five years, the last two were traditionally regarded as his real testing-time. It might thus be argued that Mayo's murder helped his posthumous reputation, in sparing him those last two critical years – as well as very likely winning for him tributes more glowing than what they might have been had he died in his bed at a ripe age. But the events of the two years following Mayo's death – which would have been the last two years of his Viceroyalty had he lived – did nothing to discredit his policies and beliefs; nor would it have been beyond his capabilities to deal with them. During those two years, India was peaceful, proving Mayo right in not making much of the Wahabi and Kuka scares; while nothing happened in the outside world to necessitate any major deviation from his foreign policy. The two great problems of those years were finance and the threat of famine, with both of which Mayo was thoroughly convers-ant. One would therefore be reasonably safe in assuming that had Mayo returned home alive and well at the beginning of 1874, he would still have ranked very high among the rulers of British India.

To speak of Mayo as the greatest Viceroy would be invidious; greatness being a quality impossible to gauge; but he could with justice be called the ideal Viceroy, as one of his most distinguished successors has called him.[34] He was fortunate, moreover, in being the ideal Viceroy at the ideal time to be Viceroy. A few years later, the telegraph – still in its infancy in Mayo's time – had robbed the Viceroy of much of his freedom of action; while the machinery of government had become so complicated that not even a ruler of Mayo's energy could supervise everything in the way that he was able to do. Those who said after Mayo's death that there would never be another Viceroy like him were right, if only for the reason that there never *could* be another Viceroy like Mayo.

'An extremely luminous
and amiable brick'

The next Viceroy, Lord Northbrook, was in complete contrast to his glamorous predecessor; rather colourless, a dry stick, shy and withdrawn. He came to India as a widower to whom the adjective elderly would certainly have applied; though he was then actually a year younger than Mayo had been when *he* arrived, overflowing with youthful high spirits. And whereas Mayo's looks conjured up youth, magnificence and strength, Northbrook was in appearance decidedly unromantic. His large, piercing eyes beneath bushy brows had a worried expression; his clean-shaven upper lip was too long to be attractive. His chin was fringed with those indeterminate whiskers – not exactly a beard – that were popular with Victorians of a somewhat older generation than his own; and he wore a small and wispy goatee.

'Just a nice, idiotic banker's clerk' [1] was how one of Northbrook's colleagues in Gladstone's Government described him; and though this was certainly unkind, it had in it more than a grain of truth. The fact that Northbrook was a Baring, a member of the famous banking family, originally German but a power in the City of London since the early years of George III's reign, would not in itself have justified this description; but he did have a mind that was slow, simple and unenterprising, as well as a concern for detail and an obsession with finance which were certainly in accordance with the popular image of a minor functionary in a bank, a sort of T.S. Eliot figure without the poetry. He also had in him something of the bureaucrat: a clerk in the Treasury, perhaps. He had, however, been neither a civil servant nor – despite his name and family background – a banker. His life up to the time of his appointment as Viceroy was divided between his Hampshire estate and politics. He held minor office in Liberal Governments, including the Under-Secretaryship for India with, as his Chief, the redoubtable Sir Charles Wood; to whom, as a young man, he was Private Secretary when Wood was President of the Board of Control.

Northbrook's Indian connection – which went further back than his association with Maharaja Wood, one of his Baring forebears having been Chairman of the East India Company and another in the

ɔrd Northbrook

Company's service – made him a less unlikely candidate for the
Viceroyalty than he might on the face of it have seemed. Another
qualification was his talent for finance; which had been the chief
problem facing the rulers of British India since the Mutiny. Then,
the fact that Northbrook, though young enough to stand the Indian
climate, was politically rather old-fashioned, no radical but a Whig in
the tradition of Palmerston, would have been an added recommendation at a time when, thanks to the statesmanship of Gladstone and
Mayo, the Viceroyalty was unusually well insulated from British
party strife. Yet another and obvious reason for Gladstone's
somewhat uninspired choice was that it cannot have been easy, in
1872, to fill a post which after Mayo's assassination seemed more

than ever ill-fated. It is significant that Northbrook was a widower; he did not have a wife whose health and safety would be a source of worry to him and who would herself be worried on his account.

Even without the misgivings of a wife, Northbrook's first reaction on being offered the Viceroyalty was to refuse it. He felt that his qualifications were doubtful; he had no ambition for high office; he did not want to leave his young grown-up daughter, Emma, nor take her with him to India and risk her health. But when the Viceroyalty was offered to him a second time, he felt it his duty to accept; and left at short notice, for the vacancy caused by Mayo's assassination had to be filled as soon as possible. On the voyage he studied Hindustani; though a knowledge of this, or of any other Indian language, was not a necessary qualification for a Viceroy.

Northbrook's arrival in Calcutta – though it made history by being the first time an incoming Viceroy arrived by rail rather than by sea – did not arouse much popular enthusiasm; which was only to be expected, for he must have seemed a poor substitute for Mayo. And he had disappointed the sportsmen by refusing to stop on his journey across India in order to shoot a tiger which had been marked down for his benefit; being impatient to get to work. The high officials, however, were quite favourably impressed by him. 'I like what I have seen of Lord Northbrook' wrote John Strachey to his brother, Richard. 'He is very well behaved to me.'[2]

Alfred Lyall, who was to be as influential as Strachey in the following decade, thought Northbrook 'cool, clever and good at business but as yet more like an English official than an Asiatic ruler'. A year later, when Lyall was Home Secretary, he wrote of him:

> Lord Northbrook is very civil and kind. I like him much as a man; having respect for his thoroughly clear head, great capacity for mastering points, governmental experience and resolution, and, above all, for his untinctured honesty of purpose. But he is a little too cautious and unimaginative; and he will insist on parliamentary expression in his writings, being always glad to get hold of a colourless or indifferent phrase . . . I could do him good by putting a little warmth and colour into him.[3]

Lyall, who was a poet as well as a great Indian administrator, fully appreciated what Mr. Philip Mason has called 'the poetry and the glory' of the Viceroyalty;[4] but Northbrook was one of those Viceroys, happily few in number, to whom the poetry and the glory meant little. He saw India not so much as an Empire to be ruled as a budget to be balanced; the very first letter he wrote to the Secretary of State after arriving in Calcutta was mostly about banks, credit and the money market: finance being a recurrent theme in his subsequent letters. To sustain him in his chief concern, Northbrook had a mastery of financial and economic facts and statistics greater than that of any other ruler of British India. He had also brought a budding financial genius with him as his Private Secretary: his cousin, Evelyn Baring, a brilliant if somewhat domineering young man who was later to become Earl of Cromer and the virtual ruler of Egypt.

However preoccupied Northbrook may have been with finance, he was no mere doctrinaire economist. His financial policy was motivated, at worst, by political expediencey and at best by humanitarianism. He was convinced, on assuming office, that India was in a state of unrest; and felt that this could be alleviated by reducing taxation. So he reduced the local taxes and in 1873 abolished the income tax altogether. In answer to the argument that the income tax affected only the rich, he maintained that it offended the particular prejudices of the Indian people; thus showing, behind all his apparent obsession with dry facts and figures, a most estimable regard for sentiment. While there may have been little connection between the abolition of the income tax and the decline in Wahabi and Kuka fanaticism, there is no doubt that Northbrook's policy had, as one Indian newspaper put it, 'a most soothing effect on the popular mind'.[5] Not only were the Indians naturally glad not to have to pay so much tax; but they were grateful for the slowing down in the process of modernisation resulting from the cuts in public expenditure which Northbrook was obliged to make in order to reduce taxation and yet maintain a surplus. Northbrook's brake on modernisation was more than just a financial necessity; he genuinely felt that the country needed a rest. In this, the great majority of educated Indians, who had suffered change and upheaval without cease since 1857, were inclined to agree with him.

If Northbrook's avowed tendency 'to let things go quietly on' [6] was welcomed by the Indians, it was naturally less acceptable to some members of the Government he had inherited from the Mayo regime; men to whom the term 'whiz kid' would now be applied. 'He hates doing *any*thing new' complained John Strachey to his brother Richard in 1874.[7] Yet such was Northbrook's tact, for all his brusqueness of manner – such was the warmth that lay beneath the 'frozen surface',[8] the dry humour that penetrated his shyness – that these men never ceased to like him. It may have been fortunate, however, that John Strachey – now Sir John – and the high-powered Sir Richard Temple both departed from the Council in the middle of Northbrook's Viceroyalty to become Lieutenant-Governors.

Northbrook's somewhat unexpected talent for making himself liked extended beyond his close associates to those whom he only met casually. His ability to put junior officials at their ease was noted by Lyall, who remembered, as a junior, being terrified in the presence of Canning.[9] He mixed no less easily with Indians, particularly with the fast-emerging educated middle classes, who liked him for his simplicity. But simple though his tastes may have been – 'Pray don't suppose' he once wrote wryly, 'that I *enjoy* an elephant procession' [10] – he accepted the fact that ceremonial was part of his duty. However much he may have husbanded the public monies, he was unsparing with his own income when it came to running the Viceregal establishment with fitting splendour. His reign saw no decline in Viceregal hospitality; though he felt much the same about grand entertainments as he did about processing on elephants: 'Ball till one, the worst part of my business this is!' [11] he grumbled in his diary. One suspects that, if he had been on his own, the life at Government House and Peterhof would, for all his good intentions, have become rather dull; he himself liking nothing better, after the long day's work, than a game of patience or 'a little mild whist' and an early bed. However, his daughter Emma, who came out to join him in his first cold weather, was there most of the time to do hostess for him; there was also a young Viceregal host in the person of his son Francis Baring, who served on his Staff as an ADC.

Francis took his father's place at the tiger shoots with which the Indian Princes so loved to regale the Viceroy. Only once did Northbrook himself go tiger-shooting, which he regarded as a waste of valuable time. On that occasion, he never got a shot; allegedly because the tiger was scared away by the snoring of his cousin and

Lord Northbrook with his daughter, Emma Baring, on his right and his cousin and Private Secretary, Evelyn Baring (afterwards Earl of Cromer) on his left

Private Secretary Evelyn Baring, who had fallen asleep. The future autocrat of Egypt denied this; while admitting to having been intensely bored by the sport.

Northbrook was more of a sportsman than might be supposed; devoted to fishing and in his younger days a keen foxhunter. Though he felt he could not spare much time for sport when he was Viceroy, he never missed the chance of a ride when he could escape from his desk; good enough in the saddle to have a go at pig-sticking on one occasion. Once at Simla he rode fifty-two miles in a day. At Simla, too, provided the weather did not bring on his asthma, he was an indefatigable walker; scrambling up and down mountains so that to be the ADC who accompanied him on these walks was a position not much coveted among his Staff. In Calcutta, he would cause anxiety to those responsible for the Viceregal security arrangements – which were now more stringent than formerly on account of Mayo's assassination – by trying to escape from his police and walk by himself to the Maidan. Northbrook rode and walked not only for exercise, and to visit out-of-the-way places on duty, but because he was a botanist and an inveterate sight-seer. His descriptions of scenery and architecture show that for all the apparent dryness of his financier's mind, he had an artist's power of observation. Thus of

Udaipur, he wrote:

> Take a lake about the size of Orta, with lower hills and of a lighter
> colour; put the walls of Verona on the lower hills with a fort or two,
> add islands smaller than those on the Lago Maggiore covered with
> marble pleasure palaces and domes, with white kiosks relieved by
> dark green trees, with a palm or two feathering above. Pile up half
> a dozen of French Norman Châteaux on the side and end with a
> piece of Venice.[12]

He was a talented watercolour painter and a connoisseur of pictures;
while he was Viceroy, he set about filling the gaps in the collection of
portraits of his predecessors at Government House. He also
commissioned his old friend Edward Lear to come out and paint a
series of Indian views for him. That Northbrook should have been
friends with the immortal Lear – who spoke of him as 'an extremely
luminous and aimiable brick'[13] – is yet another sign of his hidden
warmth. One can sense an affinity between this shy and withdrawn
financier Viceroy and the lovable misfit who wrote *The Owl and the
Pussycat*. Both were lonely men; the widower Northbrook felt
particularly lonely in his exalted and isolated position as Viceroy,
especially when his son and daughter were away in England. Like
Lear and so many other lonely bachelors and widowers, Northbrook
was attracted by children. In one of his letters to the Secretary of
State, he suddenly becomes human when he interrupts the inevitable
dissertation on banking and cash balances to tell of how he has visited
schools in Calcutta: 'The little urchins being very nice looking, like
English boys with a touch of bronze; some lighter and some darker,
and as sharp as possible'.[14]

For all his interest in the 'little urchins', Northbrook was not
inclined to do much for elementary education in India. To have
introduced any major educational schemes when he was Viceroy
would have been contrary to Northbrook's first principle of
economising in order to reduce taxation. He was only prepared to
depart from this principle when, towards the end of 1873, parts of
Bengal and Bihar were threatened with a severe famine. To the kind-
hearted and humanitarian Northbrook, the saving of life was all-
important, regardless of the cost: 'This is a case where, just as in war,
everything must go to the winds' he declared.[15] He was also
politician enough to point out that if the British were unsparing in
famine relief, it would strengthen their position in India by
convincing the Indians of their good intentions.

There were those who criticised Northbrook's methods of dealing
with the famine as unnecessarily expensive; particularly on account
of his rigid adherence to the doctrine of free trade. When the

Lieutenant-Governor wished to prohibit the export of rice from Lower Bengal, where it was in abundant supply, in order to 'force it back' north-westwards to the famine region, Northbrook was 'as much shocked as a bishop might be with a clergyman who denied all the Thirty-Nine Articles'.[16] So the export was allowed to continue and the Government paid to import rice from Burma; 'The strange spectacle was seen of fleets of ships, taking rice out from the Hughli and passing other ships bringing rice in'.[17] And the expensive imported rice was said to have been handed out too liberally by Temple, who was in charge of famine relief and set to work with all his customary abundance of zeal.

But while Northbrook's famine policy may have been expensive, at least it was successful. The scarcity was reckoned to have been the worst for a hundred years; yet there were very few deaths from starvation. And while the famine cost the Government over six million sterling, Northbrook – whose knowledge of figures was equalled only by his honesty – believed that if various mistakes and unnecessary wastages could have been avoided, there might have been a saving of half a million but no more. For all of Temple's alleged prodigality, the Government did not depart from the accepted doctrine of providing work for the able-bodied so that they could earn money with which to buy the rice that had been brought in; free food being given only to the old and infirm.

The calm, firm, business-like way in which Northbrook dealt with 'his' famine is in striking contrast to the sad ditherings of Lawrence during the previous visitation. Because of the famine, Northbrook cancelled the annual migration to Simla for the 1874 season; and apart from weekends at Barrackpore and a brief tour of Assam, he spent an entire hot weather in Calcutta; the only time after Canning that a Viceroy ever did so. It cost him dear in terms of illness among the members of his Government and Staff; though he himself suffered nothing worse than the parting from his daughter and son, whom he sent back to England for the summer. But while he did not spare his subordinates during those famine months, he afterwards praised them for their labours with a warmth of language quite untypical of him.

Northbrook's handling of the famine set the seal of success on his Viceroyalty, which was otherwise undistinguished. His temperament and his anxiety to reduce taxation and give the country a rest made for administrative inertia. In the crisis that arose over the misgovernment of the Gaekwar of Baroda, the feeble-minded Ruler of one of the most important Indian States – an event chiefly remembered for the Gaekwar's alleged attempt to poison the British Resident – Northbrook ended by doing the right thing, deposing the Gaekwar in favour of a twelve-year-old kinsman; but he did it in the

wrong way. In foreign affairs, Northbrook adhered to Mayo's policy; favouring a clear understanding with Russia, an independent Afghanistan and a well-defended North-West Frontier; but whereas under Mayo British influence in Afghanistan had increased, under Northbrook it declined. Mayo had, through the magic of his personality, kept the Amir in a good humour while giving him next to nothing. Northbrook, in continuing to refuse him any definite assurances, succeeded in making the Amir disgruntled.

Afghanistan was one of the issues on which Northbrook disagreed with Lord Salisbury, who became Secretary of State in 1874 when the Conservatives returned to power; and who favoured a 'forward' Frontier policy in accordance with Disraeli's new ideas of Empire. Another was the question of tariffs. Northbrook, though a free trader, had a very laudable desire to promote Indian manufactures – 'Whisper it not in Manchester' he drily admonished a friend.[18] He was therefore alarmed when Salisbury asked him to reduce the import duties on British cotton goods.

In September 1875, when the controversy between Northbrook

Group with Northbrook and Albert Edward, Prince of Wales, at Government House, Calcutta, Christmas 1875. Northbrook's daughter, Emma Baring, sits on the Prince's left and Salisbury over the tariffs was at its height, Northbrook asked to resign. He gave as his reason that he wished to devote more time to the interests of his son and daughter; but there seems little doubt that he decided to leave India a year before his term ended because he felt that he and Salisbury could no longer work together. Salisbury, whose brilliant and subtle intellect was hardly compatible with the slow, cautious, rather stubborn mind of Northbrook, held very definite views on India. By now, the electric telegraph was sufficiently advanced to enable the Secretary of State to govern India by remote control; though future Secretaries of State would often be happy to interfere as little as possible. Salisbury proceeded, as Northbrook put it, to 'rattle off orders from home'; which Northbrook regarded as an unconstitutional exercise of home authority.

Although Northbrook's premature departure was ostensibly for family reasons, he left India in the spring of 1876 amid some recriminations. His own feelings can be gauged from the last letter he wrote to Salisbury as Viceroy, which is curt even for him and contains none of the customary regrets expressed by Viceroys and Secretaries of State to each other at the ending of their association; there is nothing but a few last-minute points of business, the chief of them, as might be expected, to do with finance.[19] But while he may have felt some bitterness towards Salisbury and the Home Government, Northbrook left India in the knowledge that his departure was genuinely regretted not only by his Council and the majority of British officials, but also by a large part of the Indian population.

Northbrook also left with the satisfaction of knowing that the visit to India of Albert Edward, Prince of Wales, which took place during the closing months of his Viceroyalty, had been a triumphant success. He was praised not only for the arrangements of the Royal tour, for which he and his daughter were largely responsible; but also for his tactful handling of the problem of precedence arising from the fact that it was he rather than the Prince who represented the Queen. By 'quiet self-effacement'[20] the Viceroy made sure that the occasions when he was obliged to overshadow the Heir to the Throne were reduced to a minimum. Having gone to Bombay to greet him on his arrival early in November, Northbrook left as soon as possible, enabling the Prince to be lord of all he surveyed until they met again in Calcutta at Christmas. Then, after a fortnight of festivities that included balls and dinners, polo and fireworks, a Chapter of the Star of India and a State performance of a farce entitled *My Awful Dad*, the Prince set off on the next stage of his tour.

A month after the Prince's departure, Northbrook himself bade farewell to India. On his return home, despite his differences with the Government, he was given the customary promotion in the Peerage

The Indian tour of Albert Edward, Prince of Wales. The Prince serenaded by an Indian Band as he drives past at Poona

The Indian tour of Albert Edward, Prince of Wales. The Prince attacked by flies while tiger-shooting in Nepal

and became Earl of Northbrook. He was to live on into the present century, at last breaking the spell which had made the Viceroyalty fatal to British statesmen.

During the years that lay ahead, Northbrook played a part in politics and held office as First Lord of the Admiralty; but India continued to be his chief interest. No ex-Viceroy kept so closely in touch with Indian affairs for so long a period as he did – with the possible exception, in more recent times, of Lord Mountbatten. He corresponded regularly with each of the six Viceroys who came after him during his lifetime; not as a Viceregal ghost reluctant to retire from the scene of his past glory, but as an experienced elder statesman offering sound and disinterested advice. His successors valued his wisdom and found him a useful ally; he was always ready to do what he could to lessen any friction there may have been between them and the politicians at home. And while loyally supporting the British Raj, he also stood forth as a friend and champion of the Indians; endeavouring to make his successors appreciate the need to give them a fair share in the government of their country. If during his long years as an ex-Viceroy he occasionally managed, in his quiet way, to influence the affairs of India, it would certainly have been for the good. In fact Northbrook's standing among the Viceroys seems to depend as much on those later years as on his actual Viceroyalty.

6

The horse that bolted

One day in about the year 1840 the young Mr. Disraeli visited a lonely little boy at a private school and gave him a half-sovereign – the first tip he had ever received. 'Now I have tipped him again and put a crown on his head' Disraeli wrote some thirty-five years later,[1] having appointed Robert, Lord Lytton, the recipient of the half-sovereign, to be Viceroy in succession to Northbrook. One would like to think that the future Prime Minister saw a future Viceroy in that schoolboy who had suffered much as a result of the appalling marital quarrel between his politician and novelist father, the author of *The Last Days of Pompeii*, and his beautiful but neurotic mother; but in fact Disraeli chose Lytton at the instigation of Salisbury, who knew him well as a Hertfordshire neighbour. Nevertheless, Lytton seems a candidate more likely to have appealed to Disraeli's intuition than to Salisbury's commonsense; as much a stranger to politics as to Indian affairs. He had inherited his father's literary gifts; his poems, published under the pseudonym of Owen Meredith, had won some considerable acclaim; he was also a career diplomat who, at the time of his appointment to India, held the pleasant and not very exacting post of Minister to Portugal. He was indeed an even darker horse than Mayo had been seven years earlier. Unlike Mayo, he turned out to be no winner; but a horse that bolted.[2]

The racehorse analogy suits Lytton, for he had about him something of the nervous thoroughbred. Not that he could in any way have been called horse-faced; he was extremely handsome, which made up for his being rather short. He had a lofty brow and a prominent, finely shaped nose; his large, pensive eyes were of a particularly vivid blue which was set off by the darkness of his curly hair and full beard. The likeness to a racehorse lay not in any physical features – except possibly in his sensitive nostrils – but in the volatile temperament which his face somehow betrayed; as well as in his air of great breeding and distinction. The latter, like other things about him, was to a certain extent deceptive; for though undoubtedly an aristocrat, his lineage was not quite so illustrious as his father believed it to be when he decked out Knebworth, the family seat in

Lord Lytton. A portrait by G.F. Watts

Hertfordshire, with stucco battlements and 'impossible heraldries'.[3] Lytton had inherited that same slightly meretricious side to his nature which had made his father delight in genealogical pretensions and bogus medievalism; and which was responsible for the somewhat excessive glitter of his Viceroyalty.

While Lytton resembled his father in this respect and in his love of literature – and also dressed like him, in silk cravats and white bell-bottomed trousers that seemed to belong more to the days of the Dandies than to the subfusc middle years of Victoria's reign – he fortunately did not inherit any of his father's less agreeable characteristics. He was, in fact, a delightful person, 'a man full of feeling', as Queen Victoria called him[4]; whose good looks were complemented by a lively mind and a low, musical voice; and as well as being cultured – probably the most cultured of all the Viceroys – he was very clever. He was a loyal friend and a devoted husband and father. Though inclined to flirt, he was physically faithful to his wife, Edith, a tall, gentle golden-haired goddess who, for her part, adored him.

Edith Lytton, a niece of the great Foreign Secretary, Lord Clarendon, was typically English; and in this respect differed from her husband, whose years as a diplomat abroad had made him something of a Continental in outlook, manner and tastes; he wore rather more jewellery than it was customary for an English gentleman to wear at that time; he kissed ladies' hands; he was totally uninterested in sport. He had rejected Anglicanism and inclined towards the Church of Rome, while finding it hard to believe in a personal God. His spiritual home was Paris; his letters are larded with French phrases, he liked and admired everything French, even to advocating the adoption of the metric system.

The latter would also have appealed to him as a progressive, which he managed to be at the same time as being an old-world romantic. This was one of many contradictions in his nature. He was a strong upholder of aristocracy; his policies in India were to be almost a parody of the new Disraelian concept of Empire; yet he was at heart a liberal and numbered among his close friends such men as the Radical journalist John Morley and the turbulent anti-Imperialist Wilfrid Scawen Blunt. His Viceroyalty was to be criticised for its pomp and ceremony; yet he was a Bohemian whose manners were thought to be too informal for someone in his high position. 'I think I am as variable as the wind . . . I have at least half-a-dozen different persons in me' Lytton wrote of himself, towards the end of his life;[5] an accurate summing-up of his own character which tells us why, for all his good qualities, he was quite unsuited to be Viceroy. Perhaps as a result of his unhappy childhood, his temperament was unstable; he was too impulsive, too quick to take decisions.

Lytton was appalled at the prospect of going to India. He had no ambition for high office; he was happy in Portugal, living at Sintra with its delicious climate and scenery and its Byronic associations. As well as being temperamentally unsuited to the Viceroyalty and liable, for all his enjoyment of life, to fits of melancholy, he was in rather poor health. He suffered from piles, an unspeakable misfortune for a Viceroy who had to spend so much of his time sitting, whether at his desk, or in Council, or at levées and Durbars. Doubtless this complaint was the reason for Lytton's lolling attitude on the Viceregal throne, which must have contributed to the impression he gave of being an indolent, rather frivolous Viceroy. This impression was false; for Lytton took his Viceroyalty very seriously indeed; having accepted it against his will out of a strong sense of duty. He was encouraged to do so by Edith, though the Viceroyalty held as few attractions for her as it did for him. The risk of subjecting their three little girls, the youngest of whom was little more than a year old, to the Indian climate would have been particularly worrying since they had already lost two children. By the time they set out for India, Edith Lytton had the additional worry of being pregnant.

Lytton on the Viceregal throne. His lolling attitude is more likely to have been due to the distressing malady from which he suffered than to the indolence of which he was unfairly accused

However apprehensive he may have been at the prospect that lay ahead, Lytton was in high spirits on the voyage. 'We are now, I think, about half way through the Red Sea, which is in one of its most amiable moods, as blue as one of Mrs. Somerville's books and as smooth as a speech of Gladstone's' he wrote to the Queen, who found his letters so entertaining with their vivid if slightly precious descriptions that she quite forgave his solecism of writing to her in the first person instead of, as was customary, in the third. He even treated his Sovereign to a remark which many would have thought not quite proper, when telling her about Bombay: 'Its very mixed population is clad in an almost infinite variety of costume, except those who are not clad at all'.[6]

Even before reaching Calcutta, Lytton acted impulsively. He was so impressed by Sir John Strachey – now Lieutenant-Governor of the North-Western Provinces – with whom he stayed when he broke his rail journey at Allahabad, that he asked him there and then to become his Finance Member. 'With your help' he said, in language redolent of his flamboyant personality, 'I shall be afraid of nothing. You and I together shall find means to carry out everything that we desire.'[7] Strachey felt it his duty to comply with Lytton's request, though he was naturally loth to give up his Lieutenant-Governorship and go back to the Council – a step down in glory as well as in salary. In after years, he would say that he had been so captivated by the new Viceroy that he could refuse him nothing; but at the time he was inclined to mistrust Lytton's charm and compared himself to Jesus being tempted with all the kingdoms of the world by the Devil: 'I do not doubt that the hoofs and horns may protrude occasionally' he told his brother Richard.[8] The hoofs and horns did not in the event protrude; and Strachey became Lytton's right-hand man and devoted friend. That Lytton was more than the glamorous lightweight which he is often depicted as being can be seen in the fact that the masterful Strachey did not become the real ruler of India during his reign; but was content to support Lytton's policies and make the rest of the Council toe the line. Thanks to Strachey, Lytton was able to disregard the opinions of the other Members of his Council – 'the six second-rate men', as he called them.[9]

Lytton seems to have been prejudiced against these men from the very start. As loyal colleagues of Northbrook, whom they felt had been treated badly, they naturally viewed the advent of the new Viceroy without much enthusiasm; but Lytton was convinced of their hostility even before he assumed office; writing of them to Salisbury in a waspish and at times almost hysterical manner. Feeling the need to say something, as he put it, 'studiously sedative to the quills of these fretful porcupines',[10] he made a speech at his swearing-in; which was contrary to all precedent. This was only a foretaste of Lytton's unconventional behaviour. Since it was already the middle of April when he arrived, he only spent a couple of weeks at Government House before migrating to Simla, where Edith and the children had gone ahead of him; but during that time, as he told Salisbury, he 'shocked all the social proprieties of Calcutta by writing private notes to Members of Council, calling on their wives, holding levees by night instead of by day'.[11] However little he may have cared about conventions, he was extremely worried lest he should put a foot wrong in more serious matters; it seemed to him that he was 'treading on eggs at every step'.[12] In fact he worried himself sick, literally; before leaving Calcutta he was afflicted with nausea, which he failed to shake off even after he had moved into the cooler Simla air. In his position, it would have been an even more distressing malady than the piles; with incessant retching which must have been largely nervous and which his doctors feared would damage his heart.

Feeling as rotten as he did, it is no wonder that Lytton had a bad first impression of Simla, which he described to his friend Morley as 'a mere bivouac'.[13] He found Peterhof uncomfortably small, complaining that he could never be alone here. The sentries outside his window were too close; 'three unpronounceable beings in white and red nightgowns' rushed after him if he walked about indoors, and if he set foot in the garden, he was 'stealthily followed by a tail of fifteen persons'.[14] He was not much attracted to Simla society, the ladies being too virtuous for his taste. 'I do miss the pleasant scamps and scampesses of pleasant France' he said, in a letter to Lady Salisbury, 'and having seen virtue embodied in the form of Lady – – I don't agree with Schiller that if virtue were a woman, all the world would fall in love with her . . . I envy you the pleasure of living amongst so many naughty people.'[15]

Edith Lytton was likewise out of sympathy with her new surroundings. She thought that the Indian servants smelled and she found it hard to put up with the absence of water-closets. She felt she was not popular with the other Simla ladies; mistaking their shyness in the presence of the Vicereine for hostility. She seems to have been one of those women who, though loved and admired by all who knew her well, failed to get through to strangers. She certainly tried her best; and while at Simla was at home for an hour each day to any ladies who cared to come and see her; hoping in this way to share their joys and their sorrows.

Simla society for its part did not take kindly to Lytton's informality and Bohemian ways: his habit of smoking between courses and in the drawing room after dinner, his 'incessant indulgence in liqueurs'.[16] People who expected the Viceroy to be dignified did not appreciate his rather boisterous *bonhomie*. A senior officer in the Political Service was furious when, at a full-dress function, Lytton plucked him playfully by the beard with the remark: 'A virgin beard, I'll swear!' [17] It was unfortunate for Lytton that he just did not have it in him to be affable and dignified at the same time. He was also inclined to be selfish where his own enjoyment was concerned; so that if he found a lady who came up to his standards of feminine charm, he was liable to sit talking nonsense to her all evening, neglecting his more important guests. Another way in which Lytton and Edith Lytton gave offence was by inviting Indians to balls. It is certainly to the Lyttons' credit that they were totally devoid of racial prejudice; however, the fact that Indians were not invited to balls by their more recent predecessors – having been invited at an earlier period again – was due not so much to racialism as to Victorian decorum; it was thought undignified for British ladies to dance while the Indian guests, who were predominantly male, watched them, as though they were a *nautch* put on for their benefit. There had never been any objection to Indians being invited to Government House parties at which there was no dancing.

Eyebrows were also raised at the Lyttons' rather bold redecoration of the Peterhof ballroom; the Japanese wallpaper which had formerly been here was stripped and the walls painted red as a background to some fine pictures brought from Knebworth; the effect would have been good except that the walls clashed horribly with the scarlet of the officers' coats. But if people had reservations about the decor – and also the decorum – of Peterhof under the new regime, they certainly could not fault the hospitality. Though Lytton was not so well off as Northbrook, he took on the latter's excellent French chef; who invented a dish – *Quenelle à la Lytton* – in his honour. He also had an Italian confectioner named Peliti, whom he brought out with him; and he brought out some talented German musicians in order to turn the Viceroy's Band from a brass band into an orchestra; they played quartettes in the drawing room after dinner. It augured well for Lytton's Viceroyalty that he had as his Private Secretary the popular Owen Burne, who held the same post with such success under Mayo; while his ADCs included that celebrated soldier and sportsman, Lord William Beresford; whose rollicking, devil-may-care Irish gaiety and talent for handling people and getting things done was to make him the beau-ideal of Viceregal courtiers.

In the middle of the Lyttons' first Simla season, Edith gave birth to a son and heir. The Queen asked to be the child's godmother; Salisbury, who was godfather, wrote referring to the infant as the *Porphyrogenitus*. When Lytton heard the news of his son's birth, he was out of Simla, on a tour of the mountainous country near Narkunda; in wild romantic surroundings his party drank the baby's health in bumpers of champagne, though he was himself too tired and excited to eat or drink. Lytton's Viceroyalty was full of sublime

Lytton on the Viceregal
throne in Star of India
robes

moments such as this; the capacity for enjoyment, which he shared
with his entourage, frequently gave it this delightful *fête champêtre*
quality. At other times, as though to match his own fits of
melancholy, it was a nightmare. Apart from the troubles of his reign,
and the criticism which he had to endure, there was his uncertain
health. His children were constantly ill; at one time, to make matters
worse for Edith, their governess and English nurses were all down
with typhoid. In addition to these misfortunes, Lytton and his
entourage were prone to accidents which, though serious enough,
had something comic about them. His Viceroyalty nearly came to a
tragic and untimely end in his first Simla season when he and his

pony disappeared over a precipice; fortunately the ground below was so wet and soft that both were unscathed. One of his ADCs, Captain Harcourt Rose, was emasculated by the bite of a donkey; Lytton remarked rather heartlessly that he would now be well qualified for employment in any Oriental Court but his own.[18]

The pleasures and sufferings of Lytton's life in India did not distract him from his work. 'Not even constant physical discomfort can lessen the intellectual and moral relish of the work I have now in hand' he told a friend soon after his arrival.[19] Contrary to popular belief, his natural frivolity did not extend to the affairs of State: 'In spite of his tom-fooling, he is not a fool' Richard Strachey wrote of him.[20] He was as hard-working as most of the rulers of British India; and during his Viceroyalty had no time for writing poetry. But appreciating the 'poetry and glory' of his office as much as he did, he rather wasted his energies in giving a fine literary style to his minutes and dispatches and in adorning his official letters with literary quotations; in a typical letter to his Foreign Secretary, Alfred Lyall, written in his own fine hand, he begins by saying something about Afghanistan, then launches forth into a two-page extract from Dante's *Purgatorio*, then concludes with a few words more on official matters.

He also carried on a rather too extensive private correspondence, writing elegantly and entertainingly in French as well as in English: 'Comme tous les poètes, il est très nerveux et un peu bizarre' was how he described the poetic Raja of Mandi to a French friend, an aphorism that would have applied equally to himself.[21] He regaled Lady Holland with a long and highly coloured account of the palace at Jaipur, which was very different from Northbrook's throwaway impressions of the Indian scene: 'Courts of all sizes and characters, gorgeously canopied, some of them thronged with trumpeters and spearmen, horses and elephants splendidly housed . . . walls hung with the richest tapestries and silks broidered with pearls, and literally dripping precious stones'.[22]

What with his work as Viceroy, his letter-writing, his flirtations and his other amusements – which included that most time-consuming of hobbies, amateur theatricals – Lytton was obliged to burn the candle at both ends. Such a way of life cannot have made for good judgement or the clearest of heads, particularly as he took virtually no exercise. His only outdoor pursuit was sending up fire balloons, which came to be something of an obsession with him; he would send one up on every possible occasion, regarding it as a good augury if the balloon flew well.

Lytton's erratic habits must have been trying for those who worked with him; yet in most of these people, as in John Strachey, he inspired the affection which he had so great a talent for inspiring in his friends. Some of them, however, had reservations about him. Alfred Lyall got on well with him as a fellow-poet; but thought him 'an uncertain man' and felt it would be easy to fall from his favour if he were with him too much.[23] Mortimer Durand, the young rising star of the Foreign Department, thought him too picturesque in looks and dress. Both Lyall and Durand recognised the touch of genius in him and also the courage.

Lytton showed his courage early in his reign when an English barrister in Agra, whose rough treatment of an Indian servant had caused him to die of a ruptured spleen, was fined no more than the equivalent of £3 by the local magistrate. Not only did Lytton order the magistrate to be suspended, but he publicly censured the Government of the North-Western Provinces, in which the incident took place, for its failure to investigate 'a case so injurious to the honour of British rule and so damaging to the reputation of British justice in this country'.[24] This was taken as a reflection on the Civil Service and aroused the hostility of the official world; as well as causing Lytton to be abused in newspapers representative of the less reputable sections of British-Indian opinion. To Lytton, such animosity was merely 'a bore';[25] and he took comfort in the praise which his action won him in the Indian Press. The incident served to demonstrate Lytton's impartiality as between Indians and British; an impartiality which took a more positive form when he attempted to make it easier for Indians to enter the public service.

Although it had been possible for Indians to become full-blown Civilians since before the Mutiny, few of them had done so because it entailed sitting for a competitive examination in England. Since 1870, the Government of India had been able to appoint Indians to official posts even if they had not taken the examination; but little had been done in this respect by the time Lytton became Viceroy. Lytton's solution to the problem was to found a new service, the Statutory Civil Service, open to Indians of good family, character and education; its members could hold some of the posts hitherto reserved for the Indian Civil Service proper, though not the highest posts. This discrimination inevitably made the Statutory Service unattractive to Indians of the first calibre; and it consequently proved a failure, being abolished after only eight years. And while the scheme represented a genuine effort on Lytton's part to increase the number of Indians in public employment, it was also an attempt to keep out the sort of Indians whom he regarded as undesirable – the new educated middle classes described by him as 'baboos whom we have educated to write semi-seditious articles in the native Press, and who really represent nothing but the social anomaly of their own position'.[26] Lytton's idea was that the Statutory Service should be restricted to the Indian aristocracy. He saw a parallel between the

British Raj and the old Austrian rule in Northern Italy, which he had known as a young diplomat; the latter had foundered, or so he believed, because the otherwise benevolent and conscientious alien rulers had 'snubbed and repressed the native *noblesse*'.[27] Like Canning before him, he felt that Britain could best maintain her position in India by conciliating and making use of the Chiefs and nobles. Even in Canning's day, this attitude was a little out of date; now, twenty years later, the educated middle classes were fast becoming the most important element in Indian society. That Lytton should have regarded them as being of little account shows that, for all his intelligence, he failed to understand the India of his time and to see the way things were going.

What Lytton and his admirers regarded as the most significant event of his reign was a spectacular effort to unite the Indian Princes and magnates in loyalty to the British Crown. This was the Imperial Assemblage, a Durbar on an unprecedented scale held at Delhi to proclaim Queen Victoria Empress of India. Lytton had been Viceroy for less than a month when he conceived the idea of this pageant; and he wrote to Disraeli – who had just succeeded in piloting the Bill conferring the Imperial title on Queen Victoria through Parliament in the face of violent Liberal opposition – giving him his thoughts on the subject. He felt that the announcement of the Queen's new title should be accompanied by 'a few acts of liberality' to the assembled Chiefs; and proposed presenting them with banners and allowing them additional guns in their salutes; which he was convinced, after what he believed to have been 'a careful study of native character', would be 'much more effective than any political concession'.[28] Writing to Salisbury soon afterwards, he repeated this piece of wishful thinking regarding the Indian Princes: 'They are easily affected by sentiment, and susceptible to the influence of symbols to which facts very inadequately correspond'.[29]

The Assemblage lasted for more than a fortnight over the Christmas period; the actual proclamation of the Queen as Empress was on New Year's Day 1877. No fewer than sixty-three Ruling Chiefs were present, from the Nizam of Hyderabad downwards; together with some three hundred great nobles. In all, about 100,000 people converged on Delhi that Christmas. The proclamation itself took place in a great open plain where ornate pavilions with canopies and hangings of red, white, blue and gold, had been erected. Canvas cities, the camps of the assembled potentates and of the Viceroy, Governors and Commander-in-Chief, stretched in all directions. The Viceroy's camp was lit with gas manufactured by the enterprising Maharaja of Jaipur; the lamp standards were designed by Lockwood Kipling, whose son Rudyard was still only a schoolboy.

On the whole, the show was well organised, dignified and

impressive; it also cost surprisingly little. Though in the words of Mortimer Durand, 'as regards some of the details connected with it, the distance between the sublime and the ridiculous had not always been maintained'.[30] When the *feu-de-joie* was fired after the proclamation, the attendant elephants 'scampered off, dispersing the crowd in every direction';[31] luckily the plain was so large and open that nobody was hurt. A levee at which 3,000 people were presented to the Viceroy was held in too small a tent and there was a fearful crush; one portly Indian gentleman was heard crying out 'Master, O Master! I die here'; another sat on a sofa which collapsed under him.[32] More serious, the brass poles of the richly embroidered banners which Lytton presented to the Ruling Chiefs – and which he was certain they would value more than 'any political concession' – had, through an unfortunate mistake, been made much too heavy; so that it took two stalwart Highlanders to carry them. Lytton, in presenting a certain Chief with his banner, expressed the hope that it would never be unfurled without reminding him of the weight of his responsibilities. 'Yes, yes, Lord Sahib, quite true' replied the Chief in a loud voice. 'But the banner is so infernally heavy that I can never unfurl it!'[33] Lytton's other 'liberality', an increase in the number of

The Imperial Assemblage, Delhi, 1877

guns to which the Chiefs were entitled in their salutes, proved even
more of an anticlimax; for since a two-gun increase was given all
round, nobody obtained any advantage over his fellows.

Apart from the banners and guns – and gold medals designed by
the Queen-Empress herself – the Assemblage gave the Indian
notables virtually nothing. Lytton had intended that it should mark
the inauguration of an Indian Privy Council and Peerage, which
would have given prominent Indians a say in the affairs of State; but
the Home Government vetoed these proposals and substituted a
merely honorific body of 'Councillors of the Empress'. Likewise
stillborn were Lytton's romantic but incongruous schemes for an
Indian Heralds' College and for allotting to each of the greater
Ruling Chiefs a specific duty redolent of the Age of Chivalry – thus
the Maharaja of Kashmir was to be Warden of the Marches.

If the Assemblage had little enough to offer the Princes, it was of
still less significance to India as a whole. Even so staunchly pro-
British a newspaper as the Calcutta *Statesman* criticised Lytton for
the 'tinsel pageantry' of his proceedings.[34] There were more
stringent attacks in the newspapers of the Bombay Presidency on the
grounds that it was no time for pomp and circumstance when
Southern India was in the throes of a famine. This opinion was
shared by the Governor of Bombay, Sir Philip Wodehouse, who was
so taken up with famine relief that he tried to get out of coming to the
Assemblage; causing Lytton to write to him petulantly that 'the
failure of the Assemblage would be more disastrous to the permanent
interests of the Empire than twenty famines'.[35]

Though his language on this occasion was that of an irresponsible
child, Lytton took the 1877 famine as seriously as Northbrook had
taken the famine of three years earlier. One useful purpose served by

the Assemblage was that it enabled Lytton to discuss famine relief with Wodehouse and with the Governor of Madras, the Duke of Buckingham and Chandos. The measures adopted in the two Presidencies were very different; Wodehouse was increasing public works to provide employment; the Madras Government was importing vast quantities of grain and feeding the people in relief camps, where they became demoralised and diseased. As a result, the famine was costing much more both in terms of life and of public money in Madras than it was in Bombay. When the Central Government intervened, the Duke of Buckingham became touchy and unco-operative. Eventually a scheme was devised for reorganising the famine policy of the Madras Government and at the same time saving Buckingham's face; in order to persuade the Duke to agree to it, Lytton himself travelled to Madras at the height of the hot weather.

Before setting out from Simla, he was obliged to undergo a pile operation; so that he started the long and sweltering train journey in great pain. As he headed southwards, his sufferings grew less; though the prospect of his encounter with the Duke made him nervous: 'I feel like the valiant Thumb facing the Castle Glum and the Giant Fie-Fau-Fum!' he told Edith in a letter.[36] There is something rather touching about Lytton's nervousness, for he was, after all, the Viceroy; but as a child of the Early Victorian Age, he would always have stood in awe of a Duke; albeit a Duke who was somewhat impoverished.

When Lytton met the Duke, he was not at his freshest; having characteristically lain awake for most of the previous night reading a French novel; however, he had no difficulty in charming him into accepting his proposals. After he and Buckingham had conferred, Lytton toured famine districts not only in Madras but also in Mysore and the Bombay Presidency; he described the Madras relief camps with some exaggeration as being 'like picnics'.[37] While at Madras, Lytton received anonymous letters from two ladies; one of them expressing concern about his soul, the other telling him that she could not sleep for thinking of his eyes and signing herself: 'Thine for ever, even though in vain'.[38]

As well as dealing effectively with the famine which occurred during his reign, Lytton took steps to make it easier for famine to be dealt with in the future. He appointed a Famine Commission under the Chairmanship of Richard Strachey, the findings of which were adopted as a permanent Famine Code; he set up a relief organisation and instituted the custom whereby the Government set aside something like a million sterling each year as Famine Insurance. Like Northbrook, Lytton showed himself at his best as a Viceroy while combating the terrible scourge of famine.

Unfortunately for Lytton's future reputation with the Indians, his work for famine relief was overshadowed by two highly unpopular measures. The first of these was the Vernacular Press Act of March 1878. Some of the newspapers in the Indian languages were in the habit of making wild allegations against the Government; and whereas the Government had hitherto managed to keep things under control by issuing occasional warnings to offending editors, Lytton saw fit to introduce what he himself described as 'a very stringent gagging Bill'.[39] His other unpopular move was to cut down the import duties on Lancashire cotton goods; which he did at the instigation of the Home Government and by overruling the majority of his Council. The readiness with which he agreed to put British interests before those of India in this matter contrasted badly with Northbrook's determination to maintain the duties at all costs. It was particularly unfortunate in that Lytton had shown a personal interest in the Indian cotton industry and felt the need for factory legislation such as Lord Shaftesbury had introduced in Britain; in fact he made a start in this respect.

Lord and Lady Lytton, family and Staff, Government House, Calcutta, 1877. *Front row, from the left*: Mrs. Owen Burne. Sir John Strachey. Lord Lytton. Lady Lytton. Lady Strachey. Colonel Owen Burne, Private Secretary.
Second from the left in the back row is Lord William Beresford, ADC; and next to him, on his left, is the unfortunate Captain Harcourt Rose, ADC. On Captain Rose's left, in uniform, is Lady Lytton's cousin, Colonel George Villiers, who subsequently got involved in a scandal over a woman

If Lytton's popularity with the Indians declined during the course of his reign, his flaunting of the conventions prevented him from becoming really popular with the British. The stories that were told of his Bohemian ways grew more exaggerated as time went on; for example, it was said that he would interrupt his levees in order to smoke a cigarette on the Viceregal throne; whereas according to Edith, he did nothing worse than have 'a puff or two' during the customary pause in the proceedings.[40] More damaging were the rumours that began to circulate about the moral laxity of the Viceregal court; which gained substance when Edith's cousin, Colonel George Villiers, a member of Lytton's Staff, got involved in a scandal over a woman. Lytton's propensity for flirting inevitably gave rise to rumours concerning his own private life; he was alleged to be showing favouritism to the husbands of his two special lady friends – particularly to the husband of 'pretty little Mrs. Plowden', who once appeared at a Viceregal function 'with a lovely water lily stuck just where she ought to sit'.[41] In fact he went no further with these ladies than giving them the occasional kiss; but all Simla naturally believed that he was their lover; as Wilfrid Scawen Blunt – himself a seasoned womaniser – pointed out to him when staying as his guest; telling him that he was merely getting compromised without having any real fun. Lytton's friendship with Richard Strachey's wife Jane, an attractive young woman of literary tastes, has given rise to the legend that he was the father of her son, Lytton Strachey; who was his godchild and named in his honour; though at the time when the future High Priest of Bloomsbury was conceived, Lytton was in India and Jane Strachey in England.

Many of the allegations about Lytton's private life might never have been made had not his Viceroyalty ended in disaster over the Afghan question. Disraeli and Salisbury wished to assert British authority in Afghanistan in order to counteract the growing influence of Russia; Lytton was briefed by them to carry out this policy 'boldly'.[42] On assuming office, he made overtures to the Amir, Shere Ali, which brought no favourable response. Whether he began by genuinely hoping to restore the good relations with the Afghan ruler that had existed in Mayo's time, or whether he was determined to pick a quarrel with the Amir from the very start has since been a major point of contention between Lytton's apologists and his critics; certainly he was not unduly disappointed by the Amir's attitude. He blamed it on Russia, being even more Russophobe than Disraeli. The prospect of a war with Russia over Turkey, which seemed likely towards the end of 1876, filled him with excitement; he made grandiose plans for the Indian Army to take the offensive in Central Asia.

Lytton had been sent to India to carry out Disraeli's and

Salisbury's 'forward' Afghan policy by skilful diplomacy; but although he managed to score at least one major diplomatic triumph – his treaty with the Khan of Kalat, which enabled Britain to command the more westerly route into Afghanistan by garrisoning the important frontier-post of Quetta – he became increasingly convinced, as the months went by, that Afghanistan could only be satisfactorily brought under British influence by war. The Home Government – a Government reputedly jingoist, to use a word which came into the English language at that very time – was alarmed. Having so far managed to avoid hostilities with Russia over the Turkish question, Disraeli and Salisbury had no desire to be embroiled in a war of Lytton's making; whether with Russia or even only with a recalcitrant Amir. Salisbury attributed Lytton's growing belligerence to 'military seducers';[43] and in this he was probably

The Plowden family in India. Lytton was attracted by 'pretty little Mrs Plowden', who once appeared at a Viceregal function 'with a lovely water lily stuck just where she ought to sit'

right. Though himself entirely unmilitary, Lytton made friends with
soldiers in a way that he did with only a very few civilians, such as
John Strachey. So much did he allow himself to be seduced by the
military that he was alone among nineteenth-century rulers of British
India in advocating that the Army should be controlled entirely by
the Commander-in-Chief, instead of jointly by the Commander-in-
Chief and the Council, as it was under the existing constitution.

As long as Salisbury was Secretary of State, Lytton's martial
enthusiasms were effectively curbed. In March 1878, however,
Salisbury became Foreign Secretary and was replaced at the India
Office by the easy-going Lord Cranbrook, who allowed Lytton to get
the bit between his teeth. That year's war scare brought increased
Russian activity in Central Asia; which culminated in the dispatch of
a Russian mission to Shere Ali at Kabul. Lytton decided to retaliate
by sending a British mission to the Amir and demanded that he
should order the Russians to withdraw. In fact the British Government had already protested at St Petersburg about the Russian
mission; and in any case the Russians had themselves decided to
refrain from any serious negotiations with the Amir now that the
danger of a war with Britain had receded with the signing of the
Treaty of Berlin. Lytton somehow did not know about the British
Government's protest; relations between him and the Cabinet in
London were, at this crucial moment, remarkably confused; the
Cabinet, moreover, was suffering from indecision. Such was the
confusion that Lytton was able to disobey the Cabinet and order his
mission to advance; and as was to be expected, since the Amir had
firmly refused to receive a British mission two years earlier, it was
stopped by Afghan troops. This created a situation in which the
honour of British India could only be saved by a military invasion of
the Amir's territories such as Lytton had for some time been
contemplating; and to which the Home Government, albeit reluctantly, now had to agree.

And so, in November 1878, Lytton declared war. His military
commanders, including the future Field-Marshal Lord Roberts,
whom he regarded as his own particular discovery, and Sir Samuel
Browne of the eponymous belt, led a triple advance into Afghanistan;
the Amir's army quickly fell to pieces and Shere Ali himself fled
northwards into Russian territory where he conveniently died in the
following February. With Shere Ali out of the way, there was the
question of what was to be done with his kingdom. Lytton was at first
inclined to favour a policy of 'disintegration', of carving up
Afghanistan and annexing part of it to India. Instead, he decided to
come to a settlement with Shere Ali's son Yakub, whom he
recognised as the new Amir. His representative in the negotiations
was Major Louis Cavagnari, an extremely able young officer with

great experience of the Frontier tribes. The fact that Cavagnari was the son of a Genoese who had served under Napoleon would have made him doubly attractive to the cosmopolitan Viceroy; who treated him as a friend and confidant, even going so far as to criticise the vagaries of the Cabinet to him.

In May 1879, Cavagnari and Yakub concluded a treaty; according to which the British would control the Amir's foreign policy, maintain a permanent envoy at Kabul and take over three districts of strategic importance on the Afghan side of the border. Lytton appeared to have won his bold game. Disraeli, who had been extremely angry with him for bouncing the British Government into a war, now showered him with congratulations: 'It will always be a source of real satisfaction to me that I had the opportunity of placing you on the throne of the Great Mogul'.[44] Though Gladstone and other Liberal leaders and the Liberal Press had been subjecting Lytton to a campaign of vituperation ever since the start of his Afghan adventure, which they regarded as contrary to the Rights of Man and likely to discredit Britain in the eyes of the Indian people, British public opinion was turning in his favour. His settlement even met with the approval of John Morley, who earlier in the year had joined so wholeheartedly in the Liberal outcry that Lytton had addressed him pathetically as 'Dear friend of former days'.[45] Lytton felt confident that Cavagnari, whom he sent to Kabul as envoy, would soon become rather like the British Resident in an Indian State, exercising much of the Amir's authority; but Cavagnari himself put his chances of coming back alive at four to one against. And sure enough, after he had been in Kabul for little more than a month, he and his staff and almost his entire military escort were massacred by rebellious Afghan troops.

'The poor Viceroy is of course very miserable but he is very brave' wrote John Strachey after the terrible news from Kabul had reached Simla.[46] The massacre, though it was little more than a tragic accident, put an end to Lytton's settlement and brought a renewal of hostilities, which were to drag on for another year. Roberts marched to Kabul where he avenged the deaths of Cavagnari and his comrades by some eighty executions, rather to the dismay of Lytton, who had told him to be stern but not cruel. Yakub abdicated and went into exile in India. Lytton and the Home Government now decided to try the policy of 'disintegration'; the province of Kandahar was to be made into a separate kingdom under British protection, the rest of Afghanistan was to be handed over to Abdur Rahman, a grandson of Dost Mohammad known to be strong though suspected of being pro-Russian.

While everything was still in the melting-pot, the people of Britain went to the polls for the General Election which took place during

Sir Louis Cavagnari
(second from left) with the
Amir Yakub (centre) at
Kabul in 1879, shortly
before Cavagnari and his
staff and most of his escort
were massacred by
rebellious Afghan troops

the last days of March and the first days of April 1880. The Afghan question was a major issue; Gladstone had stumped Midlothian reminding the electors that 'the sanctity of life in the hill villages of Afghanistan, among the winter snows' was 'as inviolable in the eye of Almighty God' as their own.[47] Rather to people's surprise, the Liberals won a resounding victory; and when the results were known, Lytton resigned. He had little choice in the matter; for the Liberal leaders, having denounced him in terms such as had never before been used of a Viceroy – accusing him not only of dishonesty but also of bloodlust – could not possibly have supported him had he remained in office. The Viceroyalty, hitherto insulated from British politics and particularly so under Mayo and Northbrook, had now, in Lytton's own words, 'been dragged into the violent arena of party conflict'.[48]

For Lytton to have to go out with his political friends, leaving Afghanistan in dire confusion, was a sad enough ending to his Viceroyalty. But to make matters worse, it was now discovered that the cost of the Afghan war exceeded the figure budgeted for by nearly twelve million sterling, owing to a major blunder in the estimates; the mistake was the fault of the Military Accounts Department, but Lytton and John Strachey should have noticed that the estimates were impossibly low, and were thus held responsible. In fact this affair of the 'Missing Millions' was not quite such a disaster as it might have been, thanks to Strachey's reforms, which had greatly improved the Indian finances; but it provided extra ammunition for Lytton's political foes. Though Lytton stood loyally by Strachey, the two of them appear to have begged the Military Member to take more than his fair share of the blame, which is not to their credit.

Nor is it much to Lytton's credit that having asked to be replaced as quickly as possible in order that the Afghan question could be settled without delay by a successor enjoying the confidence of the new Government, he was extremely indignant on hearing, a fortnight later, that Gladstone had taken him at his word and was sending out his successor, Lord Ripon, at once. Lytton seems to have convinced himself that the new Viceroy could not possibly travel to India until after the hot weather; and that until then he would be allowed to remain as a sort of Viceregal figurehead, avoiding all controversial business; he regarded the 'indecent haste' with which Gladstone proposed to replace him as something of an insult.[49] More understandably, he did not want Edith and the children to have to travel from Simla to Bombay at the beginning of June, when Ripon was due to arrive; the plains of India would then, as he put it, be 'hotter than the furnaces of Nebuchadnezzar'.[50] Eventually it was decided that after handing over to Ripon, he should stay on at Simla in a house belonging to Roberts until the onset of the Rains made it cool enough for him and his family to travel. With feelings running so high, it was feared that the two Viceroys would be unable to endure each other's presence for this length of time; but in the event, Lytton was never anything but his usual charming self to Ripon; while Ripon, though personally disliking Lytton and sharing Gladstone's moral indignation at his alleged misdeeds, behaved towards him with 'cordial civility'.[51]

During those last weeks in India, Lytton maintained an air of courage and dignity; and was inclined to be philosophical about what he called 'the sportive elfishness of that great practical joker, Democracy'.[52] By way of consolation, there was the warm sympathy of the Queen and the knowledge that he was now Earl of Lytton; Disraeli having recommended him for an Earldom before going out of office. But it was, as Edith gloomily remarked, 'a pauper Earldom';[53] for to add to Lytton's misfortunes, his personal finances had rather come to grief while he was in India; so that he was now not at all well off. As soon as the Lyttons moved out of Peterhof after Ripon's arrival, they began to economise; getting rid of the French chef and also of the Italian confectioner Peliti who stayed on in Simla where he became well known as the proprietor of Peliti's Grand Hotel.

Lytton still had sufficient means to enjoy the life of poetic retirement at Knebworth to which he had for so long looked forward. From being the war-mongering libertine of Gladstonian demonology he became the respected former Viceroy; though this did not prevent him from falling so passionately in love with an American actress young enough to be his daughter that for a time the happiness of his married life was threatened. He managed, however, to resist the advances of that pretentious but incurably romantic woman novelist Ouida, who after feeding him with expensive early strawberries proposed that he should elope with her to some 'Sicilian palace'.[54] Such was Ouida's infatuation for Lytton that she called one day on Lady Salisbury, whose husband was then Prime Minister, and urged that he should be made Ambassador in Paris. Lady Salisbury, who had never met Ouida before, was hardly encouraging; yet it so happened that Salisbury did give Lytton the Paris Embassy; which he held with the greatest success from 1887 until his death in 1891. 'I devoted my life to India and everybody abused me' Lytton remarked while in Paris, 'I come here, do nothing, and am praised to the skies'.[55]

If Lytton was a bad Viceroy, at least he was not a colourless one; the fact that he overruled his Council and managed, despite the telegraph, to disobey the Home Government would alone give him a claim to fame. Perhaps he was not so much a bad Viceroy as a great Viceroy *manqué* – fired by the glory of his high office, motivated by a patriotism that was no less genuine for being misplaced. Though he left his Afghan policy apparently in ruins, he lived to see much of it vindicated; notably his occupation of Quetta, which was acquired on a permanent lease by his successor and made into an important British-Indian military centre. His fear of a Russian take-over in Afghanistan, however alarmist it may have seemed in 1880, has been proved right by events of exactly a century later.

If, apart from Quetta and the Famine Code, Lytton did not have much to show for his reign in terms of solid achievement, if he ended by doing little for Indian aspirations, he nevertheless lived on in the folklore of the Raj; as the Viceroy who proclaimed Queen Victoria Empress, the Viceroy who gave 'Bobs' his chance, the Viceroy who flaunted the conventions – also as the Viceroy who, in a manner of speaking, founded Peliti's Grand Hotel. Moreover, India loomed large in the destinies of two of his children, which kept his memory more than ever alive in the India of later years. His elder son was to govern Bengal; his youngest daughter Emily was to be the wife of Edwin Lutyens, architect of New Delhi. And while it is fitting that Lytton should be linked, through his daughter, to a city that is an expression in stone of the idea that inspired his Delhi Assemblage, it is very much in keeping with Lytton's paradoxical nature that this same daughter should have helped to launch the Home Rule for

India League as a friend and disciple of the Theosophist, Mrs. Annie Besant. Thus Lytton, most Imperial of Viceroys, is alone among Viceroys in having a family connection with Indian mysticism and the movement for Indian independence.

7

Ripon

Ripon resembled Lytton in being a short man with a large beard and in preferring the Church of Rome to the Church of England; but in other respects it seemed that Gladstone had chosen him for the reason that he was Lytton's antithesis. Whereas Lytton was blessed with romantic good looks, Ripon was decidedly plain; with a bulbous nose and a rather timid, donnish expression in his eyes. Whereas Lytton was inclined to be frivolous, Ripon was serious-minded; a voracious reader of books about politics and religion, noted for his sincerity and his moral earnestness. Lytton could charm individuals and hold audiences spell-bound; Ripon was prosaic, endowed with neither grace nor sparkle, wanting in tact and a dull speaker. 'His style is that of a sermon' remarked Wilfrid Scawen Blunt, who nevertheless admired him.[1] Lytton was clever but volatile; Ripon was steady-going but something of a mediocrity. His friend and Cabinet colleague Lord Granville, who was not usually uncharitable, summed him up as being little more than 'a very persistent man with wealth'.[2]

Persistence was Ripon's outstanding quality and he was certainly wealthy; probably the wealthiest of all the Viceroys if one does not count two of his successors who were married to very rich wives. He was the first Viceroy who was a real grandee; a territorial magnate in both Yorkshire and Lincolnshire, a Marquess, a Knight of the Garter; and while he bore the unassuming surname of Robinson, the name of the prosperous Yorkshire baronets from whom he sprang, his second title of Earl de Grey commemorated his descent, in the female line, from the Greys, former Dukes and Earls of Kent. He was also, like Canning, a Prime Minister's son; his father, as Lord Goderich, having headed a Government with singular lack of success for a few months in 1827, the year of his birth. But although Ripon was a wealthy grandee, he had a homespun simplicity about him which makes one inclined to forget his wealth and his rank; when, on threatening to resign from his Viceroyalty, he speaks in a letter of returning to his '*lares* and *penates*',[3] one thinks of him going back to the cosy and cluttered fireside of some impecunious Victorian sage,

rather than to the splendours of his Yorkshire seat, Studley Royal, with its eighteenth-century water gardens almost on the scale of Versailles.

Ripon was a grandee with a difference in that he had, when younger, been attracted to the Christian Socialism of his friend Tom Hughes, author of *Tom Brown's Schooldays*. He remained throughout his life very much a Radical; while keeping the inherited instincts for law and order of a great Whig landowner and making a successful career for himself in more orthodox Liberal politics. His political career seemed to have been brought to an untimely end by his conversion to Catholicism in 1874; which, given the strength of Nonconformist opinion in the Liberal Party and of anti-Catholic feeling in the country as a whole, threatened to bar him from future Liberal Cabinets. But after four years in the wilderness – during which time he immersed himself in the affairs of his adopted faith, working for Catholic education and the Catholic poor, joining with the Duke of Norfolk in obtaining a cardinal's hat for Newman – he returned to political life largely on account of what he considered to be the immorality of Disraeli's conduct of foreign and Imperial affairs. Having served at the India Office both as a junior minister under Maharaja Wood and as Secretary of State, he was particularly concerned about India and the Afghan question; which he studied closely, so as to become one of the more informed if less strident critics of Lytton's policy. He was thus well qualified to be made Viceroy; which as a way of rewarding him for his very considerable services to the Liberal cause during the 1880 election seemed less likely to offend anti-Catholic prejudice than giving him a place in the Cabinet.

When Ripon heard from his former Chief, Maharaja Wood – now Lord Halifax and a Liberal elder statesman – that he was being considered for the Viceroyalty, his first reaction was that, much as it tempted him, he would have to refuse it on account of his wife's delicate health. After talking it over with her, he was in no way reassured: 'She is very good about it but evidently dreads it so much I shall get out of it, if I possibly can' he wrote in his diary.[4] Four days later he accepted the post, planning that his wife should stay in England until the following winter in order to avoid having to share the discomforts of the journey from Bombay to Simla in the terrible heat of early June. His appointment, which made history as the first appointment of a Catholic to a high office of State since the seventeenth century, did not go without a protest from the British Reformation Society; though on the whole it was surprisingly well received.

Owing to the circumstances of Lytton's resignation, Ripon had to take up his appointment in a hurry; which may explain his otherwise eccentric choice of Colonel Charles George Gordon, afterwards famous as the hero of Khartoum, to be his Private Secretary. Even before leaving England, Ripon must have had doubts as to the wisdom of this choice when Gordon, at a farewell dinner, insisted on eating all his courses off the same plate; saying, by way of explanation: 'We shall have to rough it out in India, you know, so I may as well begin now.'[5] When, on arriving at Bombay, Gordon found not the primitive simplicity which he had expected, but State banquets beneath the crystal chandeliers of Parell, the spacious old Bombay Government House, he promptly resigned; declaring that 'he would not, could not, stay amid all this splendour and luxury, while so many millions had not daily bread'.[6] Gordon's way of atoning for his defection was to write to newspapers and public men at home predicting that the new Viceroy would 'rule in the strength of the Lord, not of men';[7] which caused Ripon much embarrassment. He did, however, perform one really valuable service to Ripon in recommending Northbrook's cousin and former Private Secretary Evelyn Baring to him as his Finance Member.

'He must have had a most fearful journey from Bombay' the now discredited Sir John Strachey wrote of Ripon when his arrival at Simla was imminent; and he added: 'We don't pretend to be sorry'.[8] In fact Ripon stood the journey remarkably well; though such was the heat that the driver and the guard of the train which left Bombay on the night before his own train left both died of heat-stroke. Ripon's chaplain, Father Henry Schomberg Kerr, was depressed by the knowledge that there were coffins in readiness at every station along the line; in case any of the Viceregal party suffered a similar fate.

Ripon's arrival at Simla was a unique occasion in the annals of the Raj; the only time a change of Viceroys took place in the cramped conditions of the hot weather capital. Instead of the great steps and portico of Government House, Calcutta, there was a tent some twenty feet square on the tiny Peterhof lawn; into which was packed the entire Government of India, together with the military High Command, the Punjab Government, the neighbouring hill Chiefs and many other dignitaries; most of them in uniform and therefore in extreme discomfort, for the heat of that June day was unbearable even in Simla. At last, after much waiting, the carriage was heard and a few minutes later the tall and imposing figure of the Lieutenant-Governor of the Punjab was seen approaching the tent, followed by the neither tall nor imposing figure of the new Viceroy; 'his London clothes looking as though they had been used as a pillow in the *tonga* on the way up, or hastily pulled out of a much-packed Gladstone bag';[9] his features – those of them that were not obscured by his beard – all but extinguished by an oversized solar topee.

In his total disregard for sartorial elegance, Ripon differed yet again from the dandified Lytton; who now stepped forward with a few well-chosen words of welcome. Ripon at once began to make rather awkward apologies to Lytton for taking his place; and with true Yorkshire doggedness he went on apologising while Lytton was endeavouring to present the notabilities to him. So small was the space kept clear in the tent for the presentations that when the tall and venerable Raja of Jhind made a deep obeisance to Ripon, and Ripon, not yet knowing the etiquette, bowed violently in return, their two heads all but collided.

After the presentations were over, Ripon, Lytton and a very select few retired into the house for the swearing-in; while the rest of the company rode homewards along the Mall. Then bang went the first gun of the new Viceroy's salute and the dignified cavalcade of gold-laced notabilities was instantly transformed into what an eye-witness described as 'a struggling mass of men and horses, all presenting the appearance of circus riders doing tricks'.[10] A portly General endeavoured to stop his pony from jumping over the railings and down the precipice; another gentleman was badly hurt while trying to discourage his horse in its attempts to climb a tree. People were seen disappearing into the distance on madly galloping steeds; horses pranced amongst topees and plumed cocked hats strewn about the ground.

Though they had regarded the advent of a Radical Viceroy with some misgivings, the high officials could not help liking Ripon when they got to know him. Even that mainstay of the Lytton regime, John Strachey, who was about to leave under a cloud on account of the 'Missing Millions', had to admit that he was favourably impressed.[11] Those who worked with Ripon found him sensible and transparently honest; as well as being unusually good-natured. Ripon himself attributed this last quality to the peace of mind that came of religious conviction; and which he regarded as an inestimable advantage to him in his difficult task. 'One thing is wonderful and is due to the influence of religion' he told his wife in a letter written to her after he had been in India for some time. 'I have not ever since I came here

Peterhof, Simla, where Ripon's swearing-in took place

been worried or snappy, and even when I have had big decisions to take involving much responsibility and criticism, I have been really *quite* quiet.' [12]

Ripon's Catholicism – which was very different from the dilettantish attraction to Rome of the unbelieving Lytton – gave him something in common with the Lawrences and their school; like them, he endeavoured to rule according to what he saw as God's will. Just as the Indians had respected men like the Lawrences for their godliness, so now did they admire Ripon for his simple piety; the very fact that on landing at Bombay his first visit was to the Catholic Cathedral was noticed by them with approval. But whereas the Lawrences' brand of evangelical Protestantism tended to be associated in the Indian mind with some of the sterner aspects of British rule, Ripon's religion was that of a million Indians, mostly in the poorer classes. The Indians came to regard Ripon as a father figure, as their own sort of holy man.

If his being a Catholic is thus likely to have helped Ripon in getting across to the Indians, it does not seem to have been any sort of handicap to him in his relations with the British. A Catholic Viceroy was certainly a new and, as it turned out, unique phenomenon; but

Lord and Lady Ripon and Staff. Lord William Beresford is standing on the left, with his dog, Ponto, on a chair in front of him. Sitting next to Ponto is Henry Primrose, who succeeded Gordon as Ripon's Private Secretary

Ripon's Catholicism only made him different from other Viceroys in that he delegated all ecclesiastical business to his Home Member and Council. There was never any suggestion of his showing favouritism to his co-religionists in India, though he did occasionally visit convents and the schools of the Christian Brothers. His devotions were mostly private; he would often start the day with early mass said by Father Kerr, a room in each of his houses being used as a chapel. The presence of a Catholic priest and a Jesuit at that in the Viceregal Household might have been expected to give rise to rumours of clerical influence and intrigue; but Father Kerr, who as well as being a saintly character was an aristocrat, a former naval officer and a good fellow, was popular with everybody.

Apart from Father Kerr, the Viceroy's entourage was not at all Catholic; nor, for that matter, was it particularly Radical. And while it was no longer the subject of scandal, as it had been under Lytton, it kept its former gaiety and glamour. Ripon was sensible enough to take on Lytton's most popular ADC, Lord William Beresford, now back from a holiday spent fighting in Zululand, where he won a Victoria Cross. The Staff maintained the smartness of the Viceregal Court which might otherwise, given Ripon's inclinations, have become a little dowdy. 'I am cutting down the swagger as much as I can' Ripon wrote to his wife, 'and walking about in a shooting jacket and dispensing with Body Guards as much as possible . . . trying to revert, as much as I am allowed, to the older and simpler precedents'. He felt that while Viceregal state might to a certain extent have been justified in Calcutta, it was absurd at Simla.[13] Lytton, who thought it *infra dig* for a Viceroy to walk, rather maliciously called on Lady Ripon when he got back to London and told her with a sweet smile that her husband, in his brave and simple way, was making a habit of wandering about the hills alone. This brought Ripon a panic-stricken letter from his wife, whom he reassured by telling her that he 'never put his nose out of doors' without being accompanied by at least one member of his Staff and a policeman.[14]

It must have been a relief to Lady Ripon to be reunited with her husband that autumn. As well as being Ripon's wife she was his first cousin; she shared his political views but not his Catholicism. She seems to have been a stronger character than her husband, and during her years in India was quite a power behind the Viceregal throne; though in her public role as Vicereine she did not make much of a mark.

Having many rich and sporting relations and friends, the Ripons were constantly entertaining visitors from England who came for the shooting. Chief among their shooting guests was their thirty-year-old unmarried son, Lord de Grey, whose life was already dedicated to bringing down game in numbers that would eventually total more than half a million. Ripon was himself an excellent shot, though not quite up to the phenomenal standard of his son; he would go shooting with his colleagues and subordinates, which enabled him to make friends with them. As a sportsman, he had more in common with the sahibs than the Bohemian Lytton.

During the first six months of Ripon's reign, Afghanistan overshadowed everything else. There was a war to be won, a pretender to be disposed of, a country to be restored to some semblance of order. Towards the end of July, the British suffered a major military defeat; Ripon remained calm in the face of this disaster and immediately saved the situation by sending Roberts on his celebrated march from Kabul to Kandahar. Throughout the crisis, Ripon drew strength from his religion: 'God is wonderfully merciful to me in the midst of all the anxieties which press upon me just now' he told his wife.[15]

Ripon came to India as one of the chief critics of Lytton's Afghan policy; but he had only been in Simla a week when John Strachey remarked of him: 'As to Afghan affairs, I can discern no difference of policy between him and Lytton'.[16] Strachey exaggerated, in that Ripon certainly did not intend to follow Lytton's policy as far as the 'disintegration' of Afghanistan was concerned; but he had resigned himself to following it in most other respects. He continued to back Abdur Rahman, Lytton's candidate for the vacant Afghan throne – though with some misgivings on account of his alleged pro-Russian sympathies – and eventually established him as ruler of the whole of Afghanistan. The resulting settlement was much the same as Lytton's settlement with Yakub in 1879; except that there was no longer any question of maintaining a British envoy in Kabul; the British were to control Afghanistan's foreign relations and to keep two of the three districts along the Frontier which Yakub had ceded. It was a settlement that was to work reasonably well for the next forty years; and which went just about as far in extending British influence over Afghanistan as Disraeli and Salisbury had originally intended, with Lytton's help, to go. From the British point of view, Abdur Rahman proved a better choice than might have been expected; though he was to rule his people with a tyranny hardly in keeping with the Gladstonian doctrine of the Rights of Man.

After Roberts had defeated Abdur Rahman's chief rival in September 1880, Ripon was able to complete the withdrawal of British and Indian troops from Afghanistan, which was one of his first objects. When it came to the evacuation of Kandahar, he found himself torn between conflicting loyalties to his Council and to the Cabinet in London. The Home Government was committed to the evacuation; the Council, backed by the majority of the British in India, was strongly against it. Ripon was obliged to overrule his

Council – this being the last time a Viceroy ever did so – but he was able to propitiate his colleagues by persuading the Home Government to allow India to keep the two ceded Frontier districts although this was contrary to Liberal policy. During the months when Afghanistan was the dominant issue, Ripon's role was very much that of a mediator between the Radicals at home who wished to return to the old policy of 'non-intervention' and the 'forward' majority of the British in India who advocated military occupation or even annexation of Afghan territory. That he ended with a satisfactory compromise between the two extremes and also managed to remain on good terms with both Council and Cabinet is a tribute to his patience and courtesy, which made up for his deficiency in tact. It was even more of a feat in that when matters were still unsettled, he was laid low, on a visit to Allahabad, with an illness which nearly proved fatal.

It was fortunate for Ripon that he managed to keep the goodwill of his Council; for as soon as he had finished with Afghanistan, he embarked on the business nearest to his heart, which was to improve the position of the Indians in relation to the British by a series of reforms. Any one of these measures by itself would have been

Interior of a tent for the Viceregal Staff in about the time of Ripon

unlikely to arouse much opposition; but coming as they did in quick succession, they proved too heavy-handed a pouring of the Radical vintage into what a later Viceroy called 'the archaic bottles' of British Indian tradition and prejudice.[17] And what was perhaps more alarming to the sahibs and memsahibs than the reforms themselves was the thinking that lay behind them: 'I get more Radical every day' Ripon wrote from India to a friend in the Cabinet, 'and am rejoiced to say that the effect of despotic power has so far been to strengthen and deepen my liberal convictions'.[18] Had Ripon been faced with a hostile Council, the difficulties of carrying out his liberal policy would have been even greater than they actually were.

But if Ripon's colleagues in Council were friendly, they mostly gave him no more than lukewarm support. The one notable exception among them was Evelyn Baring, whom Ripon had, on Gordon's advice, borrowed from the Egyptian Government to replace John Strachey as Finance Member. Baring was Ripon's right-hand man, just as Strachey was Lytton's; though in that case it was a partnership of equal intellects, whereas with the patient and painstaking Ripon and the brilliant 'Over-Baring' it was more a case of opposites being attracted to one another. 'On most points we agree in principle' Ripon wrote in 1881; but he added: 'The great distinction between us is that he is a Doctrinaire and I am not. I think a Doctrinaire policy dangerous in India'.[19] At the time when Ripon wrote this, Baring's doctrinaire approach to the Indian finances was causing him grave concern, as likely to offend public opinion; so strongly did he feel about it that when Baring's measures looked like being supported by the Home Government, he talked of resigning. The situation was saved by Baring's older and wiser cousin Northbrook, himself a member of the Government, who wrote scolding him for being so high-handed. Baring took the correction and from then onwards he and Ripon worked together in harmony.

As members of his Council retired, or were promoted to being Lieutenant-Governors, Ripon had the opportunity of replacing them with men more of his way of thinking; who were not all that hard to find among the higher officials. Instead, he mostly chose what one of his younger subordinates called 'the unsympathetic and ordinary Simla material he found ready to his hand'.[20] It was a sign of his simplicity, which made him a poor judge of men; though with some of his appointments one would suspect that his Christian meekness prompted him to turn the other cheek. Thus he gave the Lieutenant-Governorship of Bengal to his chief opponent in Council just at a time when the co-operation of the Provincial Governments was essential to the success of his policy. As it was, he had poor enough support in the provinces. The Government of Bombay actually put it on record that his measures were premature.

'If Bombay is to blow its Tory penny whistle, why should not Madras sound its Liberal trumpet?' Ripon wrote cheerfully to Mountstuart Grant Duff, a minor Liberal politician sent out to govern Madras by Gladstone;[21] but Grant Duff's Liberal trumpet-blast proved to be nothing but wind, while he weakly allowed his Government to go its own obstructionist way. The North-Western Provinces were from 1882 onwards governed by the now Sir Alfred Lyall; who though Liberal in his sympathies, felt that Ripon was going too fast. Only in the Punjab was there a Lieutenant-Governor both willing and able to make Ripon's policy work: Sir Charles Aitchison, who also took over in 1882. Ripon described him as 'a real good man of the best Scotch type, with a strong infusion of Puritan force'.[22]

If his Council and the Provincial Governors gave Ripon little enough support, it was more than what he received from his political friends at home. Once the Afghan question had been settled, the Liberal Government lost interest in India; and while the similar lack of interest in Indian affairs shown by Gladstone's previous administration had enabled Mayo and Northbrook to govern with a free hand, they were not only stronger men than Ripon but were less subject than he was to telegraphic interference from Whitehall. Ripon needed to be supported by the Government against the opposition of the retired Civilians and soldiers on the India Council; whom he spoke of, in a moment of particular frustration, as 'a set of old gentlemen, whose energies are relaxed by age, and who, having excellent salaries and no responsibility, amuse themselves by criticising the proposals and obstructing the plans of those who have the most recent knowledge of the real state of India'.[23] But that sleepy-eyed statesman, the Marquess of Hartington, who was Secretary of State during most of Ripon's reign, actually made it easier for the 'old gentlemen' to thwart the Radical Viceroy by delegating much of his own authority to them. So indolent was Hartington that he could barely bring himself to read Ripon's letters to him, which were admittedly on the lengthy side. Once, in a railway carriage with Lord de Grey, he 'suddenly drew forth from his pocket a "small volume" and said with a deep and despairing sigh: "De Grey, what do you think this is? It is one of your father's letters"'.[24]

Not only did the Home Government show a lack of interest in Ripon's policy of reform; but it actually turned down, on doctrinaire grounds, a plan of his for building more railways as a safeguard against famine. Then Gladstone, not wanting to have to ask Parliament for more money, expected the Indian taxpayer to bear the cost of the contingent sent by India to help quell the Egyptian revolt of 1882. Ripon strongly objected, regarding it as an injustice that the Indians, 'a very poor people',[25] should have to pay in order to lighten the burden of the richer taxpayers at home; but in the end the most he could get out of Gladstone was rather less than half the cost of the contingent.

If Ripon's political friends showed no real concern for India, Ripon himself was concerned overmuch with English politics. 'His constant glances over his shoulder at the state of his party interfere seriously with his usefulness as an Indian Viceroy' the clever young Under-Secretary in the Foreign Department, Mortimer Durand, complained in a letter written in 1882. In the same letter, Durand, who acted for a time as Ripon's Private Secretary, foresaw trouble ahead for the Radical Viceroy in view of his defects: 'Lord Ripon will be lucky if he escapes coming to grief before the end of his term of office here. I like him and respect him as a good and honest man, but he is painfully cautious and "funky" – and he does not support his men as he should do. He has made one or two bad mistakes of late, from sheer timidity.'[26]

While people like Durand were worried, Ripon went blithely on with his reforming policy; which was not so much a policy of innovation as of carrying his predecessors' reforms a step further. He continued Lawrence's work by giving the peasants a greater security of tenure, particularly in Oudh and Bengal; risking unpopularity with the influential zemindar class in so doing. He showed the same concern as Mayo had shown for primary education and appointed a commission to report on ways in which it could be extended. He improved on Lytton's somewhat rudimentary factory legislation. He breathed fresh life into Mayo's plan for appointing municipal committees by election, so as to enable the Indian people to take a greater part in local government; a plan which became law under Northbrook but was afterwards allowed to languish. He followed Lytton and earlier Viceroys and indeed acted in accordance with the Queen's Proclamation of 1858 in tackling the question of admitting Indians to the Civil Service.

Even allowing for the fact that in most of these matters Ripon hoped for greater advances than he was actually able to bring about, his policy was not such as would have seemed likely to arouse the storm of protest which eventually broke over his head. Behind his policy, however, lay Ripon's determination that the Indians should be better educated, more politically conscious, more capable of managing their own affairs. 'Having planted this small tree of self-government' he wrote of the municipal plan, 'we ought not always to be pulling it up to look at its roots'.[27] Others before him, such as Mayo, had thought likewise; but Ripon, in speaking his thoughts, seems to have shown less regard than they did for the feelings and prejudices of the British community. And when Ripon spoke his thoughts, he did so to a British community on the whole less friendly

Lord William Beresford and other members of the Viceroy's Staff in lighter moments

towards the Indians than in Mayo's time. That relations between the British and the Indians should have deteriorated as a result of the Mutiny is only too easily understandable. That they should have been worse in 1880 than in 1870, when the Mutiny was fresher in people's memories, can be blamed on the very process which Ripon was trying to further – the rise of an educated and politically conscious Indian middle class. The British tended to feel an antipathy to the Westernised Indian lawyer or journalist such as they never felt to the peasant or zemindar. Other factors may have helped to bring about this lamentable state of affairs; notably the growth of British society in India, which made it less necessary than it had been to get to know the Indians. Then there was the influence of the memsahibs, allegedly more given to racial prejudice than their menfolk; their numbers had greatly increased during the eighteen-seventies, after the opening of the Suez Canal and the construction of the principal Indian railways had made travel so much easier.

It is not surprising that the sahibs and memsahibs of Ripon's time should have come to detest the Radical Viceroy and the change of heart inherent in his policy; a change epitomised in his repeal of Lytton's Vernacular Press Act. Their resentment reached boiling-point over a Bill to remove the disability which Indian magistrates had hitherto suffered of being unable to try British offenders. This measure – known as the Ilbert Bill, after Ripon's Law Member, Courtenay Ilbert – was introduced largely for administrative reasons; so that Indians in the Civil Service should be on the same footing as their British colleagues in judicial power as they were in executive authority. For Indians to become full-blown magistrates was not, on the face of it, unduly radical when they could already be High Court Judges; nevertheless, the Ilbert Bill caused an outcry such as had not been heard in British India since the clamour for Canning's removal during the Mutiny.

The agitation against Ripon over the Ilbert Bill started in Bengal, among the same sort of non-official British who had denounced Canning: the planters, the Calcutta barristers, the businessmen. The planters were genuinely alarmed at the possible implications of the Bill: living as so many of them did in remote districts, they saw themselves at the mercy of the local Indian magistrate, who, they felt sure, would put them in prison on the trumped-up evidence of a disgruntled servant or tenant. The barristers encouraged the planters in their fears; being themselves angry with Ripon's Government over a reduction in judges' salaries and the appointment, during the previous hot weather, of an Indian judge to act as Chief Justice. All other sections of the non-official British community joined forces with the planters and the barristers; a monster protest meeting was held early in 1883 at the Calcutta Town Hall, which was near enough to Government House for the Viceroy to hear the shouts of applause and wrath as he was denounced in speeches 'intemperate beyond all decency'.[28]

Meetings were held all over Bengal and the agitation showed signs of spreading to other provinces. Officials sympathised almost to a man with the non-officials; the wife of the Chief Justice got up a 'Ladies' Petition' against the Bill; there were even rumours of disaffection in the Army. The malcontents were joined by Eurasians, whose own particular grievance was their exclusion from the engineering college at Roorkee, to which, according to a recent Government decision, only Asiatics of pure blood would henceforth be admitted. The English newspapers of Calcutta subjected Ripon to an hysterical campaign of abuse. The cry was raised of British womanhood in danger, which brought many progressives on to the side of Ripon's opponents.

To Ripon, the agitation over the Ilbert Bill came as a complete surprise. Neither he nor his Government had any idea that the Bill would cause so much trouble; nor for that matter had Hartington, to whom it was referred for approval before being introduced. A note of warning was sounded by the legal expert on the India Council, but his minute was somehow overlooked; Hartington is said to have stuffed it into the pocket of his greatcoat and then gone off to Newmarket, having forgotten all about it. However much Ripon could claim to have been badly advised, he as Viceroy had to accept responsibility for what Lyall called 'a horrid political blunder'.[29] The Bill had not even originated with him; but believing as passionately as he did in the principle underlying it, he felt he could not now give it up without betraying that principle. He was encouraged in his resolution by his wife. 'My Missus is very fairly well for her' he wrote in his folksy way to Tom Hughes. 'The Anglo-Indian row has done her a world of good; she is as strong and bold as a lioness, and would soon recall me to a proper frame of mind if I were in the least inclined to waver.'[30]

During the summer of 1883 there was a lull in the controversy; while Ripon and his Government obtained various opinions on the Bill. That autumn, however, the agitation started up again with renewed violence. Arriving back in Calcutta for the cold weather, Ripon was personally insulted at the gate of Government House. On another occasion, when he returned to Calcutta after a visit to Darjeeling, he was hooted at the station by a crowd of tea planters; Bill Beresford, who was with him as ADC, was with difficulty restrained from leaping out of the railway carriage and giving them a good thrashing. Government House was not only boycotted by the non-official community, but there were threats that it would have its windows broken. There was even a conspiracy to kidnap the Viceroy and put him aboard a steamer bound for England by way of the Cape.

Ripon at first was 'cool and plucky'[31] in the face of all these insults and scares; he was totally impervious to the Press campaign, believing that lies were beneath his notice. Then his colleagues in the Council began to lose their nerve; they no longer had Baring to rally them, since he had left to take up a higher appointment in Egypt. Faced with the defection of his colleagues and with the prospect of a full-scale 'white mutiny' having to be subdued by a mere sixty or seventy British police, Ripon's natural timidity got the better of him, emboldened though he may have been by his lion-hearted 'Missus'; and he agreed, as a compromise, that British offenders tried by Indian magistrates would be allowed the safeguard of a British jury.

This was virtually a surrender, a betrayal of the principle of racial equality inherent in the Bill; but it was a surrender for which Ripon himself can only be partially blamed. In the words of a modern Indian historian, 'a weak Viceroy had been betrayed by a weaker Council';[32] though Ripon's colleagues might not have been quite so weak had it not been December. According to Lyall, the compromise was 'hurriedly patched up so that Christmas Day might produce goodwill and reconciliation generally, also that both sides might rush off to take holidays'.[33] Another reason for settling matters without further delay was that the Queen's son, the Duke of Connaught, was coming to Calcutta shortly to open an exhibition.

The final act of the Ilbert Bill drama took place at Government House early in the New Year, when the Bill in its modified form was debated by the Legislative Council before an audience that included many prominent Indians as well as most of the leading British inhabitants of Calcutta and their wives; so large a gathering that the meeting was held not in the Council Chamber but in the Marble Hall. In reply to a British official who with 'wagging beard' delivered a 'violent philippic' attacking not only the Bill but also the principles of the Queen's Proclamation of 1858, Ripon said: 'To me it seems a very serious thing to put forth to the people of India a doctrine which renders worthless the solemn words of their Sovereign and which converts her gracious promises, which her Indian subjects have cherished for a quarter of a century, into a hollow mockery'.[34] Educated Indians were to remember these words for many years to come; they were to revere Ripon more for what he said when fighting the losing battle of the Ilbert Bill than for anything he was actually able to do for them during his reign. In fighting that losing battle, he was able to stand forth as the champion of their rights and aspirations in a way that would not have been possible had the peace of his Viceroyalty remained unbroken. Lyall spoke of the Ilbert Bill controversy as 'the most unlucky business that ever a Viceroy got entangled in';[35] in fact it was, for Ripon, a great stroke of luck; not a defeat but a triumph.

As well as being a personal triumph for Ripon, in winning him the everlasting gratitude of the Indian people, it was a triumph for the best traditions of the Raj over what one of his colleagues called 'the evil "nigger" tradition'.[36] The tradition that the British were in India to educate the Indians to rule themselves, the tradition of racial equality, went back to the time of Bentinck and before; they had been upheld by the Queen's Proclamation, but since then had been all too frequently forgotten, or else deliberately ignored. Ripon's battle over the Ilbert Bill gave them such publicity that they could never again be ignored or forgotten. The fact that eminent civilians like Lyall and Durand stood just as much as Ripon did for the best traditions –

Ripon's Staff and guests at Government House, Calcutta. Lord William Beresford is sitting in the centre, with his sister-in-law, Lady Charles Beresford, on his left. On Lady Charles's left is Henry Primrose, Private Secretary to the Viceroy

which were also upheld by recent Viceroys such as Mayo and Northbrook and even, to a certain extent, by Lytton – does not take away from Ripon's achievement in ensuring that these traditions would be respected by the men who came after him. Others may have felt as strongly as he did, but were either too timid or too tactful to say so; he was also timid, but he was not particularly noted for his tact.

If through his tactlessness Ripon succeeded in reminding the British of their trust, and in winning the affection of the Indians so as to strengthen their confidence in British rule – achievements which entitle him, mediocrity though he was, to a place among the great Viceroys – his Viceroyalty was a failure in most other respects on account of his timidity. He was too 'funky', as Durand would have said, to prevent his reforming policy from being watered down by the 'old gentlemen' of the India Council and obstructed by the officials. He is remembered by Indians as the 'Father of Local Self-Government'; but this is a title to which Mayo has a better claim; Ripon simply reorganised an existing scheme which was still very much in the experimental stage and was to remain so for many years to come. If we believe Wilfred Scawen Blunt, who visited India towards the end of Ripon's Viceroyalty, his Local Self-Government Bill was actually received by the Indian people with some suspicion.

The anti-Imperialist Blunt thought Ripon the most successful Viceroy or Governor-General India had ever had, 'because the most loved'; but before leaving India he saw for himself how 'funky' Ripon could be. A party of Indian gentlemen were talking to Blunt at Patna station when a Scottish doctor threatened them with a stick if they remained outside his railway carriage window. Blunt wrote Ripon a strong letter asking for action to be taken against the offending Scot; but Ripon, fearing a repetition of the Ilbert Bill row if Blunt's letter were published, begged him to tone it down. The doctor was eventually made to apologise; but one feels that he would have had shorter shrift from Mayo or from Lytton in all his Imperial glory than he had from the Radical Ripon.

Although Blunt's Indian tour convinced him of Ripon's failure to do anything tangible for the Indians, he was no less struck by the extent to which the Indians praised him. 'Wherever I went in India I heard the same story; from the poor peasants of the South, who for the first time had learned the individual name of their ruler; from the high-caste Brahmins of Madras and Bombay; from the Calcutta students; from the Mahommedan divines of Lucknow; from the noblemen of Delhi and Hyderabad – everywhere his praise was in all men's mouths. "He is an honest man", men said, "and one who fears God."'[37] Blunt may have exaggerated, but certainly Ripon's hold over the Indians was a remarkable phenomenon; while the fact that people so utterly different as the peasants of the South and the students of Calcutta were united in praising him can be taken as a sign of an emerging Indian nationhood. Such was his popularity that a municipal orator had only to pronounce the words 'Lord Ripon', however irrelevant the context, in order to raise a cheer.

Like his two immediate predecessors, Ripon resigned before his five years were up; he did so in order that his successor might be appointed by the Liberals rather than by the Conservatives, who seemed likely to be back in power by the time his Viceroyalty was due to end. The Indians showed their affection for him by giving him a send-off such as they had given to no previous Viceroy. In Calcutta, he and Lady Ripon drove to the station amidst the cheers of at least a hundred thousand people lining the streets; there were triumphal arches all along the way and every house and tree was ablaze with lamps. More crowds were gathered at stations along the line from Calcutta to Bombay, where priests blessed the departing Viceroy and merchants hung out garlands in his honour. In contrast to the Indians, the vast majority of the British felt no regrets at Ripon's departure; though the Bihar Light Horse Volunteers, a regiment made up almost entirely of planters who had been among his fiercest opponents during the Ilbert Bill controversy, sent a deputation to bid him farewell. But while some of the British community were ready to shake hands with Ripon before he left, his stock with the British was still sufficiently low thirty years later for none of them to be willing to subscribe towards the statue of him which was put up on the Calcutta Maidan in 1915. The statue was unveiled in the presence of a vast gathering of Indians for whom the name of Ripon had become the legend which it is in India to this day.

Having excited such mixed feelings in India, Ripon managed to stay clear of controversy during the quarter of a century of public life which lay ahead of him after his return to England. Perhaps the only echo of the battles of his Viceroyalty in his later career was when Queen Victoria, faced with the prospect of a Liberal Government in 1892, wrote a letter to her Private Secretary which contained the much-underlined injunction: 'Ld. Ripon *not to have anything to do with India*'.[38] Gladstone, to whom her views were communicated, took the point and gave Ripon the Colonies. After his Viceroyalty, Ripon's Catholicism was no longer regarded as a bar to his being a Cabinet Minister; and he held office in every Liberal Government from 1886 until his final retirement from politics in 1908, a few months before his death. Having first served in a Cabinet under Palmerston, he lived to be a Cabinet colleague of the young Winston Churchill.

Kipling's Viceroy

A man of the world, cultured and charming, a diplomatist with a talent for literature and the arts, a romantic and a dandy; Ripon's successor, Lord Dufferin, though a Liberal in politics and appointed by Gladstone, was possessed of most of the qualities which Disraeli had admired in Lytton. In fact there was a legend that he was Disraeli's natural son; and although this is certainly untrue, one can understand how the legend grew up. Not only did Dufferin have many characteristics in common with the great Jewish statesman – a romantic temperament, a touch of Oriental flashiness, a suave, urbane, almost purring manner – but as a young man in the eighteen-forties he bore a striking resemblance to the young Disraeli. By the time he became Viceroy the likeness was less apparent; for he now sported a curling moustache and a trim beard; while his dark hair, which in his younger days he had worn rather long, was now thin and receding. Nevertheless, there was still something Semitic about his looks: the unusually swarthy complexion, the prominent nose, the sensuous lips, the heavily-lidded eyes. His eyes were large and therefore short-sighted; being a little vain, he eschewed spectacles and made do with a monocle, which would leap engagingly from his face when he greeted someone.

It was not, however, Jewish blood which made Dufferin dark, charming and quick-witted, but Irish. Or rather, Irish and Scottish mixed; for while on his mother's side he was a great-grandson of Richard Brinsley Sheridan, his father's family, the Blackwoods, came to Ulster from Scotland early in the seventeenth century. Sir Harold Nicolson, who was his wife's nephew, speaks of the 'exquisite balance between the Scotch and Irish sides of his temperament' and reminds us that his 'much proclaimed brilliance had beneath it a hard-headed Ulster foundation'.[1] This Ulster hard-headedness was what made Dufferin so different from the volatile Lytton, despite his superficial resemblance to him; it was always there, behind the lisping, dilettantish exterior, enabling him when required to deliver a particularly tough mailed fist within the smoothest of velvet gloves. If Lytton was something of an amateur, Dufferin was very much a

ord Dufferin. A portrait
y G.F. Watts

professional; though as far as their diplomatic careers went, it was the other way round; Lytton having worked his way up in the Diplomatic Service, Dufferin being a political peer whose knowledge of the Eastern Question had caused him to be sent on a mission to Syria and more recently to be made Ambassador in St Petersburg and then in Constantinople – and to be entrusted, during the latter Embassy, with settling the future of Egypt. Though his years in diplomacy had given him the slightly punctilious manner of a man who has associated much with foreign diplomats, he did not possess the professional diplomatist's talent for languages. He was a man of the world but not a cosmopolitan; foreigners loved him not because he seemed like one of them, as Lytton did, but because he was their idea of the perfect English gentleman.

As well as holding high diplomatic posts, Dufferin had been

Governor-General of Canada. While being a constitutional Governor-General was very different from ruling India, this difference applied only to himself. As far as his wife was concerned, Canada had been the ideal apprenticeship. Hariot Dufferin, known to her husband and family as Lal, was not suited by nature to be a Viceroy's consort; though intelligent and strong-minded, she was shy and rather plain, with looks of the mouselike sort. She had grown up far from the world of Courts and Embassies, the daughter of County Down gentry; of the same Ulster-Scottish stock as her husband and in fact a distant cousin of his. But on marrying Dufferin, who was more than fifteen years her senior, she had set about overcoming her shyness in order to be a suitable spouse for a husband who obviously had a brilliant career ahead of him. So well did she succeed that she came positively to enjoy State occasions, saying the right thing to all manner of people, visiting schools and hospitals, giving away prizes; she also acquired a dignity and grace and a dress sense which quite made up for her nondescript looks; so that she had the reputation of being one of the most fascinating great ladies of her time. Her husband would proudly repeat a remark by the King of Greece, 'that there was no lady in Europe who could enter a room like Lady Dufferin'.[2]

Hariot Dufferin was without doubt the perfect Vicereine. Very many of his contemporaries, both in India and at home, would likewise have regarded Dufferin as the perfect Viceroy; and yet, for all his brilliance and charm, there was something lacking. 'Was Lord Dufferin a *great* man?' a distinguished Oxford Don once asked Sir Harold Nicolson, adding: 'I have never been sure'. Sir Harold, though he had loved and admired his uncle by marriage, was equally undecided as to his greatness. 'Did he possess vision as well as imagination?' he asked himself. 'Was he a great statesman or only a great diplomatist?'[3]

On the face of it, Dufferin was one of the greatest public servants of his time, successful in each of the high offices, diplomatic or proconsular, which he held; but his friend and fellow-Ulsterman, Lord George Hamilton, writing to a later Viceroy, suggested that this appearance of success was deceptive: 'He has never long held any post in which he has not more or less been found out'. Hamilton also called Dufferin 'a delightful literary humbug';[4] allowing that he was being unduly harsh – though he was not normally harsh in his judgements – one has to admit that there was some measure of humbug in Dufferin's nature. His vanity was not confined to his personal appearance; he loved popularity and hated criticism. Whereas to Mayo the Viceroyalty had been an unrivalled opportunity for doing good, and to Northbrook, Lytton and Ripon a task to be undertaken reluctantly out of a sense of duty, to Dufferin it was a

Lady Dufferin

prize which he had long coveted; a fitting climax to a career which had raised him from a rather obscure Irish Baron to an Earl and a statesman and diplomatist known and admired throughout Europe, North America and the Near East. There was something a little calculating about him; though this less attractive side to his nature was made up for by his genuine kindness, his consideration for others and his loyalty to his friends.

Dufferin's chief failing was his indolence; he was quite equal to the duties of an embassy or a figurehead governorship; but the work of ruling India was beyond him. He had the excuse of age; at fifty-eight he was older than any of his predecessors had been when they assumed office, while being youthful in appearance; though in 1872, when at the age of forty-six he was first considered for the Viceroyalty, the percipient Granville doubted whether he had 'sufficient stamina either of mind or body' for the post.[5] Being a man who knew well how to organise his life, he managed to work less than almost any other Viceroy; by interfering as little as possible in departmental business, paying scant attention to detail and leaving many decisions to his very able Private Secretary, Donald Mackenzie

Wallace; who had been a foreign correspondent of *The Times* and thus shared the Viceroy's interest in diplomacy. Dufferin even authorised his Private Secretary to forge his signature, which Wallace did 'with lifelike fidelity'.[6] Even delegating as much as he did, Dufferin felt overwhelmed by the work of the Viceroyalty: 'It is the greatest grind I have ever experienced' he told the Secretary of State.[7]

That Dufferin should have been prevented by his indolence from being a great Viceroy was particularly regrettable in that everything else was so much in his favour. He was a strong man, stronger than any of his predecessors since Mayo; and whereas Mayo had come to India virtually unknown, Dufferin was a widely respected public figure whose opinions carried great authority. In the words of Lyall, he 'seemed always to carry his point, yet he never seemed to be in antagonism with anyone'.[8] He was shrewd enough to make it a condition of accepting the Viceroyalty that the 'old gentlemen' of the India Council in London would not interfere with him as much as they had interfered with Ripon; and he was singularly fortunate in the Secretaries of State, Conservative as well as Liberal, under whom he served; all of whom, including Lord Randolph Churchill, were willing to give him a remarkably free hand. He might have been a second Mayo if only he had been prepared to work harder. True, since Mayo's time, the business of ruling India had greatly increased; so that it was no longer possible for a Viceroy to oversee everything in the way that Mayo had done; a certain amount of delegation was

Lord Dufferin with his family and Staff.
Lady Dufferin sits on his left; and on her left is the Viceroy's Private Secretary, Sir Donald Mackenzie Wallace. The Dufferins' daughter, Lady Helen Blackwood, is second from the left, with Lord William Beresford next to her; the two of them are holding a long-tailed monkey. Lord Herbrand Russell, ADC, who afterwards became the 11th Duke of Bedford, stands behind Dufferin, wearing a white suit. Charles Lawrence, son of the former Viceroy, John Lawrence, stands second from the left

necessary, even desirable. But Dufferin went too far in this respect.

A Viceroy who said 'My dear fellow, you can do as you like' as often as Dufferin did[9] was naturally extremely popular with his colleagues and subordinates: 'By far the best Viceroy I have seen yet' was Mortimer Durand's verdict on him.[10] Durand had a particular reason for liking Dufferin, who had made him Foreign Secretary at the age of thirty-five; but others felt the same. While liking him as a Viceroy who interfered with them as little as possible, who always considered their feelings and who backed them up loyally against any attack, Dufferin's colleagues and subordinates also, to their credit, liked him because they saw in him a strong and decisive Viceroy. 'A Viceroy who is as bold and resolute as he is patient and courteous'[11] is how he seemed to Durand, who was also impressed by 'the rapidity with which he saw the points of a case, and formed conclusions, and right conclusions, on complicated matters'.[12] And from the very start of his association with Dufferin, Durand realised that though he had 'some Blarney in him', he would 'stand no nonsense'.[13] Lyall likewise realised that while Dufferin was ready to allow his subordinates a very free hand, he would 'lay about him very disagreeably' if they blundered or 'let him in'.[14]

Dufferin also commanded respect as a very shrewd judge of character; with 'an almost uncanny "flair" for anything like insincerity or weakness'.[15] But although he could be ruthless with those who did not come up to his own high standards, his ruthlessness was usually tempered by genuine kindness of heart. When a certain officer was broken for divulging secret information, Dufferin, though he could not stand men who were indiscreet, asked for his punishment to be reduced. 'My heart, which is a great deal too soft for my present place, melted within me' he told Durand;[16] a statement which tells us as much about Dufferin's vanity as about his compassion.

Dufferin's besetting fault, his indolence, took the form not only of leaving too much to his subordinates, but of writing little, though he was possessed of great literary gifts. 'Our mutual letters are becoming shorter and shorter, which is a good sign, for happy is the country without annals' he remarked smugly to the Secretary of State towards the end of his reign.[17] Grudging as he did the hours spent at his desk, it is ironical that he should have wasted some of his time in learning Persian, which he took up under the mistaken impression that it was still spoken by all the magnates of India; having realised his mistake, he continued with his studies, though they served no purpose other than enabling him to read the Persian poets and to listen to stories from the Arabian Nights told to him in Persian by the 'learned policeman' who accompanied him on his daily walk.[18]

When Dufferin saw fit to write at length to the Secretary of State, his letters were models of what a Viceroy's letters should be. Urbane, cogent, good-humoured, they were as different from the prosiness of Northbrook and Ripon as they were from the rather hysterical if elegant outpourings of Lytton. From the very start, he showed himself to be master of the situation. On arriving for the first time in a Calcutta where there was still a smouldering resentment among the British as a result of Ripon's policy, he wrote confidently:

> I have no doubt that the British Colony will be very glad of the opportunity I propose to offer them of making their peace with Government House. It must have cost them a good deal to maintain the offensive attitude they assumed towards Ripon. Their wives and daughters will want to dance and to show off their new frocks; and being at heart, like the rest of their countrymen, reasonable and good-natured men, there is a fair prospect of my getting our party-coloured team to jog along together in peace and good fellowship.[19]

Having, in the words of his nephew, been 'sent out primarily to repair the ravages caused by Lord Ripon's impulsive optimism',[20] Dufferin was none the less committed to Ripon's policy; not only as a Liberal appointed by a Liberal Government, but also in order to maintain the continuity of the Government of India. It was a sign of his virtuosity that he was able, on his arrival, to reassure the British while at the same time convincing the Indians that he intended to follow in Ripon's footsteps. 'The Marquess of Ripon and his predecessors have prepared the soil, delved and planted' he told the Corporation of Calcutta in a speech. 'It will be my more humble duty to watch, water, prune and train.'[21]

And so he carried through Ripon's Tenancy Bill – albeit with some prunings – and he set about fostering Local Self-Government. As a new concession to Indian aspirations, Dufferin proposed raising Indian volunteer regiments; the scheme came to nothing owing to official opposition, but helped him to make friends with Allan Octavian Hume, a former Secretary to Government who had stayed on in India after his retirement working to improve the social and political standing of the Indians. Hume was the man behind the first Indian National Congress, which many would regard as the most significant event of Dufferin's reign; for in this meeting of educated Indians and British well-wishers in Bombay in 1885 lay the seeds of the Congress Party of later years. It was, however, a Congress very different from what it afterwards became; 'absolutely unanimous in insisting on unswerving loyalty to the British Crown',[22] meeting simply to draw up a programme of political reform which it commended to the Government. Dufferin gave the Congress some friendly encouragement and Hume at first responded by urging his Indian friends to put their trust in him. The friendship between Dufferin and Hume was not destined to last; for Hume, who though able and dedicated was conceited and something of a crank, soon felt that the Viceroy was not sufficiently wedded to the cause of reform and attacked him in print. Dufferin was at first prepared to tolerate Hume's vagaries, no doubt seeing in him a useful ally; but in the end Hume went too far.

Awkward though he found Hume, Dufferin was able to get on perfectly well with the Indian leaders of Congress. As a romantic, he naturally felt more attracted to the Indian Princes and nobles than to what he called the 'Bengalee Baboo';[23] nevertheless, he was percipient enough to appreciate the qualities and potential strength of the growing educated classes. He understood the educated Indians better as he got to know them; he was particularly impressed with the educated classes of Bombay, even going so far as to suggest that Bombay should be made the capital of India instead of Calcutta; though one suspects him of being to some extent influenced in this respect by what he saw of the munificence of the wealthy Parsis.

While sympathising with the Congress movement, Dufferin was well aware that it did not represent all the educated classes – let alone all the people of India. He found that it did not have so strong a following among the educated Muslims, to whom, with his knowledge of the Islamic world, he felt personally drawn. Without overtly encouraging the Muslims to stay aloof from Congress, Dufferin widened the breach between them and the Hindus by standing forth, in Mackenzie Wallace's words, as their 'benevolent protector'.[24] While Dufferin can thus be held partly responsible for the communal strife of the present century, he would have been as horrified at the idea of deliberately stirring up religious or racial discord for political motives as was his Government; which, speaking no doubt in all sincerity, called such a policy 'diabolical'.[25] Rather, Dufferin saw Muslim separatism as an existing fact and took advantage of it to further the growth of some kind of Indian conservative party; which, Liberal though he was, he felt would be more suited to the circumstances of British India than Congress with its ideas borrowed from Gladstonian Liberalism.

To associate educated Indians of moderate views with the Government, Dufferin, towards the end of his reign, put forward a scheme that had long been in his mind for introducing elected Indian members into the provincial Legislative Councils. At the same time the powers of the provincial Councils were to be increased, through decentralisation. 'Now that we have educated these people' he wrote, 'their desire to take a larger part in the management of their own domestic affairs seems to be a legitimate and reasonable aspiration,

Lord Dufferin tiger shooting

and I think there should be enough statesmanship amongst us to contrive the means of permitting them to do so without unduly compromising our Imperial supremacy'.[26] A Viceroy who thought like this, who urged the Home Government to give the Indians 'quickly and with good grace whatever it may be possible or desirable to accord'[27] and who was also endowed with tact, charm and diplomatic skill as Dufferin was, might have done much for the political development of India; but his proposal for the Legislative Councils was his only real achievement in this respect.

The truth is that Dufferin was far less interested in the internal politics of India than he was in foreign affairs. When, early in 1885, there was a major crisis with Russia, he was in his element. The Russians, who were continuing to infiltrate into Central Asia, now proceeded to occupy the district of Panjdeh which the Afghans claimed to be part of their territory. Panjdeh was also dangerously close to the important Afghan city of Herat. Since the British had guaranteed the 'integrity and independence' of Afghanistan, they were bound, if the Afghans required them to do so, to drive the Russians out of Panjdeh by force; which might have caused an Anglo-Russian war.

As luck would have it, when the news came that the Russians had entered Panjdeh, the Amir of Afghanistan, Abdur Rahman, was paying Dufferin a State visit at Rawalpindi in the Punjab. Having been Ambassador in St Petersburg, Dufferin was anxious for a settlement with Russia; he was convinced that the Russians, from the Tsar downwards, were no less anxious to be on good terms with Britain. Yet being in Durand's words 'always ready for a bold game', he was willing to send troops to Herat; but the military authorities threw 'the wettest of blankets' over this idea.[28] Nevertheless, Dufferin told the Amir that if he was anxious about Herat, the Government of India might be prepared to send troops for its defence. He knew how much the Afghans hated having even friendly foreign troops in their midst; and sure enough Abdur Rahman replied that his people would resent any such assistance. Dufferin then said quickly: 'If Your Highness rejects the assistance that we offer you under the terms of our Treaty, then Your Highness will have to make with the Russians the best arrangement you can. You will be unable, for instance, to maintain your claim to the Panjdeh district.'[29] The Amir then, to everyone's surprise, said that he made no such claim, which virtually put an end to the crisis. Britain was released from any obligations she may have had over Panjdeh without loss of face; the frontier between Afghanistan and Russia being afterwards settled by an Anglo-Russian boundary commission.

As well as settling the Panjdeh crisis, Dufferin, through his talks with the Amir at Rawalpindi, established a satisfactory relationship with him. 'It was a curious thing to see him and Lord Dufferin together' wrote Durand, who as Foreign Secretary was present at the meetings. 'On the one side the trained diplomatist with his cordial refined manner, playing a bad hand with admirable skill – on the other, the rough strong savage, never yielding the smallest of his advantages and striking home at times very forcibly'. Abdur Rahman reminded Durand of 'a sort of Afghan Henry VIII and of an old boar – the latter similitude being brought home to one by a huge single tusk which formed a marked feature in his countenance until Miller the dentist pulled it out'.[30]

The ministrations of Miller the dentist were among several factors contributing to Abdur Rahman's 'great good humour'.[31] Others included the charm of Hariot Dufferin – whom he afterwards described as 'the cleverest woman I have ever seen'[32] – the Star of India with which he was invested, the gifts lavished on him, the clocks, the musical boxes, the jewelled sword of honour; the privilege of meeting the Queen-Empress's son, the Duke of Connaught, who together with his Duchess was a guest in the Viceroy's Camp. The Amir did not seem to mind the rain which fell in torrents during most of his stay at Rawalpindi; turning the tasteful lay-out of fountains, flower-pots and beds of maidenhair fern between the tents of the Viceroy's Camp into a quagmire. Fortunately the weather improved sufficiently for Dufferin to be able to show his guest something of the military might of British India at parades held on two successive days. On the first day no fewer than 20,000 troops marched past to the highly appropriate tune of 'We don't want to fight, but by Jingo if we do'.

Before 1885 was out, Dufferin was concerned about the machinations of another European power on India's borders. This time it was Britain's old rival, France, intriguing with the government of King Thibaw, the effete young ruler of the still independent state of Upper Burma. Dufferin decided to take a tough line with the Burmese monarch, having the added excuse that Thibaw, who was completely dominated by his violent and passionate Queen Soopaya-Lât had for some time been guilty of gross misrule. He demanded that Thibaw should receive a British Resident at Mandalay and in future conduct his foreign policy according to the advice of the Government of India. When Thibaw rejected this ultimatum in highly offensive terms, Dufferin ordered his troops to march into the Burmese kingdom. 'We breakfasted at eight o'clock. At a quarter past the Viceroy signed the declaration of war with Burmah' Hariot Dufferin wrote laconically to her mother.[33]

The campaign was brief and decisive; the Burmese army fled before the British, who in ten days and with a loss of no more than twenty men made themselves masters of a country the size of France. Thibaw and Soopaya-Lât were sent to a place of exile on the Bombay coast and Dufferin annexed Upper Burma. He did so, as he said, 'with great reluctance';[34] for while annexation was the most logical step, the adjoining country of Lower Burma being already part of British India, it seemed too much like a return to a policy that had been out of favour since the time of Dalhousie; not only Gladstone but also Ripon and Northbrook viewed it with misgivings. Parliament, however, supported Dufferin warmly in his annexation, which he soon came to regard as the climax of his Viceroyalty. He asked for some place in Upper Burma to be called after him; and so a hill station was accordingly named Dufferin. When in 1888 he was given a step in the Peerage, he became Marquess of Dufferin and Ava; Ava being the ancient Burmese capital. He was not entirely happy about this title, fearing that it might appear presumptuous. His original wish was to be 'Dufferin and Quebec', having as Governor-General of Canada been instrumental in saving the old walls of that city; but the Queen wanted him to take an Indian place-name and suggested Delhi. Dufferin felt that this would be resented in India, and that a Burmese name would cause 'less inconvenient resentment'.[35] He lost no time in visiting his new kingdom; he and Hariot spent a couple of nights in Thibaw's palace of glass and gold at Mandalay and attended divine service in the Burmese monarch's Audience Hall.

To the present-day Indian historian, Dr. Sarvepalli Gopal, the acquisition of Upper Burma constitutes 'a dark shadow on an otherwise colourless Viceroyalty'.[36] From the point of view of administrative changes and the political advancement of the Indians, Dufferin's Viceroyalty might indeed be called colourless. 'I never had any ambition to distinguish my reign by a sensational policy' he told Salisbury in 1888, 'believing as I did . . . that in the present condition of affairs it is best for the country that the administration should be driven at a slow and steady pressure'.[37] But at the time, to the more conservative Indians and to the majority of the British in India, the reign of Dufferin and his 'little Lal', as he would affectionately call her, seemed nothing short of brilliant. The Viceregal entertainments in Calcutta and Simla were larger and more splendid than ever. Dufferin and Hariot charmed everybody, she managing to break through the shyness which overcame so many of the memsahibs in the presence of the Vicereine. To give added gaiety to the Viceregal establishment, there were the Dufferins' two debutante daughters; while their handsome eldest son Archie, who was soldiering in India, came on frequent visits. In the cold weather season, Government House was full of visiting swells from home together with numerous globe-trotting European royalties. At the head of the entourage was Bill Beresford, now Military Secretary. 'From the highest military affairs in the land to a mosquito inside my Excellency's curtain or a bolt on my door, all is the business of this invaluable person, and he does all equally well'[38] Hariot wrote of him, while admitting that she found driving to and from the races on his coach something of an ordeal, particularly when he had just dislocated his shoulder in a steeplechase.

Both the Dufferins appreciated the poetry of their high position as much as any Viceroy and Vicereine before them or after. Both saw romance in almost every aspect of India; though she was not quite such a romantic as he; thus Indians in their loose cotton garments reminded Dufferin of 'ancient Romans in their togas', whereas to Hariot they were just 'ordinary men in cotton sheets'.[39] Dufferin enjoyed living in Wellesley's great palace, which he adorned with mirrors brought from the palace of King Thibaw at Mandalay. Hariot liked the house too, while preferring Barrackpore and the breakfasts under the banyan tree. She was at first a little daunted by the domestic arrangements of Government House. 'The kitchen is somewhere in Calcutta, but not in this house'[40] she observed soon after her arrival; she did not exaggerate, for the Government House kitchen was in fact situated outside the grounds, in one of the narrow and inevitably squalid streets that flanked the northern approach. She also objected to having her sitting room and bedroom in opposite wings, separated by the length of two corridors and by the echoing space of the State apartments in between. So she and Dufferin abandoned the traditional Viceregal bedrooms and moved into the wing that contained her sitting room. That Dufferin should thus have slept a Sabbath day's journey away from the room in which he worked tells us much of his indolent habits; for most other Viceroys, who worked well into the small hours, would have found it intolerable having so great a distance between their desk and their bed.

If Dufferin did not spend as much time at his desk as he ought to have done – in fact he seldom did any work after dinner – he certainly did not neglect the social and ceremonial side of the Viceroyalty. He was forever visiting hospitals, schools and other institutions; he even went on foot through the worst of the Calcutta slums, to see for himself how the destitute lived. He enjoyed Durbars, receptions and Viceregal progresses; he enjoyed sitting enthroned under a canopy of State surrounded by scarlet-clad attendants bearing the peacock fans and the other emblems of royalty. He enjoyed being the honoured guest of the Princes: 'Several hundred young nautch girls danced before us' he noted with satisfaction during a visit to the Maharaja of Jaipur.[41] He enjoyed being kind to all manner of people and saying the right thing, which he did to perfection; whether it was flirting with the Dowager Maharani of Dholpur through a purdah screen or showing the requisite amount of civility to a criminal just released from prison; having been told to be very civil to this personage because he was a great man, but not too civil because he was a bad man.

Such was Dufferin's love of parties that Hariot could never drag him away from them; so that his guests were permitted to leave while he and Hariot were still there, instead of as was customary waiting for Their Excellencies to retire. He would enter wholeheartedly into the spirit of every entertainment; at a fancy dress ball at Simla he was impelled, on the spur of the moment, to get himself up as an Arab; which he did so well that even Hariot failed to recognise him. While declaring that he 'preferred men and women to trees'[42] he was not an indoor person like Lytton; but rode well, played an energetic game of tennis, went pig-sticking and also tiger shooting. 'It was too delightful' he purred, after a tiger shoot in the Terai, that pestilential jungle which killed Charlotte Canning.[43]

As well as affording Dufferin all these pleasures, India made a lifelong dream of his come true. He had long dreamt of building an enchanted castle, first on his estate in County Down, then, when he was Governor-General of Canada, at Quebec; but neither his own resources, nor those of the newly-fledged Dominion, had been up to his soaring architectural fantasies. Now, with the blessing of Lord Randolph Churchill as Secretary of State, Dufferin was at last able to build his enchanted castle on the summit of Observatory Hill at Simla; a new Viceregal Lodge, more suitable than Peterhof, something that had been talked about since the time of Lytton and before. For two of his Simla seasons, the building works were Dufferin's chief hobby. He visited them morning and evening, rather to the dismay of the Public Works Department, since he was constantly making changes. He would take his family and his guests – including the Duke and Duchess of Connaught and the Duc d'Orléans – on hazardous tours of the fabric. 'We climbed up the most terrible places, and stood on single planks over yawning chasms' wrote Hariot after one such tour.[44]

Halfway through their last Simla season, the Dufferins were able to move into their new house. They were delighted with the tall, Elizabethan-style mansion of greyish stone, its towers and cupolas rising above the trees. After Peterhof, the rooms seemed so grand and so plentiful that Hariot wondered how they would ever be filled. They were also very sumptuous, having been furnished and decorated by Maples of London. In the tremendous hall, which rose through the full height of the house, everything was of teak, walnut or deodar, elaborately carved and moulded. The big drawing room was furnished with gold and brown silks; the ballroom decorated in a lighter shade of yellow; the State dining room hung with Spanish leather in 'rich dark colours'. An unusual feature, for India, was the large, white-tiled basement kitchen, very different from the traditional cook-house. An even greater novelty was the electric light; Hariot found it 'quite a pleasure to go round one's room touching a button here and there'.[45] Yet another innovation was the indoor tennis court. In London, Lord Cross, who had succeeded Churchill as Secretary of State, was less enchanted when faced with the bill for the new house, which finally came to well over £100,000.

In one notable respect, the weather, India was a disappointment to Dufferin. Having suffered much from the cold of Canada, he was ready to enjoy the Indian heat. Arriving for the first time at Bombay, which most incoming Viceroys were apt to find oppressively hot, he pronounced the climate 'exquisite'.[46] But then, somehow, the heat failed him; so that throughout his Viceroyalty he was constantly complaining of the cold: 'Take your fur coat!' was to be his parting advice to one of his successors about to sail for India. The torrential rain which fell during the Amir's visit was no isolated occurrence; in fact so many of Dufferin's State occasions were rained upon that Hariot was to speak ruefully of 'the Viceroy's usual downpour'.[47] When the sun did appear, Dufferin was apt to bask in it at all hours, heedless of the warnings of the old India hands. Lyall attributed the severe bout of fever which Dufferin suffered while staying with him at Lucknow to his habit of choosing the hottest time of the day to inspect jails and hospitals and to his having sat outside at noon under an awning 'like a Hindu ascetic'.[48] We now know that, in exposing himself to the heat, Dufferin ran far less of a risk to his health than his contemporaries imagined; certainly less than he did when, on his visit to Burma, he wandered about the food bazaar at Rangoon tasting 'every queer sort of seed or mess he came near'.[49] Dufferin's horror of the cold – which was shared by his womenfolk – brought a hazard other than heat-stroke; for when he was in camp, the tents of the Viceregal family were rather too well provided with fireplaces. In a

Viceregal Lodge, Simla

camp at Patiala, the same thing happened to his daughter Nelly as happened to Charlotte Canning a quarter of a century earlier; she woke up in the middle of the night to find her tent ablaze. Fortunately she escaped unharmed and the fire did not spread to the adjoining tents; but she lost her entire wardrobe.

The burning of her daughter's tent was one of the many tribulations of Viceregal life recounted, along with the splendours and the absurdities, by Hariot in her letters to her mother, which she afterwards published. Much of what she tells seems frivolous, a round of balls, dinners and theatricals interspersed with jolly expeditions such as when she and her other daughter Hermie went 'roughing it' for five days in the Himalayan foothills: 'We have tried hard to see wherein lies the roughing it' she remarked ironically, 'and can only discover that we have to do without champagne and without cheese and that for three days out of the five we have had no coffee after dinner'.[50] Her letters do not, however, say much about her chief preoccupation when she was in India; which was to provide proper medical and nursing care for Indian women. The Queen had asked her to do something about this and she threw herself heart and soul into the task; launching the 'National Association for supplying Female Medical Aid to the Women of India', subsequently known as the 'Countess of Dufferin Fund'; presiding over countless meetings to raise money for it; founding hospitals and dispensaries which were to be a lasting memorial to her. Thanks to her talent for organisation and her commanding personality, her scheme had, by the time she left India, been adopted in every province and in all the principal States. Her work was commemorated on her departure in a poem entitled *Song of the Women*:

> How shall she know the worship that we do her?
> The walls are high and she is very far.
> How shall the womens' message reach unto her
> Above the tumult of the packed bazaar?
> Free wind of March against the lattice blowing,
> Bear thou our thanks lest she depart unknowing.

The poem was written by a young journalist in Lahore named Rudyard Kipling. The Kipling family, though their official standing was hardly such as would get them into Viceregal circles – Rudyard's father, Lockwood Kipling, being merely Head of the Lahore School of Art and Curator of the Museum – were taken up privately by the Dufferins at Simla; for the reason that Dufferin enjoyed talking about art and literature with Lockwood and even more so with his wife: 'Dullness and Mrs. Kipling cannot exist in the same room' he used to say.[51] The friendship survived a short-lived romance between the

Veranda at Viceregal
Lodge, Simla

Dufferins' eldest son Archie and the Kiplings' beautiful daughter
Trix; of which Dufferin made it abundantly clear that he did not
approve. As well as honouring Hariot in verse on her departure from
India, Rudyard Kipling wrote a poem entitled *One Viceroy Resigns* in
which Dufferin is made to look back on his Viceroyalty in a
monologue addressed to his successor. The monologue, as Sir
Harold Nicolson remarks, is highly characteristic of Kipling; but
'does not accurately reflect the habits, manners or phraseology of the
proconsul whom he was describing'.[52] It also shows Kipling as
having an exaggerated idea of the size of Upper Burma.

> Four years and I forget. If I forget
> How will *they* bear me in their minds? The North
> Safeguarded – nearly (Roberts knows the rest)
> A country twice the size of France annexed.
> That stays at least. The rest may pass – may pass . . .

Ballroom, Viceregal Lodge, Simla

Dufferin's decision to resign from the Viceroyalty at the end of 1888, a year before he was due to leave, took India by surprise. His resignation was entirely for personal reasons; his enjoyment of India was beginning to flag; however lightly he may have worked by the standards of other Viceroys, even that was becoming too much for him. As he remarked to a friend:

> It is an odd thing to say, but dullness is certainly the characteristic of an Indian Viceroy's existence. All the people who surround him are younger than himself; he has no companions or playfellows; even the pretty women who might condescend to cheer him it is better for him to keep at a distance.[53]

In other words, like Lytton before him, he felt starved of the sophisticated society to which he was used. He wished to return to the easier life of diplomacy; by leaving India when he did, he was able to secure the Embassy in Rome; which was near enough to Britain for him to see more of his younger sons than he would have done had he stayed a year longer in India.

These were the reasons he himself gave for his premature departure. One suspects that his vanity also had something to do with it. He wished his Viceroyalty to go down to history as successful; he felt, as he said, 'like a man engaged in riding a very dangerous steeplechase' and that he would be lucky if he completed the course without 'having a cropper'.[54] Having managed to avoid coming to grief over a four-year course, he would very likely have felt that to stay a further year was tempting Providence. 'I am truly grateful to be able to escape out of India under these tolerable conditions and without any very deep scratches on my credit and reputation' he wrote in his final letter to the Secretary of State, to whom he also declared with characteristic smugness: 'Without self-flattery, I think I can say that I shall have handed over the country . . . in a satisfactory condition. There is not a cloud on the horizon and we have succeeded in all our undertakings.'[55]

The regret shown by the British and the conservative Indians at his impending departure and the tributes they paid him were enough to confirm Dufferin in his belief that he had been a great success. Yet it would seem that he wished also to be applauded by Indians of the more radical sort, as Ripon had been; for during the last year of his reign he appears to have deliberately set out to court popularity with Congress. To this may be attributed his haste in getting his proposals for reforming the provincial Legislative Councils approved by the Home Government before he left India, which was ostensibly in order to make things easier for his successor. It is alleged that he made a covert approach to two Congress leaders, asking them to organise a send-off for him that would outdo Ripon's; but one very much doubts if, even to satisfy his vanity, he would have done anything quite so inconsistent with the dignity of his high position.

However hard Dufferin may have tried to win applause from the more politically-minded Indians, he failed to get any; though the quixotic Hume wrote a spirited defence of his Viceroyalty in a newspaper. Dufferin believed that things would have been different if the Home Government had authorised him to announce his Council reforms publicly, which it had not yet done; he nevertheless left India very much out of humour with Congress and its friends. In his last major speech as Viceroy, which he delivered at the St Andrew's Day dinner of the wealthy and powerful Scots community of Calcutta, he put Congress – 'this microscopic minority', as he called it – firmly in its place.[56]

If Dufferin left India feeling to a certain extent ill-used, Hariot was overwhelmed by gratitude for what she had done. On the afternoon of one of her last days as Vicereine, a deputation of the ladies of Bengal, Bihar and Orissa waited on her at Government House to present her with an address, something that had never been done before. She had expected a group of twenty or thirty, but 'the ladies came in crowds';[57] so that by the time they had all been assembled it was getting dark; and since out of deference to those of them who were in purdah all the menservants had been sent away, there was nobody to light the chandeliers. Hariot was 'very low' at the prospect of leaving;[58] and when she and Dufferin walked for the last time down the great steps of Government House, almost everyone present was in tears.

Dufferin was only two years in Rome before being appointed to succeed Lytton as Ambassador to France. He thus secured the highest prize in British diplomacy; but unfortunately his career did not end there. After retiring from the Paris Embassy in 1896, he agreed to become Chairman of the group of companies floated by the notorious Whitaker Wright; that this man should have taken in so shrewd a judge of character as Dufferin may perhaps be attributed to deafness and failing eyesight. In December 1900 the companies crashed; and while Dufferin was exonerated from all blame in the matter, it cast a cloud over the few months that remained of his life. The good fortune which had stayed with him for so long deserted him at last in his old age; for the year 1900 also saw the death of his beloved eldest son Archie, who was mortally wounded while serving in the South African War.

Hariot Dufferin lived to see the death of her three younger sons as well; but her spirit was never broken. She was one of several Victorian Vicereines who survived until well into the present century; she died aged 93 in 1936, a month after Edith Lytton. In the previous year she attended a celebration at the India Office to mark the fiftieth anniversary of her Fund; her speech on that occasion was full of 'that gentle but most persistent authority'[59] which had made her such a success as a Vicereine half a century earlier.

9

Imperial siesta

The year 1888, when the Dufferins left India to the plaudits of Kipling, can be seen as the high noon of the Raj; it was also a turning point in the history of the Viceroyalty. Although Northbrook had feared that the telegraph would reduce the Viceroy to being a mere puppet of Whitehall, circumstances and the character of each of the three Viceroys who came after him were such as to prevent this from happening for another decade or more. After Dufferin's time, however, the Viceroy came much nearer to being 'The Great Ornamental' – which he had certainly not been in 1880, when a satirical writer called the ruler of British India by this name.[1] To a certain extent, it was a change of circumstances which helped to bring this about. Parliament was now taking a greater interest in Indian affairs; Dufferin's immediate successor enjoyed a reign more peaceful and uneventful than that of any other Viceroy before him or after. The decade of the eighteen-nineties saw few political developments; it was, in the words of Dr. Sarvepalli Gopal, 'a period of marking time'.[2] But the decline in the influence of the Viceroyalty during this period can also be blamed on the character of the 'two acquiescent, unimaginative men',[3] as Dr. Gopal has called them, who followed Dufferin.

The first of these two Viceroys, the Marquess of Lansdowne, is now remembered as a distinguished Foreign Secretary and as an elder statesman who had the courage to advocate a negotiated peace at the height of the First World War. As a Viceroy, he is largely forgotten; one feels that he would himself have been the first to admit the justice of this, for his heart was never really in his Viceroyalty. For him, ruling India was not the culmination of his career, but a job taken on without much enthusiasm for the mundane reason that he needed the money; he hoped to be able to save some of his salary as well as to live on it during the five years of his reign. That the Viceregal salary should have been an inducement to him may seem strange, for he was one of the great territorial magnates of the United Kingdom, with estates in England as well as Ireland, where he had his roots; his paternal ancestors, the Fitzmaurices, having been

The 5th Marquess of
Lansdowne. A caricature
by C. Pellegrini ('Ape')

Lords of Kerry since the thirteenth century. His principal seat, Bowood in Wiltshire, was on a palatial scale and he also owned Lansdowne House, one of the finest of London's private palaces. But along with his great possessions he had inherited a vast debt; moreover his Irish rent-roll had been reduced almost to nothing by the agrarian unrest of the eighteen-eighties.

Coming as he did of a dynasty of Whig statesmen, it was natural that Lansdowne should have followed a political career. But after serving as a junior minister in two Liberal administrations, he left the Liberal Party because he disagreed with Gladstone's Irish policy. Soon afterwards, in 1883, he went to Canada as Governor-General;

his reason for going being the same as that which, five years later, induced him to go to India. But for his financial plight, he would never have endured these two periods of exile; for he hated being away from his estates, on which his interests were very much centred. He also hated being parted from his mother, who was a daughter of Talleyrand's natural son, the Comte de Flahault.

Lansdowne was only a quarter French, for his grandfather Flahault had married a Scottish heiress. Yet he was very much a Frenchman in appearance; a slight, dapper, small-boned figure with moustache and side-whiskers, always elegantly dressed. A picture of him as a young man, wearing a low, semi-circular bowler, might serve as an illustration to Proust. Without doubt a friend of the Duc de Guermantes, a French face of the highest breeding, with a fine bone-structure, an aquiline nose, rather piercing, twinkling eyes beneath dark eyebrows. His forehead seemed all the higher because his hair receded at an early age; it had done so by the time he went to India, when he was only forty-three.

As well as looking French, Lansdowne had the manner and ways of a cultivated Frenchman; a polished grace, an unfailing, slightly ceremonious courtesy. While being always able to converse animatedly on any subject, he had a natural reticence that discouraged intimacy. British heartiness was quite alien to his fastidious nature. But while French in appearance and manner and in his frequent use of French phrases, he was in character the archetypal British nobleman; simple, straightforward, of reasonable ability if limited imagination; with a strong sense of duty and a deep love of country pursuits. Transparently honest, he had inherited none of Talleyrand's deviousness; nor, for that matter, any of the subtlety of his other great-grandfather, the eighteenth-century Prime Minister Shelburne, who was known as 'The Jesuit of Berkeley Square'. Few if any of Lansdowne's contemporaries would not have agreed with his brother-in-law's tribute that 'he was possibly the greatest gentleman of his day'.[4]

As everyone's idea of a *grand seigneur*, Lansdowne made an excellent impression on the British in India, as well as on the Princes and other more traditionally-minded Indians. Being who he was, he was able quite unselfconsciously to be Viceregal while never losing his natural simplicity; he hated pomp and circumstance, yet performed his ceremonial duties to perfection. All this was no less true of Maud Lansdowne, who as a daughter of the Duke of Abercorn, a former Viceroy of Ireland, was in no way overawed by her high position, but took it in her stride. Though her State arrival with Lansdowne at Bombay was far from auspicious, in that the funnel of the launch taking her and her husband from the ship to the Apollo Bunder belched coal dust and steam all over her beautiful white embroidered dress, she was an immediate success as Vicereine; in no way handicapped by being the successor of so popular a Lady Sahib as Hariot Dufferin. On the face of it, the new reign seemed rather like a continuation of the popular Dufferin regime. The entertainments at Government House and Viceregal Lodge were just as brilliant, with Bill Beresford still in charge as Military Secretary.

In the Government, as at Government House, the change of regime was not much felt; Lansdowne, though more hardworking than Dufferin, was just as disinclined as he had been to interfere with the officials. Durand, who continued as Foreign Secretary, obviously liked and admired the new Viceroy; but it is significant that he mentioned him far less often in his letters than he had previously mentioned Dufferin and before that Ripon. 'So far as India is concerned, anyone who troubles us will find we have a fighting Viceroy' is the most we learn of Lansdowne from Durand; who, while clearly intending this as praise, gives the show away by adding: 'He and Bobs run neck and neck'.[5] That Lansdowne should have been called 'a fighting Viceroy' is proof not so much of his own strength as of the extent to which he was under the influence of his redoubtable Commander-in-Chief. It was through Roberts's influence that Lansdowne favoured a return to the old 'forward' policy in relations with Afghanistan; though his motives were not only strategic but also humanitarian – his aristocratic Whig blood revolted at the cruelties of Abdur Rahman's rule and made him anxious to modify them. In the event, the Home Government wisely refused to allow any major change in the *status quo* as Dufferin had left it; outstanding differences with the Amir being settled by sending Durand on a mission to him.

Lansdowne's failure to get his way over Afghanistan is one instance of his weakness in his relations with the Home Government; which in this case was a blessing in disguise. Less fortunate was the fact that it took him nearly four years to get the Home Government to agree to the Council reforms which Dufferin had promised. Lansdowne personally favoured these reforms, which he felt would enable the majority of Congress 'to shake themselves clear' of the extremists;[6] it was not merely that he was committed to them by his predecessor. His attitude towards Congress at the beginning of his reign was very much one of tolerance: he even went so far as to repudiate an order by the Government of Bengal prohibiting officials from attending its session in 1890. For a time after his courageous action Congress saw Lansdowne as a second Ripon; but by 1892, the year when the Council reforms at last became law, the Viceroy had on the one hand been alienated by the erratic British Congress leader, Allan Octavian Hume, and on the other had allowed himself to be persuaded by the officials that Congress no longer counted for

Picnic given by
Lansdowne's Staff at
Simla, 1891

anything. For the rest of his Viceroyalty, Lansdowne fell back on the
traditional policy of strengthening the landowners against the rising
educated middle classes; he became less sympathetic towards Indian
aspirations and tended to echo the more conservative official point of
view. After his return to England, when the question of having an
Indian Member of the Viceroy's Executive Council was being
discussed, he said to the then Vicereine: 'I agree that we must make
concessions, but to place a Native in the Holy of Holies I should
consider a grave mistake'.[7]

Having been a hero to Congress in 1890, Lansdowne was at the
end of his reign denounced by the more extreme vernacular
newspapers as an 'Enemy of the People and a mere puppet in the
hands of the Civil Service'.[8] He had made himself obnoxious to them
by taking effective though by no means repressive steps to curb
sedition in the Press; and by proposing to dispense with juries in
murder trials in Bengal. The latter was a purely administrative
measure; for the right of trial by jury did not exist all over British
India, but only in some parts and then only for certain offences.
Nevertheless, the measure provoked an outcry in India which was
taken up by liberal opinion in England; Lansdowne mishandled the

affair so as to incur a rebuff from the Secretary of State, to which he reacted by threatening to resign and by canvassing the support of his friends in the Opposition – an improper expedient for a Viceroy. Lansdowne eventually had to give way, though the Home Government enabled him to do so without too much loss of face.

In other less controversial measures, such as an attempt to stabilise the rupee and a proposal to introduce import duties, Lansdowne also had to give way to the Home Government. All he could do was to utter a *cri-de-coeur* to the Secretary of State: 'There is an impression in this country that HMG will not allow us to do anything'.[9] Though he suffered more defeats after the Liberals had returned to power in 1892, he had trouble enough getting the Conservatives to implement the Council reforms. The change of Government certainly made his position more difficult; for whereas in the days of Mayo and Northbrook the Liberals had been on the whole less interested in Indian affairs than the Conservatives and therefore less likely to interfere, by the eighteen-nineties an ever-increasing section of the Liberal Party was being influenced by visiting Indian extremists and held strong if misinformed opinions as to how India should be governed. 'There is, I am sorry to say, something of a dead-set by Liberal MPs against our whole administration in India' the Liberal Secretary of State, Lord Kimberley, himself admitted to Lansdowne.[10] Yet one also has the impression that by the time the Liberals came into power, Lansdowne had somehow grown weaker and less sure of himself. In the earlier part of his reign, he was much more in control; thus he dealt firmly and fairly with a minor revolt in the Eastern hill-state of Manipur in 1891, which led to the murder of two senior British officials; he insisted on executing the ringleaders contrary to the wishes of the Home Government and also of the Queen, who objected because one of them was a Prince – encouraged by her Indian servant to believe that the Indian Princes were being badly treated by the British. In this crisis Lansdowne was able to draw on his own experience, having dealt with the rising of Louis Riel in Canada six years earlier.

Lansdowne's troubles, though they not only prevented his achievement as Viceroy from amounting to anything very much – apart from the Council reforms, the credit for which really belongs to Dufferin – but left the Viceroyalty permanently debilitated, were seldom enough to disturb the unruffled calm of his reign. On the face of it, the Indian administration went on smoothly and successfully with him in charge; he was a Viceroy who did everything that was required of him and more; even going over a pilgrim ship at Bombay in order to see for himself the horrors which devout Muslims had to endure for the sake of their souls. He described it in a letter to his mother: 'The whole ship, on deck and between decks, was packed with the poor creatures . . . so close together that I had to pick my way on tiptoe, putting my foot wherever I could find room for it among the confusion of limbs and bodies. It was a blazing hot day, and although the ports were open, the smell was enough to make me sneeze.' In the same letter, he also told of how he had inspected a leper colony and a veterinary hospital; adding ruefully: 'What with emigrants, lepers and glandered horses, I ought to pick up something unpleasant as a souvenir of my visit'.[11]

A Viceroy so much to the manner born, who brought a patrician grace to the Viceroyalty and at the same time was willing to perform duties from which others might have shrunk — it is hard to know whether to count Lansdowne as a failure or a success. One would rate him higher had there not been something sadly lacking in his attitude towards his Viceroyalty: no sense of mission, certainly no appreciation of the poetry of his high office. To him it was simply a five-year stint which he longed to get over. Perhaps he was too great a swell for the job. Born to an exalted position at home, the trappings of Viceroyalty left him cold. Used as he was to the splendours of Bowood and Lansdowne House, he was not particularly impressed by Wellesley's palace in Calcutta, remarking only on 'the utter absence of anything like homely comfort'.[12] And if the Viceroyalty held little glamour for him, India as a whole does not seem to have appealed to him or won his affections. He never seems in any way to have identified himself with his Empire; his letters home were always those of an exile, an outsider, a tourist. He had quite a good eye for the Indian scenery, but in describing it to his mother had the irritating habit of comparing it unfavourably with scenery in Scotland or Ireland. 'The Indus is very well' he remarked, when travelling on that great river, 'but I wish I was dropping down to Isla Point.'[13]

His letters home are full of the discomforts, the tedium, the shortcomings and the absurdities of Indian Viceregal life; but seldom if ever contain any mention of the glories. 'The crowd of black servants oppresses me' he complained, soon after his arrival.[14] He disliked having to make a speech at a gathering 'half of which consists of native gentlemen who do not understand a word of what is being said, while the other half is mainly composed of ladies, who I always think are a most aggravating audience to speak to'.[15] When entertained by the Indian Princes, he felt disgusted at being 'garlanded and smeared with their horrible attar of roses some half dozen times';[16] though one can imagine that he might have felt out of humour during a visit to the Maharaja of Indore when another of poor Maud's dresses was ruined by having holes burnt in it by the fireworks. From Hyderabad, he told his mother how weary he was of fireworks and illuminations: 'I think I shall hate even a solitary squib

for the rest of my days'.[17] He did not think much of the sport at
Viceregal shoots: 'I don't much care if I never take part in another' he
wrote after one of them.[18] It was fortunate that he was far too much
of a gentleman to betray his true feelings to his Indian hosts. Despite
his French blood, he was bored at having to put on the customary
State reception for the Governor-General of 'Pondicherry, Chander-
nagore and one or two more ridiculous little French scraps of
territory' as he called them. But it was with some pride that he
observed 'Maud's face of mingled disgust and indignation' at the
sight of a certain French lady who came to the ball given in honour of
the French Governor-General 'apparently under the impression that
a liberal covering of paint made amends for a corresponding
deficiency in the matter of clothes'. The lady 'squirmed' beneath the
Vicereine's gaze and – as Lansdowne afterwards learnt from Bill
Beresford – was unable to eat any supper.[19]

As the end of Lansdowne's Viceroyalty drew near, his letters home
became rather like those of a schoolboy at the approach of the
holidays. 'Halleluja!' he wrote, on realising that there were only two
more months to go.[20] One doubts if any other Viceroy looked
forward to the end of his reign as avidly as he did. In fairness to him it
must be said that he was physically exhausted by his labours and
found the Indian climate very trying; he was also longing to be
reunited with his mother, his two sons and his elder daughter who
was now married and living in England. His departure was as much
regretted by the British and the more conservative Indians as
Dufferin's had been. The extremists who attacked him in certain
newspapers and also tried to prevent the Corporation of Calcutta
from giving him a farewell address he dismissed as 'a little knot of
seditious scoundrels'.[21] They failed to influence the Corporation and
one more address was duly added to Lansdowne's collection, the size
of which had already caused him to lament – rather touchingly, when
one thinks of the rooms and corridors of Bowood – 'Where I shall put
all my caskets, etc, when I get home, I don't know'.[22]

The Lansdownes left Calcutta by water from Prinsep's Ghat and
boarded a ship in the river, as their predecessors in the days before
railways had done. 'We steamed away feeling very miserable' their
younger daughter wrote in her diary.[23] She spoke for herself and
probably also for her mother; but certainly not for her father. The
Queen wanted to make Lansdowne a Duke, having always supported
him strongly except over the Manipur executions; but Gladstone was
unwilling to recommend him for so high an honour since he was no
longer a member of the Liberal Party. Although Lansdowne had
spoken of retiring into private life when his Viceroyalty came to an
end, he joined Salisbury's Cabinet as a Liberal-Unionist in 1895, the
year after his return; he became Foreign Secretary in 1900 and

continued at the forefront of politics until the end of the First World War.

If Lansdowne had it in him to be Viceroy but failed to assert himself, his successor, the ninth Earl of Elgin – son of the Viceroy whose reign was cut short by a heart-attack at Dharmsala – was weak and not quite of Lansdowne's calibre. He was earnest, sincere, conscientious, a dutiful landowner and a pillar of the Scottish Liberal Party; a good public speaker though by nature shy and reserved; in short, as he has rightly been called, 'a sound and sober Scot'.[24] But he was not really up to ruling India. He owed his appointment to his friendship with Lord Rosebery, his neighbour on the other side of the Firth of Forth, who was then Foreign Secretary and soon to succeed Gladstone as Prime Minister. It was Rosebery who thought of Elgin; one can only imagine he did so because he and the rest of the Cabinet were in a hurry to fill the post, which had already been offered to General Sir Henry Norman – an unlikely choice for a Liberal Government in peacetime, though this distinguished elderly soldier had much experience of governing India, having served for seven years as Military Member of the Viceroy's Council. Norman had actually accepted the Viceroyalty and his appointment had been announced in the Press; but he had then backed down on account of his age.

Elgin was fully aware of his own inadequacy. He had none of his father's rather calculating ambition – by all accounts, he was a much nicer person – and unlike his father had absolutely no wish to be Viceroy. Rosebery had to walk him three times round that dour mountain in the outskirts of Edinburgh known as Arthur's Seat before he agreed reluctantly to accept the post. It was typical of Elgin that while being wise enough to realise that the Viceroyalty was beyond his capabilities, he should have allowed himself to be talked into taking it on against his better judgement. Elgin seldom had the courage of his convictions, which in themselves were usually sound enough; thus Curzon, his successor as Viceroy – a man more given to criticism than to praise – was to write of him that 'he was a much more sagacious administrator than the world knew'.[25] But unless his views happened to coincide with those of the officials or of the Home Government, he allowed them to be disregarded. Far from carrying the Home Government and the officials along with him, as a successful Viceroy could do, Elgin was happy to leave the important decisions to the Home Government and the administration of India in the hands of the officials; himself acting merely as a connecting link between Whitehall and the Secretariats in Calcutta or Simla.

In fact, Elgin came even closer to being a Great Ornamental than Lansdowne had been during the latter part of his reign. But while Lansdowne really was ornamental – whatever his shortcomings as a

Lord Elgin on 'the most comfortable sofa in this part of India'. The Retreat, Mashobra, 1896

Viceroy, he looked the part – Elgin was not. He was short and bearded, lacking in personal glamour, a Ripon figure without the reforming zeal. Though not yet forty-five when he came to India, he looked considerably older; he was careless about his dress and avoided wearing uniform if he could possibly help it. Sport did not interest him and he never felt at home on the back of a horse. There is a story of how, on one of the very rare occasions when he rode a pony at Simla, the lady who was with him asked him something to which he replied impatiently: 'Can't you see that I am busy riding?' He preferred to take his exercise by going for long walks, stepping out across the Maidan when in Calcutta, scrambling up and down precipices at Simla. He was a quick and tireless walker so that his Staff often had difficulty in keeping up with him; and he frequently managed to evade the policeman who was supposed, for the sake of security, to accompany him wherever he went.

With the advent of his homely figure – and the departure of Bill Beresford, who retired from India when the Lansdownes left – Government House and Viceregal Lodge lost something of the brilliance and gaiety of the two previous reigns. A lady who sat next to Elgin at his first State dinner at Government House expressed what most people were feeling when she blurted out to the new Viceroy: 'How terribly sad it is to come here and not find the Lansdownes! But perhaps some day it will be nice again!' Elgin took her tactlessness in good part, grateful for a little light relief on an occasion which for him was something of an ordeal.[26]

The new Vicereine was possessed of more glamour than her

Lady Elisabeth (Bessie) Bruce examining a flower

husband; though she could not adequately fill the place of Maud Lansdowne and Hariot Dufferin on account of her rather poor health; she was always tired, forever suffering from headaches and insomnia. Yet she carried out her duties as best she could, even undergoing the rigours of a Viceregal tour when she was expecting a baby. The Elgins brought three young daughters with them; the eldest, Lady Elisabeth Bruce, emerged from the schoolroom towards the end of their first year in India and became an invaluable understudy to her mother. For a girl of seventeen, Lady Elisabeth – known to her family as Bessie – was remarkably mature; she could draw out the most taciturn of guests in conversation and took a serious interest in everything that was going on. She was also a born listener and very observant; so that the diary she kept for the benefit of an aunt – who had been in India during the Viceroyalty of the previous Elgin – gives as good a picture of Viceregal life as the journals and letters of Charlotte Canning and Hariot Dufferin. She adored and admired her father, so that she naturally tells us nothing of his shortcomings. She gives us, however, occasional glimpses of him which show that while he may have been a weak Viceroy, he was certainly a very human one; such as when, during an Investiture, he smiled down at the six-year-old Claud Elliott – a future Headmaster of Eton – who was one of the two little pages holding up his robes; then looked reassuringly at the boy's somewhat anxious mother.

Elgin's reign was to be described by Curzon as the 'apotheosis of bureaucracy'.[27] Unfortunately, it was an apotheosis in which the deities were a rather poor lot compared with the gods of yesteryear –

The Retreat at Mashobra

A snapshot taken by the Elgins' second daughter, Lady Christian Bruce, at a picnic in Baghi Forest in September 1895. Lord Elgin is in the centre, leaning against a tree; Lady Elgin sits in a *dandy* on the right, and between them sits their third daughter, Lady Veronica. Sitting on the left of the picture smoking a pipe is Henry Babington Smith, Lord Elgin's Private Secretary who afterwards became his son-in-law

the Temples, the Stracheys, the Lyalls. Perhaps the only outstanding figure among the top civilians in Elgin's time was Sir Anthony Macdonnell who left the Council in 1895 to become Lieutenant-Governor of the North-Western Provinces. Durand was still Foreign Secretary when Elgin arrived; but went to Teheran as Ambassador a couple of months later. Elgin fondly imagined that by allowing himself to be ruled by his somewhat undistinguished Council he would have 'a strong and united Government'.[28] Instead, he had a Council that was not only undistinguished but also disorderly, each Member tending to go his own way; even with the Home Government behind him, Elgin was unable to control it. A lack of discipline was also noticeable at this time in relations between the provinces and the Centre; in particular, the two Presidencies of Madras and Bombay, which had always enjoyed a measure of independence, now tended to act as though Calcutta or Simla did not exist.

Elgin and his Government appear at their worst over the perennial question as to whether or not import duties were to be imposed on cotton goods brought into India from Britain. It was a question of conflicting interests, Indian and British; in happier days, Northbrook and his Council had been as one in staunchly upholding the interests of India. Now, the top civilians as well as the Viceroy were indecisive in the matter and even inclined to favour the interests of Britain. Elgin was told by the formidable head of the India Office, Sir Arthur Godley, that although the Home Government had refused to allow the import duties when Lansdowne was Viceroy, it would have to agree to them if they were urged again; but instead of taking his cue from Godley, Elgin simply left the decision to the Home Government. The Liberals were then still in power, so that there were men such as Ripon and Kimberley in the Cabinet who would have supported Elgin if he had really insisted on the duties; but as he did not, the interests of Manchester prevailed and the duties were vetoed. And what was worse, both the Liberal Government and its Unionist successor took advantage of Elgin's timidity to bring in a series of measures designed not only to prop up the ailing Lancashire cotton industry at the expense of India, but to stifle the growth of Indian manufactures which were still in their infancy.

This is one of the darkest chapters in the history of Britain's Indian Empire; a real case of India being exploited for the benefit of Britain; something which happily occurred much less frequently than is now popularly supposed. It brought protests from all over India – from the non-official British as well as from Congress and other sections of Indian opinion – but public attention was largely distracted from it by the terrible visitations of famine and plague which began in 1896. The famine, the worst ever known under the British Raj, was dealt with as well as could be expected; Elgin has been praised for his calmness and patience during the crisis, as well as for continuing the good work of Mayo and other Viceroys before him in building railways to facilitate famine relief. The plague, which was mainly centred on the Bombay Presidency though it affected other parts of India, was handled less efficiently. The more stringent anti-plague measures offended the religious susceptibilities of the Hindus; the provincial authorities and the Central Government were not in agreement as to how far religion could safely be disregarded in the interests of public health and Elgin vacillated between the different points of view. In the Bombay Presidency the anti-plague

Lord Elgin at the Tin Tall Caves, Aurangabad

campaign was conducted without much tact; causing resentment which erupted into violence on the night of the Queen-Empress' Diamond Jubilee, when two British officials were murdered at Poona.

At about the same time as the Poona murders, severe rioting occurred in Calcutta. There had been a feeling of unrest in India at the beginning of Elgin's reign, but it had soon died down; now it was noticeable once again. Newspapers became increasingly violent in their attacks on British rule; but Elgin did not believe that the Government should be given any more power to curb the Press than what it possessed already. Nor was he inclined to take any action against Congress, although many of the British from the Unionist Secretary of State downwards were convinced of the 'seditious and double-sided character' of its leaders for all their protestations of loyalty.[29] Elgin's attitude towards Congress was consistent; he did not regard it as a danger and was prepared to cultivate friendly relations with it; but the troubles of his reign prevented him from making any sort of progress in this respect.

Lady Elgin in a silver
anjan at Gaya, December
1896

To add to Elgin's troubles, his reign was marked by disturbances in the tribal territory along the North-West Frontier, which necessitated several costly and difficult military campaigns, notably the Chitral Expedition of 1895 and the Tirah Campaign of 1897. After the Chitral Expedition, Elgin so far forgot his Liberal principles as to advocate a 'forward' policy; a sign of how quickly he had, like Lansdowne before him, fallen under the influence of the High Command – albeit a High Command without the dominant personality of 'Bobs', whose Indian career ended in 1893. 'The usual Viceroy is a mere puppet in the hands of his military advisers' Curzon was afterwards to write. 'The tunes to which my two predecessors were induced to dance would constitute a page of history that I hope for their sakes may never be written.'[30] Yet Elgin at any rate did not allow himself to be persuaded by those military hawks who, believing Abdur Rahman to be the instigator of the Malakand disturbances of 1897, called for a march to Kabul. 'Honestly, I feel that an incautious word or act on my part might land us in an Afghan war' he told the Secretary of State.[31] That was a calamity he was able to avoid.

There are occasional echoes of the troubles of Elgin's reign in his daughter's diary. During the famine, which was caused by drought, there was great excitement at Government House when the sky suddenly darkened and there was thunder. 'Is it raining yet?' Lady Elgin asked anxiously. 'I wonder how many thousand pounds rain would give to the famine fund?' It did rain, a proper downpour; and the Viceroy and his family 'were all too happy to . . . do anything but watch it'. When reports reached the Viceroy at Simla of panic in

Calcutta following the riots there, he remained unperturbed; that evening he 'sang Scotch songs . . . and seemed very cheerful'. The outbreak of hostilities on the Frontier in 1897 saw the departure of several of the ADCs to the Front. One of them, Lord Fincastle, came back with a VC; he had served with the Malakand Field Force, along with another young officer mentioned by Bessie as having come to stay at Barrackpore: 'Mr Churchill (in Captain Baring's regiment) . . . He is short, with reddish hair and face, blue eyes and "some of his father's characteristics", I have been told'.[32]

On the whole, Bessie avoided writing about affairs of State, except in so far as they impinged on the day-to-day life of her family. One is left with the impression that it was a simpler life than that of the Lansdownes and Dufferins. One is also regrettably struck by how little the Elgins mixed socially with Indians – much less than the Dufferins had done in the previous decade. After nearly two years in India, Bessie wrote of the young Maharaja of Gwalior: 'He is the first native I have seen whom I can feel really quite fond of'.[33]

Bessie's activities were not so much those of a princess as of the Squire's daughter in a large and rather sociable village. She made dolls' clothes for innumerable charity bazaars and sales of work; she took part in amateur theatricals; she practised the Scottish reels that were a feature of balls at Government House and Viceregal Lodge during the Elgin regime. She attempted to list and draw all the wild flowers of the Simla region. She also performed the homely task of darning her father's stockings, the ones he wore when going for his walks; the Indians being apparently incapable of darning them properly. Such was Elgin's love of walking – which Bessie shared – that he took every opportunity of getting out into the country when at Simla; acquiring a small house known as The Retreat at Mashobra, five miles away, where he and his family spent their week-ends. One spring they went on an adventurous three-week march through the Himalayan foothills, Lady Elgin being carried in a *dandy* or litter, her husband and eldest daughter mostly walking. Their route took them to Dharmsala, where they visited the previous Elgin's grave; its tall Gothic monument as yet undamaged by the earthquake which happened a few years later. It was a poignant and historic moment, a Viceroy doing homage at the grave of another Viceroy who was his father.

The tenor of the Elgins' Viceroyalty was interrupted by two important family events. There was the safe arrival of the baby; when the birth was registered and the occupation of the child's father put down as 'Viceroy', it was noticed that the father's occupation in the entry immediately above was 'sweeper' – which to Bessie seemed an excellent example of 'democracy in action'.[34] The second event was one in which Bessie was herself the central figure: her marriage at

The young Winston Churchill in India

Simla in 1898 to Henry Babington Smith, her father's unusually young Private Secretary. After the service at Christ Church, the bride and bridegroom and the Viceroy and Vicereine drove back to Viceregal Lodge in carriages, splendidly escorted by the Bodyguard and a detachment of the Punjab Light Horse. They were followed by the carriages of the Commander-in-Chief and the Lieutenant-Governor of the Punjab and their respective wives; and then – since carriages were permitted to nobody else in Simla, owing to the narrowness of the roads – by a rather comic procession of guests in rickshaws and on horseback, jockeying to keep up with the illustrious carriage-folk. In the dining room of Viceregal Lodge a wedding cake nearly six feet high awaited them; it had taken Tancredi, the Viceregal chef, two months to make.

Bessie's wedding took place during the Elgins' last Simla season. As the sands of her father's Viceroyalty ran out, a wistful note crept into her diary; whether or not her father was conscious of the poetry of India and of his high position, there is no doubt that she was. She recorded the enchantment of the drive to Barrackpore when they went there for one of their last visits: 'The stars were sparkling and the fireflies shone among the dark trees . . . I wished that Virgil had been in India to describe the beautiful nights.' Back in Calcutta a few days later, she and her parents went to the Fort to say goodbye to the retiring Commander-in-Chief, Sir George White, who was laid up after a fall from his horse while paperchasing. 'It was growing dark and Sir George was laid on his long chair underneath a banyan tree on the ramparts . . . it was curious to sit there and watch the carriages with their lights hurrying along the dusty red road and think that by next year we too shall be part of the past.'

And then came the evening at Simla when Elgin learnt who his successor was to be. An office box was brought to him in the drawing room, where he was playing patience; it contained a single telegram which he read and then held folded in his hand. As he left the room he said to his wife in a low voice: 'Curzon – confidential'. He repeated this information to his daughters on the way upstairs. 'I cannot explain to you his beautiful expression' Bessie told her aunt. 'It seemed a mixture of feelings, of a sense that his own work seemed more nearly at an end, of happiness about being soon to see home, and also a thought of that rash man and of to what he was leaving all India. Where will it go if Mr. Curzon is impetuous?'[35]

Curzon

'That rash man.' Elgin's daughter, in speaking thus of George Nathaniel Curzon, hit on one of his chief defects; one of those flaws in his character which, for all his outstanding qualities – his encyclopedic knowledge, his limitless capacity for work, his sense of duty, his drive and efficiency, his dazzling powers of elucidation – made him not the greatest of all the Viceroys but only the best-known of them. 'Too much hubris' was the inevitable answer when Curzon asked his friend and Private Secretary, Walter Lawrence, what was wrong with his Viceroyalty; and he would make no attempt to deny this. 'I was born so' he would say, 'you cannot change me.'[1] As well as being rash, Curzon lacked vision and was incapable of understanding other people's psychology. He was too masterful, too certain that he was right; too ready to score off his opponents rather than win them over. 'He has a great deal of industry and courage and also of sterling qualities' another of Curzon's friends wrote of him, 'but it isn't a fine nature.'[2]

Those who worked under Curzon often found him aloof, ill-tempered and lacking in manners; but this was due not so much to his arrogance as to the pain he suffered owing to a weakness of the spine; which makes the Herculean labours of his career seem all the more remarkable. The fact that he never minced words – he did not mind if others treated him with equal bluntness – also tended to give offence, as did his well-known pomposity; though he was born pompous just as he was born rash. 'Had he spoken simply, it would have been affectation' remarked yet another of his contemporaries, who also said of him that his 'unique achievement was to combine this pomposity with humour'.[3] Curzon's sense of fun was one of his outstanding characteristics; at the slightest provocation his shoulders would shake with infectious laughter. The more extreme manifestations of his pomposity, the extravagantly class-conscious sayings with which he is credited, were mostly part of an elaborate joke against himself.

Curzon has frequently been called an eighteenth-century aristocrat born out of his time. He certainly resembled an eighteenth-century aristocrat in being in the grand manner, in his love of great entertainments and splendid houses and gardens as well as in his speech; which contained archaisms such as his much-imitated pronunciation of words like 'glass' as though they rhymed with 'lass'. He also belonged to an earlier age in suffering, as Viceroy, from the Napoleon Complex, the belief that one man can, so to speak, run an empire single-handed. In most respects, however, Curzon seems to belong more to the later twentieth century than to the eighteenth; he was very much a modern in his striving after a somewhat soulless efficiency.

As the first twentieth-century Viceroy, it was fitting that Curzon should have been clean-shaven and absurdly young in appearance. The stately, portly Curzon who looked, in Sir Harold Nicolson's words, 'as if he were carrying his own howdah',[4] belongs to a later period; Curzon the Viceroy was a slender, boyish figure, which was to be expected since he was not yet forty when he assumed office. Out of his robes, he did not look particularly aristocratic, except that he was tall. 'I've sometimes been mistaken for a parson, and at others Have recognized in butlers and in waiters long-lost brothers' the young Curzon wrote of himself in a comic verse;[5] and like all caricatures this has in it more than a grain of the truth. 'God's Butler' was to be a nickname for him in later years; and though he was not an orthodox Christian, he had a clerical air in keeping with his intellectual prowess and his rather schoolmasterish way of dealing with people.

Curzon was in fact a parson's son; his father, Lord Scarsdale, was in Holy Orders. His ancestral home, the palatial eighteenth-century mansion of Kedleston in Derbyshire, Robert Adam's masterpiece, had, during his childhood, not so much the atmosphere of a palace as of a parsonage. As a house, Kedleston had always been rather too grand for his forebears, who were, as he himself put it, 'just ordinary country gentlemen'. Curzon thus grew up far from the charmed circle of the great ruling families; so that there was some truth in his oft-asserted claim that he was a self-made man. His relatively obscure and austere background would also explain why, although undoubtedly an aristocrat by birth – descended from one of William the Conqueror's knights, heir to a peerage and to an estate which his ancestors had held since the time of Henry I – he was no more typical of the aristocracy in temperament than he was in looks. Whereas the true aristocrat tends to delegate, Curzon would insist on doing everything himself. The aristocrat is concerned with broad issues rather than with detail; for Curzon, detail was all-important. Curzon would attribute his success to what he called his 'middle-class method';[6] there was nothing of the aristocrat's air of easygoing amateurishness about him, but a punctilious professionalism. His

'Curzon the Viceroy was a slender, boyish figure'

outlook was that of what would now be called the 'meritocracy', the class to which belonged most of the friends he made at Balliol, where he went after a brilliant Eton career. Though lampooned in undergraduate verse as 'a most superior person' – a label which, in the words of one of his biographers, 'was to stick to him through life like a burr'[7] – he did not, at Oxford, mix so much with the gilded youth as with clever young men of varied background who afterwards achieved distinction. Typical of them was Walter Lawrence, his future Private Secretary; no relation of John Lawrence, but destined, like him, to become an eminent Indian Civilian.

After leaving Oxford, Curzon kept in touch with academic circles by winning a Fellowship of All Souls. At the same time he entered fashionable society, the doors of which were thrown wide to him as the heir to a peerage, a fascinating talker and a charmer of women; he became a leading spirit in that group of intellectual but light-hearted young aristocrats of both sexes known as the 'Souls'. And yet he was never entirely of that world; so that it seems fitting that he should have married an American from Chicago rather than one of the many daughters of the nobility with whom he flirted. Mary Curzon's father, Levi Zeigler Leiter – who despite his first name was not Jewish – had made a vast fortune in real estate; but although Curzon cannot have been unaware of the advantages which this would bring him, there is every reason to believe that he married for love and not for money. He found he had more in common with Mary than with any other girl he had met; she was highly cultured and came near to being his intellectual equal. She was also extremely beautiful, tall and dark, with violet eyes and a smile of singular sweetness. While she was an immediate success in Britain, she helped to widen the temperamental gap between Curzon and his friends by bringing out some of his more un-English characteristics. Viewing the English political scene through her American eyes, she caused him to see intrigues and jealousies where none existed. She encouraged him to be rather too blatantly ambitious; so that, as has been written of another and later Viceroy, Mountbatten, he sought and won the prizes of life 'untrammelled by diffidence'.[8]

The prize which, from an early age, Curzon sought above all others was the Viceroyalty. According to one of two different accounts which he afterwards gave, he was first fired with the ambition to rule India when he visited Government House, Calcutta, in 1887 as Dufferin's guest. So impressed was he by the splendours of the house and its much-exaggerated likeness to his Derbyshire home that he vowed there and then that he would one day 'exchange Kedleston in England for Kedleston in India'.[9] According to his other account, his ambition to be Viceroy dated back to when, as a boy at Eton, he heard a lecture by Mayo's Law Member, FitzJames Stephen.

Having made up his mind that he would be the ruler of British India, Curzon set out to qualify himself for the post in a way that no other future Viceroy ever did. In order to acquire a first-hand knowledge of Asian affairs – in which he had a passionate interest quite apart from his ambition – he travelled extensively; some of his journeys being hazardous in the extreme. He went four times to India and explored the most inaccessible outposts of the North-West Frontier. He ventured into Afghanistan and became personally acquainted with the Amir. His journey to Samarkand and Tashkent bore fruit in a book entitled *Russia in Central Asia*; his travels in Persia enabled him, at the age of little more than thirty, to write what would long be the definitive work on that country, in two massive volumes.

As well as during his travels, Curzon made a close study of Indian problems when he was at home; and he gained some experience of Indian government by serving for a short time as Parliamentary Under-Secretary at the India Office. By 1897, when he was Under-Secretary for Foreign Affairs, he felt sufficiently sure of himself to put his own name forward to the Prime Minister, Lord Salisbury, as a successor to Elgin. In the following year he was duly appointed; achieving his great ambition at the age of thirty-nine. Walter Lawrence became his Private Secretary; the young Winston Churchill nearly became one of his ADCs. Since he did not yet possess a title of his own, his father being very much alive, he was made Lord Curzon of Kedleston; but only in the Peerage of Ireland so as to enable him to sit again in the House of Commons after his return. Amidst the plaudits, Curzon's friends were worried about his health. They knew that he would never give his troublesome back sufficient rest; one of them, calling at his London house shortly before he left, found him moving dozens of bottles of wine with his own hands.

On arriving in India, Curzon threw himself into his work as wholeheartedly as Mayo had done thirty years earlier. He set about overhauling the entire machinery of government; and within three months of taking office had drawn up a programme of reforms ranging in scope from agriculture to education, from currency to municipalities, from the Army to the Archaeological Department, from the North-West Frontier to the Calcutta Imperial Library. As in Mayo's time, the strong personality of the Viceroy soon came to be felt in every branch of the administration; minutes on every subject flowed from his pen, clearly and accurately summarising masses of detail. While the task he set himself and his way of tackling it inevitably confined him to the great room in the south-western wing of Government House for even longer hours than his predecessors had spent there, he had no intention of being a remote bureaucrat, but followed Mayo's example and went about the country as much as he could to talk to the men on the spot. During the terrible famine of

Curzon in Star of India
Robes

1899 and 1900 he inspected the relief works and toured some of the
worst affected regions. In the July heat, when he was far from well, he
undertook a long journey on horseback through an area where, in
addition to all the other horrors of famine, cholera was rampant; a
ride which severely tested the endurance of the District Officer who
accompanied him. He likewise toured areas stricken with the plague
which had continued to rage since it broke out in Elgin's time. These
visits on the whole had an excellent effect, though Lawrence wished
that Curzon could have shown a little more tact. 'He will notice
trifling defects, and his remarks perturb and confuse the overworked
officials.'[10]

Lawrence's criticism unfortunately applied to all Curzon's dealings with the officials, who found him overpowering and lacking in
consideration for their feelings; though if they met him off duty they
were often pleasantly surprised by his humour and kindness of heart.
Where Mayo had inspired the officials to give of their best, Curzon
simply bullied them into doing what he wanted; he dominated his
Council rather than carrying it along with him. 'Mary is adored by
everyone here, and I am regarded with mingled bewilderment and
pain' he wrote with some complacency soon after his arrival.[11]

Certainly British India was in need of a new broom when Curzon
took over; the administration being more than a little run down. But
as an eminent Civilian of a later period wisely remarked: 'It is not
enough to do the right thing. You must do it in the right way.'[12]
Curzon all too frequently did things the wrong way and he drove the
machinery of government too hard; not listening to Lawrence who
would tell him that 'India worked all right at half speed'.[13]

'I am prodding up the animal with most vigorous and unexpected
digs, and it gambols plaintively under the novel spur' wrote the
newly-fledged Viceroy in typically Curzonian language. 'Nothing
has been done hitherto under six months. When I suggest six weeks,
the attitude is one of pained surprise; if six days, one of pathetic
protest; if six hours, one of stupefied resignation.'[14] He tended to
regard the Civilians as a lot of fuddy-duddies, which was hardly fair
seeing that the oldest of them were little more than ten years his
senior. 'One cannot expect these old birds out here, whose feathers I
stroke the wrong way, not to cackle home by post to the other old
birds who have preceded them to the gilded aviary in Charles
Street.'[15]

Like so many Viceroys before him, Curzon was frequently
exasperated by the denizens of the Charles Street 'aviary', the retired
Civilians and soldiers of the India Council; who vetoed some of his
reforms, albeit minor ones, and slowed down the progress of others.
To Curzon, it was unthinkable that the Government of India should
be directed in detail by Whitehall; he could never quite accept the

fact that, as Viceroy, he was the servant and instrument of the British Government. It is an exaggeration to say, as has been frequently said, that he regarded himself as an independent potentate; but he certainly did not see the Viceroy as the Great Ornamental; believing that 'he and he alone' was 'the Government in its personal aspect'.[16] In his attitude of 'l'état c'est moi', Curzon was trying to put the clock back to before the advent of the telegraph; or at any rate to before the days of Lansdowne and Elgin.

During the earlier part of his reign, Curzon was singularly fortunate in having Lord George Hamilton, a brother-in-law of Lansdowne, as Secretary of State. Hamilton had asserted himself with Elgin; but now that Curzon was Viceroy he wisely felt that 'India was in good hands and that he had not much to say to it'.[17] He allowed Curzon to lay down his own policy and take the big decisions, a freedom of action which no Viceroy – except in the abnormal circumstances of Mountbatten's reign and at one other brief period – would ever again possess. Hamilton's tact did much for Curzon's relations with Whitehall and Westminster; just as the no less tactful Lawrence helped to oil the wheels in India. The letters of Hamilton to Curzon contain many sound pieces of advice, such as 'Try and suffer fools more gladly, they constitute the majority of mankind'.[18] And when he heard that Curzon was working eleven hours a day, Hamilton admonished him sternly against 'continuing to attempt a daily task which is beyond the power of almost anyone to accomplish in a tropical climate'.[19]

Hamilton's remonstrance about overwork – like most of his good advice – unfortunately went unheeded. Curzon, whose maxim was 'Do everything yourself',[20] was attempting to run India single-handed. No other Viceroy did so much. He would attend to the most trifling details, such as whether or not visitors to zoological gardens should be allowed to carry cameras; and not content with trying to be a one-man Government, he kept his own household accounts instead of leaving them to his Military Secretary. He worked through most of the day and long into the night, returning to his work-room after dinners and State balls. Mary would sometimes find him still writing at his desk at five in the morning and beg him to come up to bed. Often he wrote lying down, being unable to sit on account of his bad back; he was once ill in bed for three weeks, but kept on working without a break, receiving Councillors and secretaries in his bedroom. It is remarkable that his Viceroyalty did not end prematurely in a nervous breakdown; but though he managed to keep going, his health suffered and so did his temper. He began to indulge in self-pity. 'Grind, grind, grind, with never a word of encouragement; on, on, on, till the collar breaks and the poor beast stumbles and dies' he wrote during the hot weather of 1901 to Mary, whose

Lady Curzon in her celebrated peacock dress

own not very robust health had obliged her to return to England for the summer months.[21]

But while Curzon was all too apt at times to think of himself as ill-used, he enjoyed being Viceroy none the less; especially when Mary was with him, for he missed her acutely when he and she were apart. Fascinated as he was by the East, believing as passionately as he did in Britain's Imperial destiny – 'To me the message is carved in granite, it is hewn out of the rock of doom, that our work is righteous and that it shall endure' he once declared in a speech – his high position afforded him the utmost fulfilment. He was a romantic; he was second to none in being aware of the poetry and glory of ruling India; he also took a keen interest in the traditions, customs and ceremonials of the Viceroyalty, of which he made a close study. It was his sense of tradition and his desire, as a perfectionist, to bring the running of the Viceregal Court up to the very highest standards which gave him his reputation for being over-fond of pomp and ceremony; a reputation to which his majestic diction and his preternaturally stiff and erect bearing – due largely to the steel corset he was obliged to wear on account of his defective spine – likewise contributed. In fact, Curzon disliked most ceremonial occasions, regarding them as a waste of valuable time which might otherwise have been devoted to work; they also caused him much discomfort, if not pain, on account of his back.

He did, however, enjoy the simple and imposing ritual which took place when a Chief came to Government House to pay him his respects. The Viceroy would await the arriving potentate on the steps of the Throne, attended by his Staff and by servants bearing the emblems of royalty. From here, in Curzon's own words:

> he looked down the long vista of the Marble Hall with its gleaming white pillars, absolutely empty save for the Bodyguard in their magnificent uniforms, standing like statues on either side . . . An intense silence prevailed, broken at length by the crunch of wheels on the gravel and the horse-hooves of the Bodyguard, as they escorted the carriage containing the Prince to the foot of the steps. At that moment thundered out the guns from the distant Fort, giving to the Chief his due salute. One- two- three, up to a total of seventeen, nineteen, or twenty-one, the reverberations rang out. Not until the total – carefully counted by the Chief himself – was completed, did the procession . . . attempt to move forward. Then he would be seen to advance along the crimson carpet laid outside and to enter the Marble Hall in all his panoply of brocades and jewels, the Foreign Secretary leading him by the hand. As they approached at a slow pace along the polished floor, not a sound was heard but the clank clank of the scabbards on the marble.[22]

Curzon loved Wellesley's great palace and was probably the first Viceroy to appreciate the house as a work of architecture; doing what he could to restore its original character, as well as improving the furnishings and filling the gaps in the collection of portraits. At the same time he introduced modern comforts, electric light and fixed baths instead of the old green-painted wooden tubs. He also installed electric lifts and electric fans, while keeping the old hand *punkahs* in the Marble Hall and the other State apartments, preferring their 'measured sweep' to what he called 'the hideous anachronism of the revolving blades'.[23]

The entertaining at Government House when Curzon was Viceroy was on an unprecedented scale. During each of his winter seasons there were two Levees, a Drawing Room, a State Ball, a State Evening Party, a Garden Party, several lesser balls and a number of official dinners; together with an informal dance and two or three smaller dinners every week. Calcutta society was still growing. There were now 1,600 guests at the State Ball, 600 at each of the lesser balls, 120 at the large dinners and 1,500 at the State Evening Party which was given mainly for Indians who did not dance. Perhaps the most spectacular Government House function of the reign was the fancy dress ball of January 1903 at which the costumes were meant to recreate Wellesley's famous ball of exactly a hundred years before. On this and similar occasions Curzon found time, amidst all his other labours, to supervise the details himself.

Against the background of pillars, lustres and scarlet uniforms, Mary Curzon appeared as a 'vision of loveliness'.[24] Everyone who saw her was enchanted by what a journalist called the 'fragile beauty of her countenance';[25] people also found her voice attractive and spoke of her kindness of heart. Yet as time went on, Lawrence heard reports of her growing unpopularity. That she was not an unqualified success as a Vicereine may perhaps have been for the reason that many of the more senior memsahibs may have resented having to bow the knee to someone so young – she was not yet thirty when Curzon became Viceroy – who was also an American. As the first American Vicereine – and in the event, the only one – she did her best to conform to protocol. 'Being a Yankee I can't understand it' she told a friend, 'but I manage to assume the necessary amount of awful respect for His Ex. when we appear in public'.[26] It is possible that in her anxiety not to be accused of Transatlantic informality she was a little too correct.

The tragedy of Mary Curzon was that at heart she disliked and dreaded India, which did not agree with her indifferent state of health. It had the opposite effect on her to what it had on her husband, who, when he was not driving himself too hard, tended to feel better in India than he did at home. Since she hated being

separated from him as much as he did from her, she did not return to
England as often as she might have done; her determination not to
fail him made her carry out her Viceregal duties even when she was
feeling far from well. 'I believe absolutely in my power of "coming
up to time" or "answering my ring" as an actor does in the wings of a
theatre' she told him in a letter; while adding, with an un-
characteristic disregard for his feelings: 'Some day, though, the bell
will go and I shall not appear, as India, I know, slowly but surely
murders women. But I suppose many humble and inconsequent lives
must always go into the foundations of all great works.'[27]

Mary's likening of herself to an actor is significant, for she seems to
have been most successful as a Vicereine when appearing before the
multitudes. Her husband shared her gift in this respect; the two of
them would drive in a phaeton through the poorer streets of Calcutta,
cheered by crowds of Bengalis. However distant and unbending
Curzon may have appeared to the senior officials, he could be very
genial when mixing with people lower down the social scale. At a
gathering of Indians which he attended when touring the Central
Provinces he was so friendly to everyone that the local Commissioner
had to hint that 'condescension was pressed too far when it shook
hands with men who drew less than £300 a year'.[28] When he was not
harassing the officials with orders and criticisms, Curzon was at his
best on tour. As a seasoned traveller, he was ready to put up with
discomforts; he saw the funny side of those mishaps and absurdities
from which Viceregal progresses were seldom entirely immune;
whether it was finding himself sitting on the head of a Maharaja in a
ditch when the landau carrying the two of them overturned, or
making a State entry into a city beneath a triumphal arch bearing the
inscription 'God Bless our Horrable Lout' which was meant to be
'Honourable Lord'. It did him good to get away from his desk and
into the open air; tours afforded him opportunities for shooting – he
was a first-class shot – as well as for sight-seeing, of which he never
tired. With his great love of architecture, it distressed him to see the
state of neglect into which India's architectural heritage had been
allowed to fall – even the Taj Mahal was neglected – and he lost no
time in setting on foot a programme of restoration which he
personally supervised. His concern was not limited to Hindu and
Islamic monuments; he was in advance of his time in also taking an
interest in British-Indian buildings of the Georgian period.

Just as Curzon admired the classic splendours of Government
House, so did he also admire the simpler Georgian elegance of
Barrackpore, to which he and Mary would escape on Saturday
evenings. Years later, he would remember those evenings with
pleasure: the peaceful twilight journey up river in his steam launch,
the walk from the landing-place to the house, 'hand-borne lanterns

twinkling in the darkness ahead'.[29] Very different were his feelings
for Viceregal Lodge at Simla which seemed to both him and Mary to
be in rather bad taste. 'A Minneapolis millionaire would revel in this'
Mary wrote on seeing the house for the first time; and she lamented
of the Dufferins' glowing interiors: 'Oh, Lincrusta, you will turn us
grey! It looks at you with pomegranate and pineapple eyes from every
wall.'[30] Curzon replaced some of the Lincrusta with damask; but his
efforts to improve Viceregal Lodge did not alter the fact that he
disliked Simla intensely. Like so many people before him and after,
he felt it was not India. Even in his spacious and luxurious eyrie,
surrounded by a hill-top garden of terraced lawns gay with banksia
roses and by many acres of steep but private woodland, he could not
forget that he was on a narrow mountain ridge crowded with officials
and their wives whose spare time was chiefly taken up with petty
gossip. During the hot weather season, he and Mary escaped from
Simla as often as they could; going not to the Elgins' retreat at
Mashobra but further away to Naldera, where they lived in a
permanent camp among the deodars, high above the valley of the
Sutlej. Naldera was to be one of the names given by the Curzons to
the youngest of their three daughters, who was born in 1904.

To make Simla even more disagreeable for Curzon, there was an
unhappy quarrel between him and the Lieutenant-Governor of the
Punjab, Sir Mackworth Young. This arose as a result of one of
Curzon's reforms, his creation of a new North-West Frontier
Province out of territory hitherto under the jurisdiction of the Punjab
Government. It was a wise and farsighted measure, bringing the vital
Frontier territory more directly under the control of the Government
of India; but the way Curzon carried it out offended the susceptibilities of the rather touchy Lieutenant-Governor and still more
so those of his wife. When Lady Young and the Viceroy were in
adjacent boxes at a performance by the Simla Amateur Dramatic
Club, she gave him, as Curzon himself put it, 'a Medusa-like bow
which would have frozen most people to stone'.[31]

Having gained first-hand experience of the Frontier on his travels
before he became Viceroy, Curzon regarded it as his special preserve.
'I am never so happy as when on the Frontier' he wrote, in his self-
confident way. 'I know these men and how to handle them. They are
brave as lions, wild as cats, docile as children. You have to be very
frank, very conciliatory, very firm, very generous, very fearless.'[32]
He was the first Viceroy to address the tribal leaders, which he did on
a visit to Peshawar; speaking to them courteously but plainly.

Like other Viceroys before him, Curzon was convinced that
Russia intended to get to India; and to prevent this from happening
he aimed at strengthening the Frontier and increasing British
influence in the neighbouring States. His relations with his old

acquaintance the Amir of Afghanistan, Abdur Rahman, and with Abdur Rahman's son Habibullah, who succeeded to the Afghan throne in 1901, were not very satisfactory; but he made some progress towards bringing southern Persia into the British sphere. At the same time he established a lasting British ascendancy over the sultans and sheikhs of the northern Arabian coast. In order to visit these potentates, and to boost Britain's prestige throughout that region as a whole, he went, towards the end of 1903, on an unprecedented three-week cruise in the Persian Gulf; it was such a success that the Gulf became known to Whitehall as 'The Curzon Lake'.

As a romantic and an autocrat, Curzon had a natural sympathy for Eastern potentates; and he aimed at enhancing, rather than depreciating, the role of the Indian Chiefs. For this reason he felt that they should be obliged to stay among their people and carry out their duties as rulers, rather than enjoying themselves in Europe as all too many of them were apt to do. He therefore made it necessary for them to obtain his permission before travelling abroad: Hamilton jocularly compared him to a headmaster stopping his pupils' exeats. He was quite prepared, however, to allow those many Princes who wished to do so to serve in the South African War; and deplored the decision of the British Government not to take advantage of their loyalty on the grounds that it would offend European opinion if Britain were to employ Indians to fight against the Boers. Curzon had offered to send an Indian contingent to South Africa; as it was, Indians were only allowed to take part in the war as camp followers of the British troops from the Indian establishment whom he sent in very large numbers to help Britain in her hour of need. These troops had to be paid for by the Indian taxpayer; so that the people of India had to carry some of the burden of the war without being able to share in the glory.

This was one of several instances in which Curzon believed the British Government to have treated India shabbily. As Viceroy, he saw his first duty as being to the Indians; he would never stand by passively while their interests were sacrificed to those of Britain. His championship of the Indian people went beyond the shores of India to the Indian immigrants in South Africa, whose numbers greatly increased after the war ended. He protested vigorously at the way they were being treated by the whites, thereby earning the gratitude of the young Indian lawyer in South Africa named Mohandas Gandhi who had espoused the immigrants' cause. 'The name of South Africa stinks in the nostrils of India' Curzon wrote;[33] and the future Mahatma wrote of Curzon as 'the strong and sympathetic Viceroy'.[34]

Curzon was as quick to condemn ill-treatment of the Indians by his fellow-countrymen in India as by the South African whites. He took steps to ensure that when an Englishman assaulted an Indian – an all too frequent occurrence at the beginning of his reign, particularly in the tea-gardens of Assam – the culprit would be brought to justice instead of being let off lightly by a European jury as usually happened. And when he discovered that the officers of the West Kent Regiment were guilty of hushing up the systematic rape of an elderly Burmese woman by some of their men, and that men of the 9th Lancers who had beaten an Indian cook to death were likewise being shielded by their officers, his indignation knew no bounds; he ordered the offending regiments to be punished and publicly censured. He was also shocked by the casual attitude of the military authorities to the growing number of fatal accidents to Indians caused by the carelessness of British soldiers out shooting for sport; and dealt with this matter no less sternly. 'These cases . . . eat into my very soul' he told Hamilton;[35] and in a minute on the 9th Lancers' outrage, he wrote: 'If it be said "don't wash your dirty linen in public", I reply "don't have dirty linen to wash"'.[36] Curzon's treatment of the West Kents and the 9th Lancers made him extremely unpopular with the Army and caused an outcry among the whole British community. There were repercussions in fashionable circles at home, for the 9th Lancers was one of the smartest English cavalry regiments. On the other hand, the Indian vernacular newspapers applauded Curzon's action and likened him to Ripon.

The affair of the 9th Lancers cast a shadow over the most memorable ceremonial event of Curzon's reign, the great Durbar which he held in January 1903 to celebrate the Coronation of Edward VII; a gathering modelled on Lytton's Imperial Assemblage of 1877 but on a much larger scale. The Durbar was also spoilt for Curzon by the Home Government's refusal to allow him to mark the occasion by announcing a reduction of the salt tax; it being customary in India for a potentate's accession to be celebrated by some grant of material advantage to his subjects.

By the end of 1902, relations between Curzon and the Government at home had changed for the worse; they would never again be the same as they were during the first three years of his Viceroyalty. The trouble started when the British Government rather meanly expected India to pay for entertaining the Indian guests at the Coronation; Curzon insisted that Britain should pay, and in this, as so often, he was in the right. But as so often, he put himself in the wrong by the way he handled the matter; sending home a violent protest which offended even the good-natured Hamilton and which he obstinately refused to withdraw although the Home Government agreed to pay up. He would not withdraw it even at the behest of his old friend and fellow-Soul Arthur Balfour, who succeeded Salisbury as Prime Minister in the midst of the controversy. Curzon had felt confident of getting his own way all the more easily with 'Dear Arthur' at the helm; but the new Prime Minister proved less indulgent than he expected.

Three months later, Balfour and his Cabinet rejected Curzon's proposal to announce a tax reduction at the Durbar; to which Curzon reacted by not only taking the unconstitutional step of appealing against the Government's decision to the King, but threatening, rather hysterically, to resign. Balfour was within an ace of accepting his resignation; but instead attempted to smooth him down with a kindly letter. Curzon continued to sulk; setting out for Delhi, as he told Hamilton, 'without the slightest ray of pleasurable anticipation, and with a feeling of indifference'.[37] Mary, too, did not much look forward to the great Durbar. 'Every bit of my vitality has gone' she complained a few days before it was due to start, 'and I am iller than I have ever been and simply can't get back to life.'[38]

Nevertheless the Coronation Durbar was, in most respects, a resounding success; a triumph of organisation for which Curzon was mainly responsible having seen to every detail himself: 'The design of a railing, the width of a road, the pattern of a carving, the colour of a plaster, the planting of a flower bed, the decoration of a pole – all this alongside of big questions affecting the movement or accommodation of tens of thousands of persons.'[39] He also more or less designed the vast horseshoe-shaped amphitheatre, which he insisted should be 'built and decorated exclusively in the Moghul or Indo-Saracenic style'.[40] As an added source of satisfaction to Curzon, the Durbar was, for all its magnificence, remarkably cheap; thanks to clever management it cost no more than £180,000, apart from military expenses.

For the State entry into Delhi, Curzon and Mary rode at the head of a picturesque elephant procession. This was, as Curzon afterwards remarked, the only occasion during his whole reign when he rode an elephant for show as distinct from as a mode of conveyance on shooting expeditionss and in country impassable to any other form of transport; whereas the English Radical Press was fond of depicting him as riding in state on elephants 'promiscuously and habitually'.[41] In fact Curzon hated the jerky motion of an elephant's back; and did not, as Viceroy, own so much as a single elephant; the old Viceregal *hatikhana* or elephant stud having been finally given up in Elgin's time. The elephants which he used at the Durbar were all borrowed from the Indian Princes.

Another myth that grew out of the Coronation Durbar was that Curzon deliberately slighted his Royal visitor, the Duke of Connaught, in order to enhance his own position. The opposite was the case; Curzon made as much of the Duke as he possibly could,

Lord and Lady Curzon
making their State entry
into Delhi for the
Coronation Durbar

regarding it as somewhat absurd that he himself should have been the
central figure rather than the King-Emperor's brother. It would,
however, have been quite improper for Curzon not to take first place;
for it was he as Viceroy and not the Duke who represented the King-
Emperor. The Duke understood this as well as anybody and had
nothing but praise for Curzon when he returned to England.

If anyone stole the show at the Durbar, it was Mary, who looked
ravishing in a dress of peacock feathers. Despite her misgivings, she
stood up well to the ordeal and played her part to perfection; winning
the admiration and applause of the Indians and also of the British,
whatever they may have felt privately about the American Vicereine.
Their feelings about Curzon, however, were made all too clear
during the military review; as the 9th Lancers came riding past,
almost every Briton present cheered loudly and pointedly. Curzon
afterwards claimed to have been in no way discomforted by this

display of bad manners; but rather to have felt, as he sat stiff and silent on his horse, 'a certain gloomy pride in having dared to do the right'.[42] But it must have been galling for him to reflect that the 9th Lancers would not have taken part in the Durbar had he not magnanimously overruled the military authorities' decision to exclude them. It was even more galling that his own personal guests, on whose entertainment he was spending something like £3,000 out of his own pocket, joined in the unseemly demonstration. Among them were some of the Souls, from whom Balfour heard reports of the Durbar when they got home. 'They seem unanimous on two things' Balfour wrote, '1) the show was the best show ever shown, 2) that George was the most unpopular Viceroy ever seen.'[43]

Balfour exaggerated the extent of Curzon's unpopularity; but certainly by the time of the Durbar he had not only made himself disliked by a large section of the British but was also losing the goodwill of the educated Indians. Curzon had no prejudice against the educated classes as such. He knew that the advance of education and the spread of Western ideas among the Indians was inevitable; it was necessary for the achievement of one of his avowed objects, which was to bring the Indians and the British in India closer together, or as he put it in a memorable speech, 'to build a golden bridge between East and West, which even the roaring floods of time shall never sweep away'.[44] He knew that as they became more educated, the Indians would grow more conscious of what he called 'individual rights and the equality of one man with another';[45] but he failed to see that this consciousness would develop into an active and organised opposition to British rule. It was an instance of his hubris

General view of the arena, Coronation Durbar, 1 January 1903

and his disregard for human emotions that he should have supposed that the Indians could be raised to a high degree of political awareness and yet be content to remain indefinitely in a situation that stopped short of self-government.

The idea that it was the duty of the British to train the Indians to govern themselves was, to Curzon, repugnant. The Indians were, in his view, a congenitally inefficient race; and to him good government meant efficiency. So while being prepared to allow Indians to serve in greater numbers as High Court Judges, in the Legislative Councils and on various Government bodies, he was opposed to any increase in their entry to the Civil Service and considered that the highest administrative posts should, as a rule, remain closed to them. In answer to the suggestion that a prominent Indian should be made a Member of the Executive Council, he replied categorically: 'In the whole continent there is not one Indian fit for the post'.[46]

Curzon therefore had little use for Congress, with its demands for a greater share in the government of the country. He regarded it as being not in any way representative and so not worth bothering about; he made no attempt to win it over, although when he first became Viceroy it was in a conciliatory mood. He admired the political skill of one of the Congress leaders, Gopal Krishna Gokhale, who was a member of the Central Legislative Council, and honoured him with a CIE; but another leader he dismissed contemptuously as a 'vitriolic windbag'.[47] While generally regarding his Indian critics with an Olympian disdain, he did go to some trouble to answer the criticisms of Romesh Chandar Dutt, a writer and Congress leader who was a former Civilian, in a document of which Mr. Philip Mason

succinctly observes: 'Every paragraph makes a telling point and every other alienates the reader'.[48]

Curzon's attitude and the tactlessness which characterised his dealings with the educated Indians – such as his notorious remark, in a speech to Calcutta University, that truth was a Western concept – inevitably gave offence. To add to his unpopularity with the educated classes, there was his well-intentioned scheme for University reform, which was accused unfairly of being a deliberate attempt to bring the Universities under tighter Government control. By 1903 the vernacular newspapers, which had formerly praised him, were subjecting him to 'incessant abuse';[49] he was to be denounced even more violently the following year over the partition of Bengal. The reduction of this unwieldy province was no more than an administrative measure, originating from the Government rather than from Curzon himself; but it was greatly resented as destroying the

The Coronation Durbar: Reading the Proclamation

unity of the Bengali people and seen as an attempt to weaken their political power. The resulting agitation gave a new vigour to the Indian nationalist movement; the ill-feeling caused by the partition left a smouldering unrest in Bengal which broke out into violence after Curzon had departed from India. Curzon was warned of this unrest during his last months as Viceroy; but being very much the opposite of an alarmist, he made light of it.

The partition of Bengal would not have been blamed on Curzon had he left India at the beginning of 1904 when his original five-year term ended. But he tempted Fate and asked for an extension to enable him to complete his reforms. This Balfour granted him, though not without misgivings, which seemed justified as Curzon continued to expect the Prime Minister and the Secretary of State to let him have his way over everything and to be peevish and hurt if they did not. From September 1903 onwards the Secretary of State was no longer the patient and diplomatic Hamilton, but St John Brodrick, whose tactlessness and obstinacy were proverbial. Brodrick, like Balfour, was one of the Souls and an even older friend of Curzon's than Balfour was, having been his contemporary at Eton and Oxford. There was a time when Curzon had looked up to Brodrick, who was more than two years his senior; but by 1903 the position was reversed. Curzon's brilliance was now universally acclaimed; Brodrick, on the other hand, had revealed himself to be no more than a plodder, one of those mediocrities who somehow manage to survive the ups and downs of political life and attain Cabinet rank. There seems little doubt that Brodrick now suffered from an inferiority complex in his relations with Curzon; and that Mary was for once right in detecting a note of envy in the cordiality which this 'true old dear', as she called him, continued to show to his friend.[50] Brodrick suspected that Curzon looked upon him as little more than his representative at the Court of St James's, and meant to make it abundantly clear that as Secretary of State he was the Viceroy's constitutional superior.

There was a coolness between Curzon and Brodrick by the spring of 1904, when Curzon went home on leave, the first Viceroy ever to do so. Curzon's holiday in England, far from producing any sort of reconciliation, saw a widening of the breach owing to differences between him and the Cabinet on two major issues of foreign policy. One was to do with Afghanistan; the other was the controversy over Colonel Francis Younghusband's recent military and diplomatic mission to Tibet, the object of which, though ostensibly commercial, was to force the Dalai Lama and his government to throw in their lot with Britain rather than with Russia. The terms imposed by Younghusband on the Tibetians were more stringent than what had been originally intended; the Cabinet therefore blamed him for

disobeying orders and publicly repudiated him. Curzon, on the other
hand, entirely approved of what Younghusband had done and was
determined to stand by him through thick and thin.

Frustrated though he was by the behaviour of the Cabinet, Curzon
might still have enjoyed his English holiday had not Mary fallen
desperately ill with peritonitis and pneumonia, so that at times she
was not expected to live. Her recovery was painfully slow; she was
still far from well in November when Curzon, with a heavy heart, left
her bedside to return on his own to India. At Bombay, when the
Governor, who had been his best man, referred to Mary's illness in
proposing his health, Curzon sobbed uncontrolledly. Back in
Calcutta, in the familiar surroundings of Government House, he
wrote in a letter to Mary: 'I have not dared to go into your room for
fear that I should burst out crying'.[51]

As it happened, Curzon did not have to endure the agony of
separation for very long; for in January, to his amazement and
delight, there came the news that Mary was now well enough to
travel and was on her way to join him. To welcome her, he wrote her a
love-song in the Indian manner.

I would have torn the stars from the Heavens for your
    necklace,
I would have stripped the rose-leaves for your couch from all
    the trees,
I would have spoiled the East of its spices for your perfume,
The West of all its wonders to endower you with these.[52]

Lord and Lady Curzon on
board ship in the Persian
Gulf, 1903

Curzon with the Raja of Nabha. On the Raja's left is Colonel Dunlop Smith, who afterwards became Private Secretary to Curzon's successor

He took time off to travel to Bombay to meet her. On the way back to Calcutta, the Viceregal train broke down; knowing that an enthusiastic reception awaited them, Curzon and Mary continued their journey at sixty miles an hour with a single engine and carriage, in order not to disappoint the populace. At the station, the Corporation presented Mary with a jewel paid for out of their own pockets; the route to Government House was packed with cheering crowds. It was a reception such as no woman had ever before been given in India; all the more remarkable in that Curzon had already lost much of his popularity on account of the partition of Bengal.

Mary's return afforded her husband a temporary relief from the controversy that was to end his Viceroyalty in sorrow and anger. It was a controversy in which he was undoubtedly in the right, though he could be said to have brought it on himself by his hubris in pressing for the appointment of that illustrious but dictatorial soldier, Lord Kitchener of Khartoum, as Commander-in-Chief. 'Give me the best man' Curzon insisted,[53] heedless of his friends who warned him that Kitchener would be more trouble than he was worth. Kitchener, who arrived in India towards the end of 1902, got on surprisingly well with Curzon; but lost no time in pressing for the abolition of the existing system in which the Military Member of the Viceroy's Council was responsible for the administration of the Army in India independent of the Commander-in-Chief who had only executive functions. Kitchener described the system as 'extraordinary', forgetting that it was, in its essentials, no different from what prevailed in Britain and most other civilised countries; the Military Member being simply the equivalent of a war minister. The fact that the Military Member was by custom not a civilian, but a senior Army officer often of inferior rank to the Commander-in-Chief, might have seemed an anomaly; but if it offended the Commander-in-Chief's vanity to have to defer to an officer junior to himself, his actual power was far greater than that of his counterpart in the British Army. Not only was he also by custom if not by right a Member of Council, which gave him a considerable say in Army administration; but his exalted position in the order of precedence meant that he was on very close terms with the Viceroy and frequently able to influence him.

Curzon was a strong supporter of the existing system, which, with the sole exception of Lytton, every previous Viceroy had upheld; and which was in accordance with the basic constitutional principle that the military power should be subordinate to the civil. Until the summer of 1904, the controversy did little more than smoulder. Then, when Curzon was on leave in England, Kitchener threatened to resign if he did not get his way. Balfour's Government was on its last legs; the Prime Minister and his colleagues knew that Kitchener's resignation might lose them the forthcoming election, for he was regarded as a national hero by the British public. He had to be placated, even at the cost of sacrificing Curzon.

Brodrick accordingly asked for opinions on the existing military system from the Commander-in-Chief and the Military Member. The battle was joined; on the one side was Kitchener, a lonely giant at Council meetings, alternating between 'incoherent garrulity' and brooding silence.[54] On the other side was Curzon, the Military Member and the rest of the Council. Calcutta society divided into two camps; though the two chief antagonists maintained outwardly cordial relations. For his part, however, Kitchener made no attempt to disguise his true feelings. A young peeress staying at Government House, who on account of her rank found herself sitting between Curzon and Kitchener at dinner, was taken aback when Kitchener asked her brusquely, as his opening gambit: 'What do you think of your next door neighbour?'[55]

In the following May the Home Government decided on a scheme which in effect gave Kitchener everything he wanted; though it had the appearance of a compromise in that it did not actually abolish the

Lord Kitchener of
Khartoum, recently
appointed as Commander-
in-Chief, at the Coronation
Durbar

Lord Kitchener of Khartoum, recently appointed as Commander-in-Chief, at the Coronation Durbar

Military Member, while transferring most of his powers to the Commander-in-Chief. 'A disembowelled Military Member has been left to prevent me from resigning' Curzon remarked bitterly.[56] The controversy dragged on through those summer months of 1905, becoming increasingly acrimonious. Curzon was at times hysterical; Brodrick was unfair and even dishonest and seemed as though he deliberately intended to cause Curzon pain. Having himself not been above running a Press campaign against Curzon over the Younghusband affair, he now accused Curzon of manipulating the newspapers in India and remained convinced of this even after the charge had been satisfactorily refuted. If Curzon was innocent of dealings with the Press, Kitchener did not scruple to enlist journalistic support. A master of intrigue, he pulled strings through his many powerful friends at home, who ranged from military correspondents to great ladies.

In the end, Curzon resigned not over the major principle; but simply because the officer whom he wished to have as the new Military Member was not appointed. As the appointment of Members of Council was the prerogative of the Home Government and not of the Viceroy, he managed, by resigning over this issue, to put himself in the wrong. He had been outmanoeuvred by Kitchener and the Home Government, who were able to represent his departure as being on account of his own unconstitutional behaviour; though not everybody was deceived in this respect. 'The military element is triumphant, the civil element is discredited' the former Viceroy Ripon observed with dismay.[57] Winston Churchill praised Curzon for his 'gallant stand' against 'the wholesale transference of the Government of India to the military power'.[58] Even so military a personage as Lord Roberts felt that Curzon was right.

Curzon's resignation left him feeling betrayed and ill-treated; but it did not to any appreciable extent cut short his work in India. He had intended, at all events, not to stay on after the spring of 1906; as it was, he resigned in August 1905 and left in the following November. He made the most of his last three months as Viceroy; those who met him at that time found him in excellent health and spirits and not at all the mentally and physically broken man he is generally supposed to have been. His departure coincided with the arrival of the Prince and Princess of Wales on a tour of India; it was arranged, at the King's special request, that Curzon should have the honour of greeting them at Bombay, where he would remain until the arrival of his successor before embarking. He gave the Prince and Princess a charming welcome; but treated the incoming Viceroy, Lord Minto, to one of those displays of childish pique in which he all too frequently indulged. Not only did he cancel the official reception of Lord and Lady Minto at the Apollo Bunder; but instead of greeting them at the top of the steps of the Bombay Government House, as indeed Mary did, he waited until they had been in the drawing room for some minutes and then sauntered in, wearing a shooting jacket and bedroom slippers.

Thus on a note of farce as incongruous as it was characteristic of its author ended the Greek tragedy of Curzon's Viceroyalty; the hero had offended the Gods with his hubris and been punished. It was a tragedy with an even more tragic epilogue: only a few months after Curzon arrived back in England, Mary died of heart failure. As well as being bereaved, Curzon found himself, on his return home, estranged from some of his closest friends; not just from Balfour and Brodrick but from others who sided with them. He was also in the political wildnerness; he had chosen to be made an Irish peer so that he could go back to the House of Commons; but the King now felt it was unseemly for a former Viceroy to face the hustings. The quarrel with Balfour and the advent of a Liberal administration at the very moment of his return deprived him for the time being of the Earldom which, as a former Viceroy, he should have been given as a matter of course. An Earldom, however, came his way in 1911 and he was afterwards promoted to a Marquessate; he eventually married again, to another American; he resumed his political career, becoming Foreign Secretary immediately after the First World War. In 1923 he all but achieved his second great ambition, which was to be Prime Minister; so cruelly was he disappointed in this respect that his death, which occurred less than two years later, was believed by many to have been caused by a broken heart.

Curzon lived just long enough to see the completion of the great domed edifice of white marble which he bequeathed to Calcutta: the Victoria Memorial Hall. It was his idea; he had raised the money for

Group at the Curzons' farewell ball at Simla, October 1905. Standing on the extreme left is Mrs Montagu Butler, wife of an up-and-coming Civilian and mother of 'Rab'

it as Viceroy; intending it to be not only a memorial to the Queen-Empress but a Valhalla of the Raj. To posterity, it has seemed more than anything else like a memorial to Curzon himself; helping to keep his memory alive in an India where he is now largely forgotten except as the restorer of the Taj Mahal and of other monuments. The Indians of today still feel the benefit of some of his administrative reforms; their failure to remember him in connection with them can best be explained by what Brodrick, that snake in his Viceregal grass, wrote of him: 'He achieved successes, but not success'.[59] Curzon's achievement lay in the mechanics of administration rather than in the minds of men – except in so far as his contemptuous attitude to Congress is now believed to have done much to turn what had been a fundamentally loyal organisation into a revolutionary movement.

The gentleman who jumped hedges

'Isn't that the gentleman who only jumps hedges?'[1] Curzon is reputed to have asked on being told that the Earl of Minto – great-grandson of the Governor-General of a century earlier – was to succeed him. Minto, when he heard this, was delighted; for he took more pride in his fame as a gentleman rider known throughout the sporting world as 'Mr. Rolly' than he did in his later success as a soldier and as Governor-General of Canada. And indeed, the courage and nerve which he had shown as a young man in riding in a steeplechase at Sandown only a few months after literally breaking his neck in the Grand National were perhaps the best qualifications he possessed for being Viceroy of India in what proved to be difficult times. Despite his Canadian apprenticeship and the fact that he already knew India at first-hand, having served on the Frontier in 1879 – he nearly went with Cavagnari's ill-fated mission – Minto was, as a Viceroy, very much an amateur, just as Curzon was a professional. He lacked any sort of political experience: 'The Turf is purest gold compared with politics' he once declared.[2] But while Curzon's career showed that even the most brilliant professional has his shortcomings, Minto's was to show the abundant resources of the aristocratic amateur at his best.

Like Ripon and others, Minto might have been chosen for the reason that he was in every respect the opposite of his predecessor. Curzon was the youngest Viceroy; Minto was one of the oldest, being over sixty when he took office. While Curzon's scholarship was prodigious, Minto was completely unintellectual; at Cambridge he had devoted himself wholeheartedly to sport to the virtual exclusion of learning; one of his closest undergraduate friends was renowned for possessing not so much as a single book. Curzon at times behaved caddishly; Minto could never be anything but a gentleman through and through: 'His Excellency rained gentlemanliness upon me'[3] was how an Afghan noble spoke of an interview with him. Curzon was pompous and frequently disagreeable; Minto had not a trace of pomposity and was affable and pleasant to everybody. One Simla season during Minto's Viceroyalty, a small boy aged five surprised

his mother with an abstruse piece of information on Indian politics, which he said had been told him by the friend he met out riding. When the mother asked her son's *syce* who this friend might be, he replied: 'Lord Sahib'.

Minto's face, with its fine bone-structure, large eyes beneath low and dark eyebrows, greying military moustache, always had a reliable, reassuring, dog-like expression. With his military moustache went a soldierly bearing, which appealed particularly to the Indian Princes. The fact that Minto was a soldier – though he had given up his regular commission at the age of twenty-five, he had afterwards taken part in several campaigns and attained the rank of Brigadier-General through his service with the Scottish Volunteers – recommended him to the Balfour Government as a Viceroy likely to tolerate the ascendancy of Kitchener; and there can be little doubt that he was also appointed because the Cabinet wanted someone amenable after the difficult Curzon; a mediocrity even, as a change from too much brilliance.

Being by nature modest, Minto was himself fully aware that he fell far short of his predecessor in talents and abilities; but unlike his fellow-Scot, Elgin, he did not feel that the Viceroyalty was beyond him. He had actually rather hoped for it, and was pleasantly surprised when it came his way. The fact that he was not well off may have had something to do with it, but not as much as in the case of Lansdowne; Minto was chiefly attracted by the honour and glory of the appointment and by the prospect of following in the footsteps of his great-grandfather, whose memory he revered. He knew that he was no Curzon, but felt that this could be an advantage; 'My racing days have taught me that many a race has been won by giving the horse a rest in his gallops' he said at a farewell dinner before he left for India.[4]

Yet as a Viceroy Minto was to be far from mediocre. People were soon to recognise in him that 'quiet courage' and the power to make men trust him and believe in him, which had been characteristics of Mayo;[5] as well as the ability to make quick decisions which, as in Mayo's case, was almost certainly acquired in the saddle. Unlike Curzon, Minto 'always knew when to lead and when to stand aside' as Joseph Chamberlain said of him.[6] 'Not a great man in some ways, but . . . a very straight one who saw things simply and clearly and saw them whole'[7] was how Minto would be summed up by the rising star of his Council, Harcourt Butler, an uncle of 'Rab' – another of whose uncles, James Dunlop Smith, was, by coincidence, Minto's Private Secretary. Dunlop Smith, who had long experience of India as a soldier turned Civilian, wrote of Minto on the voyage out: 'He is much impressed with the bigness of his task and is so humble about it all'. A month later, when the new Viceroy and his Staff were duly

Lady Minto

installed in Government House, he wrote: 'I can only say that Lord
Minto means to be Viceroy, and his Council, his Secretaries and
Kitchener, who hitherto have seen little but his courtesy and great
charm of manner, will find out that his backbone is of steel'.[8]

Kitchener came up against this steely backbone only a day after
Minto's arrival when he tried to make the new Viceroy sign a paper
giving him wide powers. Minto firmly refused to sign and did not send
home Kitchener's proposals for the final settlement of the military
controversy until the Commander-in-Chief had acknowledged the
supremacy of the Viceroy and the civil power in writing. The new
system, which came into being early in 1906, could have caused
trouble if Kitchener had taken the bit between his teeth; instead,
having got his way over the Military Member, he became surprisingly docile and worked off his energies harmlessly if expensively
building grand additions to his houses in Calcutta and Simla.

Minto's backbone of steel made for satisfactory relations with his Council; and more important, it enabled him to hold his own with a masterful Secretary of State. An electoral landslide brought the Liberal Government of Sir Henry Campbell-Bannerman into power a fortnight after Minto became Viceroy; and Brodrick was replaced at the India Office by Lytton's old friend John Morley, a Radical journalist and man of letters turned politician. Morley, though not far off seventy when he became Secretary of State, was to continue in that post under Asquith right up to the end of Minto's reign. As time went on, he grew increasingly autocratic and subjected Minto to 'perpetual interference';[9] yet Minto was not only able to gain his point with him in all major issues but struck up a friendship with him that endured, even though Morley was a most difficult person to deal with, exceedingly touchy and enormously vain. 'He tells me he is not a vain man. Oh Himmel!'[10] the long-suffering Viceroy was once driven to exclaim. Minto also wrote of Morley: 'Our Secretary of State seems the most loveable individual, but he gives me endless worry in constantly guarding against wounding his feelings'.[11] Morley, for his part, came to admire Minto in a somewhat patronising way; remarking on one occasion: 'It is extraordinary to me that he should write the letters of a statesman without the schooling of the House of Commons'.[12]

The friendship between Minto and Morley was all the more remarkable in that the two of them were as different in character as they were in background and interests. They also, of course, differed politically; though not as much as might be supposed, for while Minto had been appointed by the Balfour Government, he was not a Conservative but a Liberal Unionist, being by family tradition a Whig; as was his wife, who was a grand-daughter of Earl Grey of the Reform Bill. Mary Minto was in her late forties when she became Vicereine and looked younger; in beauty she did not fall far short of her predecessor, having large eyes, a well-shaped nose and a long and graceful neck. She had an air of great distinction, dressed well, was highly intelligent and charmed everybody – including Morley, with whom she discussed affairs of State on her two visits to England during her husband's Viceroyalty.

She also possessed the inestimable advantage which poor Mary Curzon had lacked of being a woman of robust health and boundless energy. Like Minto, she spent as much time as she could spare from her Viceregal duties in the saddle, being as keen and fearless a rider as he was. Just as the sexagenarian Viceroy was fit enough to go in for the jumping at the Simla Horse Show of 1907, and after being thrown was able to remount and take his horse the whole way round once again, so did Mary, already a grandmother, ride over a steeplechase course one morning during her last Calcutta season; and

then, having come 'a fearful smash',[13] breaking her hand and bruising herself badly, was able to entertain 2,300 guests at a garden party that afternoon. As well as riding, this most sporting of Vicereines shot tigers and bears. The sporting prowess of Minto and Mary Minto was shared by their three good-looking grown-up daughters, whose presence brought back an element of gaiety and informality to Viceregal life which had been absent during the Curzon regime when the daughters of Government House were to be found in the nursery rather than in the ballroom.

If their qualities were such as appealed primarily to the British and to the Princes and the aristocracy, the Mintos also managed to win the affections of some of the more radical elements of Indian society. When the Prince and Princess of Wales came to Calcutta soon after

Minto with the Maharaja
of Patiala, 1906

Minto had assumed office, the Congress leader Gopal Krishna Gokhale planned a boycott of the Royal visit on account of the partition of Bengal. Minto, however, sent for Gokhale and pointed out that, having only just arrived, he could not form an opinion regarding this measure; Gokhale was so completely won over by the Viceroy's sympathy and understanding that he not only agreed to call off the boycott but for the rest of Minto's reign believed in him implicitly. At the same time as he won the heart of Gokhale, Minto captivated the Indian Association by receiving an address from that body which the officials had regarded as seditious; and by replying to it with what Dunlop Smith called his 'great frank charm . . . as if he were talking to a friend over the breakfast table'.[14]

Minto's attitude to Congress was sensible and realistic. 'We must recognize them and be friends with the best of them' he wrote, 'yet I am afraid there is much that is absolutely disloyal in the movement.' [15] Unlike Curzon, he was convinced that 'the fellow-service of British and Indian administrators' [16] was essential for the future political happiness of British India. He also saw the importance of breaking down the social barriers between the Indians and the British. Other Viceroys before him had felt the same; but he made a practical contribution towards bringing this about; helping to found the Calcutta Club which was open to Indians as well as to British; doing away with anything that might have seemed a slight to the Indians in Viceregal protocol. When visiting the Indian States, the Mintos really tried to make friends with the Chiefs and their families; Minto even sang *Comin' thro' the Rye* with the Maharani of Gwalior, he on one side of the purdah screen and she on the other.

The Mintos made friends with the Amir of Afghanistan, Habibullah, when he came to India on the Viceroy's invitation in 1907. The fat, cheery little Amir, who wore English clothes, sometimes appearing in knickerbockers and a Norfolk jacket, enjoyed every minute of his stay; which began with a Durbar at Agra and ended in Calcutta with a State Ball and a spending spree at Mary Minto's mammoth Fête in aid of her Nursing Association. He was so captivated by the European ladies that he seriously contemplated marrying at least one of them and had ideas of carrying off the Mintos' eldest daughter, Eileen; he also tried to find a wife for Kitchener, whose celibacy grieved him. On a more serious plane, the visit enabled Minto to reconcile the Amir to the Convention about to be signed between Britain and Russia which established once and for all that Afghanistan was a British sphere of influence. So well did he succeed in this that Habibullah became wholly attached to Britain and abandoned the traditional Afghan policy of giving military support to the Frontier tribes in their attacks on British outposts.

Two of the tribes gave trouble in 1908; Minto had to obtain Morley's grudging permission to send troops against them, which Kitchener did with immediate success. Far more serious than these Frontier raids was the threat of anarchy within India itself. Such was the discontent over the partition of Bengal that there were rumours of an actual rising staged to take place in May 1907, the fiftieth anniversary of the Mutiny; this never materialised, but from then onwards there was a wave of terrorism; British officials and Indian police officers were murdered, two English women died in a bomb outrage. At the same time as Bengal boiled up, there was serious unrest in the Punjab, largely caused by the passing of a Bill by the Government of that Province which introduced various unpopular measures in the administration of a district known as the Chenab Colony. The campaign of violence spread to other parts of India;

The Amir of Afghanistan,
Habibullah, playing
croquet with the Mintos'
eldest daughter, Lady
Eileen Elliot, Barrackpore,
1907

Minto at Simla Horse
Show, 1907

when the Mintos visited Ahmadabad in 1909, bombs were thrown at their carriage which, however, failed to explode; though one of them did so later, killing an Indian. Minto also had a narrow escape in Calcutta, when a brick was thrown through the window of his motor car, missing his head by an inch. Stones were thrown at his car on other occasions; while a poisonous snake which the Viceroy and his daughter Violet encountered in the lift at Government House was thought to have been put there deliberately. Violet's wedding to a son of the former Viceroy Lansdowne which was the chief social event of the 1909 Calcutta season came near to being marred by tragedy; for a bomb was discovered in a flower-pot in the Cathedral just before the ceremony.

Minto was completely unmoved by threats to his personal safety; but he was determined to do everything he could to maintain law and order. He deported some of the worst agitators; others were imprisoned. In 1908 Bal Gangadhar Tilak, the leader of the extremists in Congress who a few months earlier had broken with the moderates under Gokhale, was sent to jail for six years on a charge of incitement. As well as making full use of the powers which the Government of India already possessed, Minto introduced some new legislation to deal with terrorism and sedition. It was a sign of his popularity that he was able to get these measures through the Legislative Council with remarkably little criticism; his Criminal Law Amendment Act, which enabled certain offences to be tried more speedily, received practically unanimous support from the Indian members as well as from the Europeans.

At the same time as he strengthened the hand of the administration, Minto sought to remove the causes of the unrest. Realising that the trouble in the Punjab was largely due to the Chenab Colony Bill, and regarding that Bill as 'very faulty' in itself, he refused to give it his assent. This was to cast a slight on the otherwise admirable Government of the Punjab; but he declared that 'if it was an unjust Bill he did not care for the prestige of fifty Punjab Governments'.[17] His veto of the obnoxious Bill had a wonderful effect in easing the trouble; giving the Viceroy, in the eyes of the people, 'the repute of a just and beneficent divinity'.[18] It was typical of Minto that he should have spoken rather apologetically of his enlightened gesture as playing to the gallery: 'a thing I have always inveighed against, but which in this strange country at a critical moment might prove a winning card'.[19]

As a remedy for the troubles that affected the country as a whole, Minto was determined to give the Indians a greater share in the government. Out of his thinking came the constitutional reforms of 1909, of which the most significant was the admission of an Indian to the 'Holy of Holies', the Viceroy's Executive Council: an innovation rejected categorically by Curzon and opposed by the diehards as well as by the King-Emperor. The reforms also brought Indians into the Executive Councils of Madras and Bombay – the only two Provinces then possessing them – and increased the elected Indian membership of the Central and Provincial Legislative Councils. The system by which the members were to be elected was complex, ordinary manhood suffrage being still out of the question in India; and as a further complication it provided separate electorates for the Muslims, in order that they might be adequately represented. This principle of separate electorates was later to be regarded by Hindus as a deliberate scheme on Minto's part to provoke communal strife and thereby perpetuate British rule; but while Minto may have been short-sighted in not realising that 'communal representation' would cause trouble in the future, his motive in adopting it was no more sinister than a genuine desire to safeguard the interests of the Muslim community which was known to be largely pro-British.

The constitutional changes of 1909 have gone down to history as the Morley-Minto Reforms; but they originated with Minto and the most important innovation, the Indian Member of the Viceroy's Council, was his idea. Morley naturally favoured the reforms and carried them through Parliament; but at times he showed himself to be less enthusiastic about them than Minto. Of the two, it is Minto

Minto and Lady Minto (sitting in a *dandy*) on the North-West Frontier

who stands out as the practical reformer; Morley appears to have been more concerned with trying to curb what he regarded as Minto's policy of repression, which seemed like a betrayal of his own liberal principles. On one of the numerous occasions when he scolded Minto for his toughness in dealing with the anarchists, he declared, in the manner of a schoolmaster threatening to deprive his pupils of a whole holiday: 'If you push me into a position of this sort, then I drop Reforms'.[20]

The reception given to the reforms in India far exceeded Minto's hopes. A congratulatory address was presented to him by a deputation representing all classes and all shades of political opinion; its members ranging from the wealthy zemindar, the Maharaja of Burdwan, to Rabindranath Tagore, the poet; and including even the editors of two extremist Bengali newspapers. The reforms were also surprisingly well received by the Europeans, who did not, as had been feared, raise an outcry about the presence of an Indian in the Viceroy's Council. In order not to trespass on the preserves of the Civil Service, it was decided that the Indian should be the Law Member, who by custom was not a Civilian. An eminent barrister and moderate Congressman, Satyendra Prasanna Sinha, was appointed; he subsequently became the first Indian to govern a province as well as being the first – and so far the only – Indian to serve in the British Government and to be made a peer.

Minto had been anxious to get his repressive legislation over before the announcement of the reforms. 'We must give the medicine first' he wrote, 'and then do all we can to take the taste away.'[21] Unfortunately, having taken away the taste, he was obliged to administer more doses of medicine; though as a gesture to mark the opening of the new Legislative Council in January 1910 he did, much to Morley's delight, release the agitators who had been deported. By then it was nearly a year since the reforms had been passed by Parliament and the country was still in a state of unrest; like other rulers before him and after, Minto learnt the melancholy truth that concessions seldom placate the extremists.

For all the troubles of their reign – and as if bombs were not enough, they were both of them bitten by a rabid dog one Simla season and had to undergo the lengthy and depressing Pasteur treatment – the Mintos were very sad when their time in India came to an end in November 1910. Despite the unsettled state of the country, they had enjoyed their Viceroyalty to the full, rather in the same way as the Dufferins had; and they had grown to love India. 'A Viceroy's period of office is too short' Minto lamented. 'Still, it would be almost impossible for any human being to continue to support the constant strain of work and responsibility as it is now. I wish I could found a dynasty!'[22] It would certainly not have been possible for

Lord and Lady Minto with the veiled Begum of Bhopal

Minto to stay on much longer; for by the end of his reign he was completely worn out, not only by work but also by social life; the scale of Viceregal entertaining being now greater than ever.

Many people wept as the Mintos left Government House for the last time; Mary and their one remaining unmarried daughter Eileen nearly broke down and did so when they reached the station. 'No Viceroy has ever had a more genuine exhibition of sorrow at his departure' Harcourt Butler wrote after seeing Minto off. 'People felt that they were losing a personal friend, who had set a high example of calmness and courage, and who had behaved throughout as a straight gentleman . . . when the Viceroy said to me, "Goodbye, Butler old chap, I'm awfully grateful to you" I nearly broke down myself.'[23] Butler also remarked on how much older Minto was looking; and indeed, he had only a little more than three years to live. Mary, on the other hand, was to survive into the Second World War.

Minto's remarkable success as Viceroy can be attributed to his character and to the fact that he was, so to speak, all things to all men.

To the sporting British, he was the intrepid Mr. Rolly who jumped hedges. To the Army, he was a brother-officer, who on ceremonial occasions would ride forth resplendent in General's uniform. To the Indian Princes, he was the perfect sahib. To Indians of more radical views, he was a sympathetic reformer. His reforms did not take the Indian people very far along the road to *swaraj* or self-government, which he himself spoke of as 'an impossibility in our time and for generations'.[24] They were, however, a step forward; and more important than the actual reforms was the spirit in which they were given. 'Lord Minto has given back self-respect to Indian discontents' Cornelia Sorabji, the authoress and legal adviser to the purdah women, wrote towards the end of his Viceroyalty.[25] But for Curzon, there might have been fewer extremists among the educated Indians of the last four decades of the Raj. But for Minto, there might have been fewer moderates.

Delhi, dyarchy and disobedience

After Curzon and Minto, the next three Viceroys seem something of an anticlimax; though two out of the three were men of great distinction. They were, however, less distinguished as Viceroys than in the careers they followed before going to India. The first of them, Lord Hardinge of Penshurst, is an elusive figure. As Sir Charles Hardinge, he was one of the most brilliant diplomatists of his time and a close friend and trusted adviser of Edward VII. It is hard to decide whether, as a Viceroy, he was a success or a failure; whether he was more liked than disliked; whether he was a strong and energetic ruler or a clever civil servant out of his depth. To a certain extent this ambiguity can be attributed to a psychological change in him due to personal misfortune; yet even allowing for this, one still finds his character contradictory. At times he was cool, austere and hard-headed and at times impulsive. He could be charming, modest and open-minded and also autocratic and arrogant – though people who served under him found him not nearly so arrogant or so autocratic as his own memoirs make him appear. At least one of his colleagues in India found him rather too open-minded; and believed this to be a habit acquired in diplomacy, when he would have had to be constantly revising his opinions.

Having satisfied himself that the Viceregal salary would adequately support the dignity of the office – for as a younger son he had little or no private means – Hardinge had no misgivings as he forsook the courts and chanceries of Europe, which he knew so well, to govern India. It was his life's ambition to follow in the footsteps of his grandfather, who was Governor-General at the time of the First Sikh War. He arrived in India in November 1910 full of enthusiasm for his 'great undertaking';[1] a supremely self-confident figure, tall, spare, upright, with a high forehead and a trim moustache, looking younger than his fifty-two years. At his side was yet another beautiful Vicereine, who was to acquire the reputation of being even cleverer than her husband.

Hardinge intended to be even more conciliatory than Minto had been, hoping thereby to put an end to the sedition and terrorism

Lord Hardinge of Penshurst with Lady Hardinge (left) and their young daughter, Diamond, at Government House, Malabar Point, Bombay

which were still casting a shadow over the Indian scene. He had not been Viceroy long when Lord Crewe, who had succeeded Morley as Secretary of State, suggested the bold step of modifying the partition of Bengal, which was the prime cause of the unrest. This was taken up by Hardinge and his Council and it was eventually decided that the two halves of Bengal should be reunited to form a Presidency under a Governor sent out from home. Out of the problem as to where the seat of government of the new Presidency was to be situated came the momentous decision to move the Imperial capital from Calcutta to Delhi, leaving the Government of Bengal in Calcutta. The change of capitals was to become Hardinge's chief preoccupation and would be the principal legacy of his reign;

though the idea of the move originated not with him but with his Finance Member, Sir Guy Fleetwood Wilson.

The decision to make Delhi the Imperial capital and to end the partition of Bengal was announced by the King-Emperor, George V, at a Durbar held at Delhi in December 1911 to celebrate his Coronation earlier that year. This third and last of the great Delhi gatherings was on an even more gigantic scale than that of 1903; whereas Curzon had spent £180,000 on his *tamasha*, Hardinge's cost £660,000. Two vast concentric amphitheatres were constructed for the Durbar itself, the larger one to hold 100,000 spectators, the smaller to accommodate the Princes and other notables; with, in the centre of all, the thrones of the King-Emperor and Queen-Empress on a marble platform beneath a golden cupola.

When Hardinge went to greet the King-Emperor and Queen-Empress at Bombay, the Royal entourage, knowing that he had ceased to be Viceroy the moment the Monarch sailed into Indian waters, treated him cavalierly; forgetting that they still had to show due deference to him as Governor-General. Apart from this contretemps – and George V's insistence on making his State entry into Delhi on horseback, instead of on an elephant, which meant that

Durbar Throne, Delhi, December 1911

The King-Emperor George
V and the Queen-Empress
Mary appearing to their
Indian subjects on the
ramparts of the old Mogul
palace at Delhi, December
1911

the crowd hardly noticed him – everything went splendidly. In the
Durbar amphitheatre and on the ramparts of the old Mogul palace,
the King-Emperor and Queen-Empress appeared to their Indian
subjects in robes and regalia; the King-Emperor wearing the
Imperial Crown of India which had been specially made for the
occasion. Curzon and others had wanted the Imperial Crown to
remain permanently in Delhi or Calcutta after the Durbar was over;
but Hardinge, in the somewhat whimsical belief that the presence of

the Crown in India would serve as a temptation to would-be usurpers of the Throne, insisted that it should be taken back to England.

The announcement by the King-Emperor that the partition of Bengal was to be ended was received with jubilation by the Bengalis; but the proposed move of the capital to Delhi met with a mixed reception. It was welcomed by the majority of Chiefs, whose States were closer to Delhi than to Calcutta; and by the people of the North-West. Some of the radical middle classes criticised the scheme on the grounds of cost; though the new capital was intended to be a symbol of Indian nationhood as much as of confidence in the future of the Raj. The strongest opposition naturally came from the inhabitants of Calcutta, Indian as well as European, who objected to their city being deprived of its pride of place; they were supported by influential opinion in Britain, notably by Curzon and Minto. There was much airing of the old superstition that the move of the seat of government of a ruling power to Delhi was inevitably followed by its downfall.

As the chief advocate of the move, Hardinge became very unpopular in Calcutta, particularly with the Europeans. During the early months of 1912, which were the last he was to spend at Government House, he was subjected to violent attacks in the Press. Lady Hardinge shared in his unpopularity, though she went out of her way to be pleasant. 'There is no doubt that the Viceroy is most cordially disliked' Harcourt Butler observed shortly before Hardinge left Calcutta for good. 'He is hasty and impetuous. He has been so successful all his life that he can't stand criticism easily. He is a fighter by nature but very susceptible to criticism.'[2] Hardinge took comfort in planning his new capital. 'He is mad on Delhi at present' Butler complained. 'I am afraid we shan't get much of a policy out of him, as he can think of little except Delhi.'[3]

The Hardinges left Government House for the last time at the end of March, in the midst of a thunderstorm; the legend that at the moment of their departure the flagstaff on the dome was struck by lightning is not, however, true. A few days later, Government House was taken over by the new Governor of Bengal; Barrackpore being retained by Hardinge for when he went to Calcutta on visits. For the next seventeen years, the winter residence of the Viceroys was to be the former Circuit House at Delhi which was renamed Viceregal Lodge. It had been built to accommodate Curzon when he came for the Durbar of 1903 and was a typical Indian bungalow of the grander sort writ large; surrounded by arcaded verandas and with a pillared *porte-cochère*. It contained a few spacious rooms for entertaining and for the Viceregal family; the Staff and guests being relegated to tents in the grounds.

The officials of the Government of India who descended on Delhi in the autumn of 1912 were housed in a temporary capital hastily run up to the north of the old walled city. Meanwhile, a Commission set to work choosing a site for New Delhi; one of its members was the forty-three-year-old Edwin Lutyens, an architect whose genius was widely if not yet universally acknowledged. As well as working on the layout of the city, Lutyens became the architect of the new Government House, which was to be a palace to compare with Versailles, Schönbrunn or Caserta. His relationship with Hardinge was to develop into what his biographer has called 'one of the classic conflicts in architectural history, comparable with that of Michael Angelo and Pope Julius II'.[4]

In his first dealings with the Viceroy at Simla during the summer of 1912 he found him 'delightful to work with, wide-viewed – non fussy and autocratic'.[5] Although Hardinge had imagined that the new Government House would cost no more than £200,000, and was shocked when Lutyens told him that £1,000,000 was nearer the mark, he agreed to spend this amount. He also appeared to have been won over to the synthesis of Eastern and Western styles which Lutyens hoped to achieve. The Viceroy had originally wanted a style that was wholly Oriental, though this would have meant 'grafting Eastern excrescences on to a Western building'.[6] Hardinge was a man of taste; it was he who first suggested the site eventually chosen for Government House, and who recommended that the new city should be laid out on a triangular rather than a rectangular plan. His ideas as to what constituted good architecture were, however, very different from those of Lutyens, with his 'infinitely finer sensibilities'.[7] Then there was the Viceroy's insistence on economy, in order not to exceed the original and as it turned out quite unrealistic estimate; which was hardly conducive to creating timeless architecture in the grand manner. No less of a scourge to his architects was Hardinge's demand for speed; though in the event it was only through his urging that some tangible progress was made before the outbreak of war, which would otherwise almost certainly have caused the new Imperial capital to be dropped altogether.

In December 1912 Hardinge and Lady Hardinge entered Delhi in state, followed by Chiefs and high officials in a long procession of richly-bedecked elephants. As they passed through the crowded streets of the old city, Hardinge suddenly said to his wife: 'I am sure something dreadful is going to happen'.[8] A few moments later he felt as if he had been hit very hard on the back and at the same time scalded; his sun helmet was blown from his head and the elephant stopped abruptly. 'I am afraid that was a bomb' he told his wife, though neither of them heard any explosion.[9] It seemed as if no harm had been done; Hardinge retrieved his topi, which was passed up to him on the end of a lance, and called to the mahout to urge the elephant on. Then Lady Hardinge glanced round and saw that the

Hardinge, after the attempt on his life, being taken from the scene of the outrage in a motor car, at the door of which stands Lady Hardinge. The trunk of the elephant on which the Viceroy and Vicereine were making their State entry into Delhi can be seen on the right of the picture

attendant who held the umbrella of state was dead, his shattered body entangled in the ropes of the howdah. She looked at her husband, who sat pale and erect, and noticed a rent down the back of his tunic, from which blood was flowing. Another instant and he fell forward unconscious. Lady Hardinge kept calm and with the help of an ADC managed to get her wounded husband down from the elephant, which was too frightened to kneel; so that an erection of packing-cases had to be hastily built up alongside the animal to serve as steps. As he lay on the pavement, Hardinge came to for long enough to order the procession and ceremony to carry on as though nothing had happened, with Fleetwood Wilson standing in for him. He then fainted again and a motor-car took him and Lady Hardinge to Viceregal Lodge. They arrived to find the house deserted, the servants having all gone to watch the procession; so that their twelve-year-old daughter Diamond had to make up a bed for her father and get him a hot-water bottle.

Hardinge's wounds proved more painful than dangerous; the bomb had contained screws, nails and gramophone needles which were embedded in his shoulders and the back of his neck. It took several operations to remove them all and he was laid up for ten weeks; though he insisted on leaving his bed for a couple of hours at the end of January to open the Legislative Council. He had also suffered a burst ear-drum from the explosion, which he and his wife never heard because it was so close to them; though people heard it up to six miles away. More serious than his physical injuries was the psychological effect the bomb outrage had on him. He lost much of his self-confidence and also some of his nerve; so that, in Butler's words, he did 'jumpy things occasionally'.[10] And apart from its actual trauma, the attempt on his life made a mockery of his belief that his policy had put an end to violence; which had indeed appeared to be the case during the deceptively quiet earlier months of 1912. He tells us in his memoirs that when he first realised the implications of the Delhi bomb, he 'literally wept with disappointment'.[11] The thought that the improvement on which he had set so much store had proved illusory left him dispirited, making him more than ever austere and remote. 'The Viceroy inspires so little personal feeling' Butler lamented in the spring of 1914. 'He lacks humanity.'[12] Hardinge's disillusionment over the bomb did not, however, affect his policy; he appeared more than ever anxious to be conciliatory, encouraged by the widespread rejoicing among Indians at his recovery from his wounds. In the autumn of 1913 he made an unexpected and unprecedented dash to Cawnpore, in the former North-Western Provinces – now known as the United Provinces – to settle a dispute over a mosque which had caused serious riots there and was inflaming Muslim opinion all over India. He addressed the entire Muslim population of that city of sinister memories; repro-ached them severely for their misbehaviour and then held out the olive branch by ordering the release of more than a hundred of them who had been imprisoned for rioting. In thus going over the heads of the provincial authorities he had the excuse that the Lieutenant-Governor of the United Provinces was away on leave; his action was nevertheless much resented by the local Civilians, particularly as he was almost rude to them; he also annoyed them by asking the leading agitators to luncheon. 'He is playing hard to the Indian gallery' wrote Butler, who was himself by no means insensitive to Indian public opinion. 'This is a mistake from every point of view, especially just now. But Viceroys will be Viceroys!'[13] Butler was inclined to attribute Hardinge's Cawnpore escapade to the effects of the bomb, which had made him more than ever impetuous.

If the bomb outrage made Hardinge more troublesome to his colleagues and subordinates, so too did it affect his relations with Lutyens, who believed that, as a result of it, he had 'lost all energy of mind'.[14] He now proceeded to go back on his agreement to spend a million on Government House and announced that half a million would be the most it would cost. In his weakened condition he wavered between Lutyens's aesthetic principles and his own idea that New Delhi should look more Oriental to appeal to Indian aspirations. 'He . . . talks the wildest stuff about architecture' a colleague remarked of him when he was still laid up with his wounds.[15] He came increasingly under the influence of Herbert Baker, the architect brought in by Lutyens to help him with the layout of the city and to design the two Secretariats; who was soon behaving more like Lutyens's rival than his collaborator. 'I had no trouble with Baker' Hardinge tells us pointedly in his memoirs. He could not see that whereas Lutyens was arguably the greatest English architect since Wren, Baker was little more than a competent practitioner good at giving officialdom what it wanted.

Lady Hardinge, who knew more about architecture than her husband, recognised Lutyens's genius and did everything she could to make his task easier. In the spring of 1914, however, she went to England for a rest. In July, when Europe was on the brink of war, she had to undergo a major operation. At Simla, Hardinge and his young daughter Diamond, who had remained with him in India, anxiously awaited the outcome. At first the news of the Vicereine was good; then complications ensued and they heard that she had died. His wife's death was a fearful blow to Hardinge, as unexpected as the anarchist's bomb which had deprived him of the strength he needed to bear this far greater shock. He was afterwards to maintain that he was only saved from total collapse by the kindness and sympathy of

Viceregal Lodge, Delhi

the fourteen-year-old Diamond, who from now on thought of nothing else but how to comfort her father. Before the year was out, Hardinge had suffered a second cruel bereavement: his elder son was mortally wounded fighting in France. As well as losing his son, the unhappy Viceroy lost three of his ADCs, who went off to the war and were all three killed within a few days of each other.

For the rest of his Viceroyalty, which was extended by six months on account of the war, Hardinge was a lonely figure; relying for companionship on Diamond, and on a number of Indians whom he cultivated, having few friends among the British. Adversity, according to Butler, made him 'much more human'.[16] To distract him from his sorrows, there was the mammoth task of organising India's war-effort. He sent large numbers of Indian troops to Europe soon enough for them to help slow down the first German advance on Paris. He also sent away as many British troops as he could; reducing the British garrison in India to what might have been regarded, in view of the unsettled state of the country, as a dangerously low level. His trust in the loyalty of the Indian people was, on the whole, justified; though there was a resurgence of unrest in Bengal and the Punjab which Hardinge dealt with by bringing in a more stringent Indian equivalent of Britain's Defence of the Realm Act.

Hardinge was also responsible for organising the transport, supplies and medical services for the campaign in Mesopotamia. The notorious mismanagement of this campaign served to vindicate the old military system which Curzon had fought to maintain; though at the cost of untold suffering and the loss of many thousands of soldiers from cholera, gangrene and heatstroke. Now that the Commander-in-Chief had to do the Military Member's work as well as his own, it was impossible for him, in wartime, to keep properly in touch with affairs at the front; particularly when he was someone as ineffective as Sir Beauchamp Duff – described by Butler as 'a white babu'[17] – who, largely on Hardinge's insistence, had been appointed Commander-in-Chief in 1914. In so far as he trusted Duff too much, Hardinge can to some extent be blamed for the Mesopotamian nightmare; though when he realised how bad things were, he went to Basra himself to do what he could to improve the conditions of the troops. When, after he had ceased to be Viceroy, there was a Commission of Inquiry on Mesopotamia, it looked as though he might have had to resign from being head of the Foreign Office, to which post he had returned having held it before going to India. He was, however, exonerated, the blame being laid entirely on the Indian military authorities, in particular on the hapless Duff, who eventually committed suicide.

'Charlie is very lucky' Lady Hardinge used sometimes to say of her husband;[18] and although it seemed as if his luck had deserted him for good after the Delhi bomb outrage, it was certainly in again during the final phase of his career, which ended in 1922 after he had attained the very pinnacle of the Diplomatic Service, the Paris Embassy. But fate dealt him yet another cruel blow in 1927 when he lost his beloved Diamond, who died at the age of twenty-six. Bereft of his wife, his elder son and his only daughter, Hardinge lived on into his late eighties, dying in 1944. In 1931 he saw his dream of a New Delhi come true, when he returned to India for the inauguration of the Imperial city.

If Hardinge, however one may judge him as a Viceroy, was in himself a very distinguished man, his successor, Lord Chelmsford, was little more than a nonentity. The grandson of a Lord Chancellor

Lord Chelmsford

who before being made a peer was Sir Frederic Thesiger – the family having originally come from Dresden – Chelmsford was a public figure of sorts, having been a member of the London County Council, governed two Australian provinces in succession and been considered for the Governorship of Bombay; but there was nothing in his past career that would have suggested him as a possible ruler of India. It seems that Asquith chose him because he was a Liberal and a Fellow of All Souls and also for the reason that he happened to be in India at the time, having gone there after the outbreak of war as a Territorial captain. He is said to have had Asquith's letter in his pocket when his colonel told him that, as a man of nearly fifty, he ought to be doing something better than commanding a company.

Chelmsford's Fellowship of All Souls is perhaps the most significant thing about him, for he was in manner and appearance very much an academic; though not so much a don as a type of rather superior schoolmaster; a master, perhaps, at Winchester, which was actually his old school. His head had that forward tilt, his handsome, bony, clean-shaven face that patient look that suggests a master listening intently to a pupil; he also had a slight look of bafflement as though suspecting his class of ragging him but at a loss to know in what way. His fine, well-dressed, athletic figure had the stylish dignity of the Headmaster at Eton Match without quite achieving a Viceregal presence. Like many schoolmasters he was outwardly frigid, while being kind and conscientious and possessing a dry sense of humour. He had other virtues that one would expect to find in the best sort of schoolmaster; he was hardworking, a good judge of character and a keen churchman. He also had the schoolmaster's, or more correctly, the don's fault of being rather too cautious; on which can be blamed what Edwin Montagu, who was Secretary of State during most of his reign, called 'his lack of constructive ability'.[19]

'I should imagine he is very conscientiously honest with himself and others but rather lacking, I will not say in human sympathy, but in the power of conveying to others that he feels it' was how Chelmsford's successor was to sum him up.[20] With his chilly voice and his lack of charm and geniality, Chelmsford did not easily get through to people. The Indian Princes found it hard to talk to him. The senior British officials, however, liked him for his simplicity and found him a patient and sympathetic chief; though many of them feared that, having been soldiering at Simla before his appointment to the Viceroyalty, he knew more about them than it was good for a Viceroy to know. But while Chelmsford on the whole made a good first impression, his wife – a first cousin of Winston Churchill – did not. Delhi and Simla society found her dull. She instituted a rather stiff regime at the two Viceregal Lodges and during her time the houses themselves were not well run; though this was to some extent due to wartime economies and afterwards to Chelmsford's public-spirited refusal to have his allowances increased, despite the post-war rise in costs. If she neglected her duties as a hostess, Lady Chelmsford threw herself heart and soul into war-work and social welfare, helped by her three grown-up daughters. The Chelmsfords also had a much younger girl; someone once met her out riding on her pony at Simla and asked her who she was; to which she replied: 'My name is Margaret St Clair Thesiger, my Daddy works very hard and my Mummy is the Viceroy'.[21]

It was a sign of Chelmsford's sense of humour that he should have told this story against himself in an after-dinner speech; yet the five-year-old Margaret's words were not so very far from the truth. Lady Chelmsford, in her various activities, was a leader in a way that Chelmsford, as Viceroy, was not; *he* just worked very hard. He was, in Harcourt Butler's words, 'too much of a machine';[22] he dutifully kept the wheels of Government turning without either giving a lead to his Council or, for that matter, thinking for himself; his views being generally, as Montagu put it, 'collected from his surroundings'.[23] For example, in the controversy which had arisen between Lutyens and Baker over the gradient of the approach to the as yet unbuilt palace in New Delhi, he simply followed the recommendations of Hardinge and the officials while listening with apparent sympathy to Lutyens; his successor was to do the same, so that Baker prevailed and the approach was spoilt. It would have been natural for Chelmsford to feel unsure of himself at the beginning of his reign, having become Viceroy so unexpectedly; yet as time went on he became weaker rather than stronger, perhaps on account of the blow he suffered in 1917 when his elder son died of wounds received in Mesopotamia.

To Chelmsford and his Council must, however, go the credit for initiating the reforms for which his Viceroyalty is now chiefly remembered. In the autumn of 1916, Chelmsford wrote to the Secretary of State of the need for a definite promise of further constitutional reform to placate Indian opinion. His Council, he said, was worried about the Indian Home Rule Movement, which during the past year had been gaining ground under the leadership of an elderly Englishwoman, the Theosophist Mrs. Annie Besant; who had since been interned or, as Chelmsford put it, placed 'in *villeggiatura* in the Nilgiris'.[24] To grant all that Mrs. Besant and her followers wanted was clearly out of the question; but Chelmsford wished to give India 'the largest measure of self-government compatible with the maintenance of the supreme authority of British rule'.[25]

This objective was announced by the Home Government a year later. By then, the Secretary of State was Edwin Montagu, a thirty-

Edwin Montagu (left) and Lord Chelmsford (right) in Calcutta. Between them sits the Countess of Ronaldshay, wife of the Governor of Bengal. Lady Chelmsford sits on her husband's left, with, on her left, Lord Ronaldshay, who as Marquess of Zetland was Secretary of State for India twenty years later

eight-year-old scion of a wealthy Jewish banking family who had been appointed to the office in July 1917 by the new Prime Minister, Lloyd George. Montagu was the antithesis of Chelmsford, a politician to his fingertips, quick, mercurial, imaginative, charming but also erratic and arrogant. On Chelmsford's invitation, he came to India in November 1917 and stayed nearly six months, working out his plan of reform. It was an unprecedented situation for the Viceroy to be thus overshadowed by his constitutional superior; and served to make Chelmsford more than ever a cipher.

During the months that they were together, Chelmsford and Montagu managed to get on surprisingly well; despite their temperamental differences and the stresses to which they were subjected. 'I like Chelmsford more than ever' Montagu wrote in his diary in December. 'Fatigue cannot stale the courtesy of his manner or the inherent honesty of his character.'[26] At the same time, Montagu complained that Chelmsford showed little or no initiative and that he could not find 'any vigour or personality in him'.

In 1910, when he was Morley's Under-Secretary, Montagu had annoyed Minto by speaking of the Viceroy as the Secretary of State's 'agent'; but even as a mere agent, Chelmsford seemed to him unsatisfactory; always taking up an attitude of 'I wish it were possible, but I am afraid . . .' He never, according to Montagu, attempted to argue with people or tried to persuade them: 'The trouble about him is that although he agrees, he cannot get things done'.[27] And as time went on, Montagu began to wish that Chelmsford would not agree with him quite so readily, but would show a little independence. 'I really find myself despairing of this man' he wrote in February 1918. 'Here he is, faced with the greatest issue of his life . . . he has had ten days away from me; I have sent him new suggestion after new suggestion, and I find that the ten days has produced no corresponding thought of any kind whatever from him. He has done nothing, except sit and wait to be fed, and then even does not criticise.' Chelmsford had just asked Montagu to postpone his departure; having already gone so far as to say to him: 'I should like you to stay here for ever'.[28]

Montagu writes of the occasions when Chelmsford did show a little spirit as though they were a nine days' wonder. There was the admirable way in which he dealt with Mrs. Besant, now released from her '*villeggiatura*', who asked him whether she would be allowed to return to India if she went home to attend to her Theosophical commitments. 'His face broke into a sweet smile and he said: "Well really, Mrs. Besant, you know that my desire is to get you safely out of India. Do you think it is likely, if I ever achieved this great end, I should let you come back?"' Then Montagu records with some amazement that the Viceroy, in an after-dinner speech, had actually made a *risqué* joke. There is no mention in the Secretary of State's diary, however, of a speech in which Chelmsford directed a schoolmasterish sally at Montagu, who was present. Having re-marked on how Montagu's flights of imagination usually came to him in his bath, he went on to say: 'Well gentlemen, when Mr. Montagu took one bath a day, according to British habit, we could keep abreast of him. But now he has fallen into our Indian habit of two baths a day it is more difficult. And, good heavens, what will happen to the Indian Empire if Mr. Montagu decides to take three baths a day?'[29]

'Chelmsford's great good temper does make one weep sometimes' Montagu lamented in January;[30] but by the beginning of March even Chelmsford's temper was beginning to get short; and by the end of the month relations between him and Montagu were showing signs of strain. But the two men soldiered on and by the middle of April the Montagu-Chelmsford Report had been finally drawn up. There was the problem as to whether Montagu's signature or Chelmsford's should appear first on the document. Chelmsford felt he should sign first, on account of his position in India; but Montagu asserted his own constitutional precedence to which Chelmsford had to agree, though 'he looked rather sorry for himself'.[31] In the end, the signatures appeared side by side. The signing, at Viceregal Lodge, Simla, was quite an occasion; Lady Chelmsford, in Red Cross uniform, stood by her husband. When Montagu signed, he found that Chelmsford had already done so in private, as though determined to have the satisfaction of signing first. Four days later, Montagu left Simla on his way back to England; remarking in his diary that 'even Chelmsford looked happy'.[32]

The Montagu-Chelmsford Reforms introduced into the Provincial Governments a system known as dyarchy. Certain departments were entrusted to Indian Ministers, responsible to an enlarged and more democratically elected Provincial Legislature. Other departments, notably finance and police, continued as before to be administered by officials responsible only to the Governor – the Reforms gave the heads of the former Lieutenant-Governors' Provinces the same title as those of the Presidencies. The Governor thus acquired a dual personality; he continued to be an autocrat in some departments but in others became a constitutional monarch – not entirely, for in the last resort he did not have to take his Ministers' advice. There was no dyarchy in the Central Government, which remained much as it had been; except that three out of the six Members who, together with the Commander-in-Chief and the Viceroy himself made up the Executive Council, were henceforth to be Indians. The Central Legislature also became larger and more democratic; and a Chamber of Princes was established as an advisory body.

The new system was a significant step forward in that it gave the Indians for the first time a measure of responsible self-government; previous reforms having given them little more than the right to advise and to criticise. Nevertheless, the Montagu-Chelmsford Reforms were not nearly so well received as the reforms of Morley and Minto. In fact, the publication of the Report in July 1918 marked a sudden change for the worse in the feelings of the politically-minded Indians towards the British, with whom they had up to now been co-operating amicably in the war-effort. Not only did it give them far less than what they expected, but it offended them by showing all too clearly that Britain still did not have much faith in the Indian leaders. A Viceroy with more personality than Chelmsford might have encouraged the Indians to see the Reforms in a more favourable light; but Chelmsford was quite incapable of appealing to Indian opinion in this way.

To the feeling of disillusionment over the forthcoming reforms was added the resentment caused by a Bill to prolong the Government's wartime emergency powers to deal with conspiracy. This measure, known as the Rowlatt Act, was in itself nothing very significant and considerably milder than its wartime progenitor, but it provoked an outcry. As a protest against it, Gandhi, who since his return to India from South Africa in 1915 had been helping to recruit troops to fight in the Army of the King-Emperor, launched a campaign of *Satyagraha* or non-cooperation in February 1919. 'Dear me, what a d——d nuisance these saintly fanatics are!' Chelmsford wrote in April. 'Gandhi is incapable of hurting a fly and is as honest as the day, but he enters quite lightheartedly on a course of action which is the negation of all government and may lead to much hardship to people who are ignorant and easily led astray.'[33]. This was a sound enough judgement; but at the time when Chelmsford wrote these words, Gandhi's campaign was causing riots in Delhi which went on for three weeks in defiance of the Chief Commissioner and indeed of the Viceroy himself.

At the time of the Delhi riots, there were worse outbreaks of violence in the Punjab, notably at Lahore and Amritsar; which Sir Michael O'Dwyer, the hard-headed Irishman who governed the province, dealt with quickly and effectively. Unfortunately at Amritsar the troops under the command of Brigadier-General Reginald Dyer continued to fire on a mob for longer than was necessary to disperse it, killing over three hundred people; an episode which outraged Indian opinion and is still remembered with bitterness. Chelmsford began by approving of Dyer's conduct, having been assured by the Anglican Bishop of Lahore that 'if Dyer had not acted so promptly and vigorously the outbreak would have assumed dimensions vastly larger than those it actually assumed'.[34] Later, he admitted that Dyer was guilty of an error of judgement.

When, in December 1919, Montagu ended one of the many telegrams with which he was harassing Chelmsford by wishing him a merry Christmas, Chelmsford retorted drily: 'I wonder if you really believe that in times like these a Viceroy's Christmas is likely to be merry'.[35] Certainly 1919 was, without doubt, the worst year in the history of British India since the Mutiny; a year in which the Raj, weakened as a result of the war, was in real danger. As well as the troubles in the Punjab and elsewhere, there had been an invasion by the irresponsible young Amir of Afghanistan, Amanullah, who sought to take advantage of the Punjab disturbances. He had been quickly repulsed, but it had added to the tribulations of the Viceroy.

That Christmas of 1919 was not without its pleasures for the Viceregal family, who spent it amidst the civilised opulence of Calcutta. Whereas Hardinge had wisely kept Barrackpore as an occasional Calcutta residence, believing that he would there be far enough away from the former capital not to overshadow the Governor of Bengal, the Chelmsfords preferred to have a house in Calcutta itself. So Barrackpore became the Governor of Bengal's weekend retreat and the Chelmsfords took over Belvedere, the former residence of the Lieutenant-Governors of Bengal, in the fashionable residential quarter of Alipore. A mansion in a rather Italianate style, with pillars, balustrades and arcaded verandas surmounted by ornamental plasterwork, it mostly dated from the middle of the nineteenth century and was therefore less historic than Barrackpore; though it probably incorporated an eighteenth-century house in which Warren Hastings had lived for a time. Its grounds were spacious, with mahogany trees and a lotus-covered lake; but

Belvedere, Calcutta

they were nothing as romantic as the Barrackpore park; and the house, though imposing, was inconveniently planned and short of accommodation. It was also situated rather too close to the Zoological Gardens, so that its inhabitants were sometimes kept awake at night by the roaring of wild animals. From now on it became the custom for the Viceroy to go into residence at Belvedere at Christmas; which meant that during the height of the Calcutta season there were two rival courts within a short distance of each other.

Throughout the following year, 1920, India continued to be in a serious state of unrest. Gandhi's primarily Hindu agitation was allied to what was known as the Khilafat movement among the Muslims, who were angry at the treatment of Turkey by the victorious Allies. The Muslims became increasingly turbulent; resolutions were passed all over the country putting loyalty to the Sultan before loyalty to the King-Emperor. The situation was exacerbated by a bad monsoon and a threat of famine. There was a feeling that things were getting out of control, that the whole authority of the Government was breaking down. At all events, British India needed a stronger hand than Chelmsford was capable of providing.

By the end of the year, Harcourt Butler was writing of Chelmsford: 'The sooner he goes, the better. No one any longer has any confidence in him . . . no Viceroy has failed as he has failed'.[36] And in the following spring, when Chelmsford's time was up, Butler wrote: 'The present Viceroy leaves unwept, unsung. A complete failure. He has failed signally to impress India.'[37] However, in January 1921, a couple of months before he left, Chelmsford had a brief moment of glory when the new Legislatures and the Chamber of Princes, set up under the Reforms, were inaugurated by that veteran Royal visitor to India, the Duke of Connaught; though the Reforms had not got off to a very good start, for the elections had been boycotted by Congress.

The Chelmsfords' departure from India was spoilt for them by an unfavourable Press and by the news that as a reward for his labours as Viceroy, he was merely to be promoted from Baron to Viscount; just one step in the Peerage, whereas according to precedent he should have been given an Earldom or the Garter. So Chelmsford arrived back in London upset and resentful: 'Rather sloppy ice' was Montagu's somewhat unkind description of his mood.[38] Apart from a brief period as First Lord of the Admiralty in the first Labour Government, Chelmsford from now on played little part in public life. He ended his days in the academic world for which he was temperamentally so well suited; becoming Warden of Winchester in 1930 and then, shortly before his death in 1933, Warden of All Souls. Lady Chelmsford survived until 1957; at one time during her widowhood she lived in Italy, where she was known as 'La Contessa d'India'.

One of Montagu's favourite criticisms of Chelmsford as a Viceroy was that he came from 'the wrong class'.[39] Given the radical ideas of the Secretary of State and also of the Prime Minister, Lloyd George, it was generally expected that Chelmsford's successor would be unconventional; there was talk of Winston Churchill; it was also thought that one of the Provincial Governors might be promoted. 'I feel that the new Viceroy will be a surprise to us all – someone like Sir Philip Sassoon' Harcourt Butler, himself a possible candidate, had written towards the end of 1920.[40] In the event he was proved right, at any rate in his guess that the new Viceroy would be of the same race as Montagu; for the man chosen was Rufus Isaacs, Earl of Reading, an eminent lawyer who was also a politician and an expert on finance. On the face of it, Reading was appointed in order that the constitutional reforms should have the benefit of his brilliant legal mind during their first few critical years; a lawyer Viceroy was particularly appropriate since the Indian political leaders were mostly lawyers themselves. The appointment was also influenced by the belief, which Montagu held, that a Jew, being in a sense an Oriental, had a natural bond with the Indians.

As well as being the only Jewish Viceroy, Reading was the only Viceroy who did not come from an aristocratic or at any rate a Service background; for even Plain John Lawrence was a colonel's son. His origins were not, however, as humble as might be inferred from the

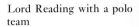

Lord Reading with a polo team

story – which as Viceroy he told rather too often – of how he had his first sight of India as a ship's boy on the deck of a merchant vessel in the Hughli. He was the son of a London fruit merchant and the nephew of a Lord Mayor; he became a ship's boy not of necessity, but because he took little interest in the family business. Later, he turned to the Bar where he achieved a phenomenal success; earning £28,000 a year by the time he entered Parliament as a Liberal in 1904. By 1913 he had become Lord Chief Justice, having already been in the Cabinet. During the War, he was what *The Times* called the 'Government's financial right hand'; in which capacity he was sent to Washington as Ambassador. Having started life as plain Mr. Isaacs, he had by 1917 risen to being an Earl.

'He will restore respectability to the Viceroyalty' Butler wrote on hearing of Reading's appointment.[41] Certainly Reading was as distinguished a figure as Hardinge; and in addition to his remarkable intellectual gifts he had an attractive speaking voice and was tall and splendid-looking, his clean-shaven features handsome in a typically Semitic way. Yet there were many who did not regard him as wholly respectable, on account of the so-called 'Marconi Scandal', which arose eight years earlier, when it was found that he and his friend Lloyd George and a third member of the Government had bought shares in the American Marconi Company at a time when the English Marconi Company was obtaining lucrative Government contracts. Although a Select Committee of the House of Commons had acquitted the three Ministers of any impropriety, the Unionists had not been satisfied; and in 1915, when Reading was Lord Chief Justice, he had been attacked by Kipling in a cruel poem, *Gehazi*:

> Well done, well done, Gehazi!
> Stretch forth thy ready hand,
> Thou barely 'scaped from judgement
> Take oath to judge the land . . .

However much one may dismiss this as mere anti-Jewish mud-slinging, it was unfortunate for the Viceroyalty, which was meant to be above reproach, that its new incumbent should have been attacked in this way by, of all people, the Poet Laureate of the Raj. The mere fact that Reading was a Jew was inevitably a disadvantage to him in his high position; it antagonised some of the Muslims as well as certain Princes, who were also prejudiced against him because he was not an aristocrat; they had heard how, on being appointed Viceroy at the mature age of sixty, he had to learn to ride and to shoot. They were similarly prejudiced against Lady Reading; the Maharaja of Bikaner, while liking the new Vicereine as a person, was to comment adversely on the fact that 'she had eaten cheese on her knife'.

The British were on the whole more favourably disposed towards Reading than some of the Indians: 'Everyone feels that he would be better if he was not a Jew, but is willing to give the Jew a trial' was how their attitude was summed up.[42] Their anti-semitism generally went no further than making the most of such incidents as when Lady Reading stopped the Viceroy from eating pork chops at his own table; though some of the more orthodox Anglican ladies of Simla were shocked to see the Jewish Viceroy and Vicereine at church and there was a worse commotion when Reading showed his impartiality by asking the Catholic Archbishop instead of the Anglican Bishop to say grace at the State Dinner – having already caused a sensation that evening by appearing in his judge's robes and wig. Whatever their prejudices concerning the Jewish race, most people found Reading impressive. 'I have never met such a smooth-working quiet mind'

Butler wrote after his first meeting with him. 'He has a big brain. Curzon is a child beside him.'[43]

Lady Reading made a no less favourable first impression; she seemed kind and simple and also rather brave, for she suffered from deafness and looked ill and frail, yet was clearly determined to make the most of her time as Vicereine. In fact her health was so poor that she was obliged to bring a trained nurse out from England with her; before her husband's Viceroyalty ended she was to undergo an operation for cancer which though successful did not give her more than a few years' reprieve. She came from the same intelligent and well-to-do Jewish world as her husband, whose devotion to her was touching.

After the rather stiff Chelmsford regime, the Readings seemed delightfully informal, not to say unconventional. Reading at first could not be serious when the ladies curtseyed to him; he would make exaggerated bows to those of them who went down particularly low; and when his wife curtseyed to him he would wave his hand at her. Although some people were inclined to grumble that the new Viceroy and Vicereine invited all and sundry to their parties, their entertainments were at any rate fun and regardless of expense; the French chef was wonderful. To make up for the Readings' lack of daughters, there was Lady Reading's secretary, Yvonne FitzRoy, a charming and clever young lady who was a cousin of the Duke of Grafton.

Reading became Viceroy in extremely difficult circumstances, with the new system of government as yet untried and the non-co-operation movement and the Khilafat agitation not only showing no sign of abating but gaining additional strength from an agitation among the Sikhs. At first he attempted to pacify India by the arts of persuasion. In May 1921, soon after his arrival at Simla, Reading received Gandhi at Viceregal Lodge. Lady Reading, Yvonne FitzRoy and some ADCs, who were busy preparing for a ball, supervising the moving of furniture and the construction of a bower of bougainvillea, geraniums and Canterbury bells for the band, paused in their labours to peep into the hall and catch a glimpse of the 'slim, spare figure in the coarse white wrappings of the Hindu holy man'.[44]

While Reading was negotiating with Gandhi, the situation continued to deteriorate. Those who had hoped that the new Viceroy would take a strong line began to be disappointed in him. In August, violence erupted in the deep South, where the fanatically Muslim Moplahs rose against their Hindu neighbours, committing wholesale murder and all kinds of other atrocities. In order to please certain elements in the Legislative Assembly, Reading and his Government began by trying to conciliate the insurgents; with the result that their reign of terror lasted for several months and far harsher measures had eventually to be taken against them than were taken in the Punjab in 1919.

By the end of 1921, Reading had made up his mind to deal sternly with disorder. Gandhi's two principal lieutenants, Motilal Nehru and his son Jawaharlal, were arrested. Gandhi himself followed them to prison in March 1922, even though he had suspended his campaign; British opinion demanding that he should be punished as the instigator of the disturbances and for having called for a boycott of the recent visit to India of the Prince of Wales. It was hard on Reading to have to be responsible for the safety of the Heir-Apparent in addition to all the other worries of his first cold weather as Viceroy. In the event, the Royal tour went off without any untoward incident; and while the Prince was given no more than a lukewarm reception in some places, he was greeted with great enthusiasm in others. The Prince's suite included his handsome young sailor cousin, Lord Louis Mountbatten, who became engaged to Edwina Ashley, one of the girls in the Viceregal house party. Lady Reading, in a letter to the girl's aunt, said of the engagement: 'We would have preferred her to get engaged to someone with a more promising career'.[45]

The Prince's visit was followed in March 1922 by the downfall of Montagu, who came to grief through publishing, without the Cabinet's permission, a dispatch from Reading deprecating the Government's policy of supporting the Greeks against the Turks, which had further inflamed Muslim opinion in India. There was a general feeling that Reading would also have to go; it was reported that the Home Government already regarded him as a failure. His position became more than ever difficult in the autumn, when Lloyd George's Coalition was succeeded by the entirely Conservative Government of Bonar Law. But he carried on; he and Lady Reading were beginning to 'love the position and the pomp of power'.[46]

The Readings had not been in India four months before Yvonne FitzRoy was complaining of a 'bad fit of being Viceregal' which had come over Lady Reading that morning.[47] After a year, it was generally agreed that they were no longer the 'simple people' they had been when they first came.[48] '*Plus royal que les royaux*' was how a lady who stayed with them later in their reign described them to the present writer. But it was not just the pomp of the Viceroyalty that the Readings loved: they loved almost everything else about it. They loved the Viceregal progresses; they loved entertaining celebrities, ranging from the King and Queen of the Belgians to Melba, whose rendering of *Home, Sweet Home* reduced the Commander-in-Chief, Lord Rawlinson, to tears. Sir Harry Lauder came to a memorable Christmas dinner at Belvedere and obliged with *Auld Lang Syne*.

Lady Reading liked giving parties that were both dazzling and exotic. During the 1923 Simla season there was the Moonlight Revel when the garden of Viceregal Lodge was turned into an Old English Fair with booths, merry-go-rounds, a baked potato stall and an Aunt Sally. The high spot of the evening was when the Viceroy, the Commander-in-Chief and the Governor of the Punjab went down the chute together. Most spectacular of all was the Feast of Lanterns, also at Simla a year later. All the guests wore Chinese costumes; the ballroom was hung with scarlet, the hall with bright blue; the monsoon mist was pierced by rows of Chinese lanterns along the

The Prince of Wales with Lord Louis Mountbatten during his Indian tour

veranda. A seven-foot dragon with motor lamp eyes made its appearance, and out of it came a pretty girl who did a Chinese dance. Then Miss Megan Lloyd George in Burmese garb entered in a rickshaw, pulled by Miss FitzRoy and another young lady dressed as *jhampanis*. When this cabaret was over, the guests danced to such tunes as *The Junkman's Holiday*, *Behind the Lacquer Screen* and *Pagoda Bells*.

Both the Readings took to modern dancing with enthusiasm; one of the Viceroy's dancing partners was Melba. There was a celebrated occasion when Lady Reading asked an ADC to tell her the name of a dance tune that was being played. It happened to be called 'I shall remember your kisses when you have forgotten my name'; but the ADC, a rather nervous young man, replied: 'You will remember my kisses, Your Excellency, when I have forgotten your name'.[49]

Dancing was not the only recreation of the energetic Viceroy and

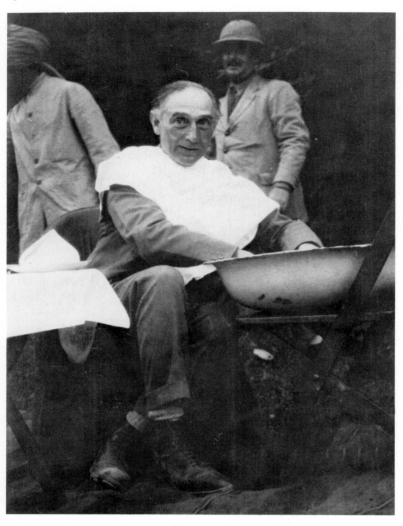

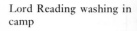

Lord Reading washing in camp

Vicereine. 'Life with HE makes one consider anything under 75 as barely middle-aged'[50] Yvonne FitzRoy declared towards the end of 1921; she had the Viceroy in mind, but the remark could equally well have applied to *Her* Excellency, for all her infirmities. If the Viceroy's riding never went beyond the quietest horse in the Viceregal stable – and even then he had a nasty fall – he took 'furiously' to big game shooting and eventually got a tiger which was not, however, as large as his flatterers made it out to be.[51] When not shooting, he played golf and bridge, both of which he loved. Lady Reading also had her game; it is touching to find her husband, the ruler of a sub-continent, beginning a letter to her with the words: 'So

Polishing the ballroom floor, Viceregal Lodge, Simla

you were in great form at ping-pong!'[52]

To pastimes of a more intellectual sort, the Readings were not much addicted; Yvonne FitzRoy found them 'surprisingly unliterary for Jews'.[53] Lady Reading did, however, read E.M. Forster's *A Passage to India* when it first came out in 1924. She did not care for it at all, and happened to say so when the Maharaja of Diwas Senior was dining at Viceregal Lodge. The Maharaja mentioned that the author had been his private secretary; at which the Viceroy interjected: 'That comes of Chiefs getting the wrong kind of Europeans around them'.[54]

It was ironical that Reading should have said this, since he was himself criticised for being surrounded by the wrong kind of Indians. 'That dreadful group' was how Butler spoke of the three Indian liberals – Sir Tej Bahadur Sapru and two others – who together with the now somewhat mellowed Mrs. Annie Besant were known to be very close to the Viceroy; and yet these people served as a valuable link between the Government and Congress. By the end of 1922, Congress was split between those who wanted to persist with non-co-operation or 'civil disobedience' and those who favoured a return to consitutional opposition. The latter had their way and Congress duly took part in the 1923 elections, emerging as the largest party in the Central Legislative Assembly as well as in some of the Provincial Legislatures. Motilal Nehru, whose imprisonment, like that of his son, had been of short duration, became in effect leader of the opposition in the Central Assembly. It was, on the face of it, a triumph for the Reforms. The new Legislatures had become the centre of gravity of India's political life, though the policy of the Congress leaders was not to make the new system work but to obstruct it. This policy on the whole met with a very limited success; but in the Central Assembly Congress was able, with the support of

The hall at Viceregal
Lodge, Simla, decorated
for Lady Reading's Feast
of Lanterns, 1924

Lady Reading's Feast of
Lanterns, Viceregal Lodge,
Simla, 1924. Lady Reading
in the centre, Lord
Reading on her right with
Megan Lloyd George
sitting on his knee

other groups, to pass votes of censure against the Government and also resolutions calling for complete autonomy. In response to Motilal Nehru's celebrated resolution of 1924, which came to be known as the 'National Demand', Reading set up a committee to consider what changes could be made in the new constitution to make it more widely acceptable. There was statutory provision for an overhaul of the Reforms after ten years; Reading now pressed for this overhaul to be carried out sooner.

At the same time as Reading endeavoured to speed up constitutional progress, the Congress opposition began to lose some of its force. There was growing dissension within the party itself; Gandhi had temporarily retired from the political scene after his release from prison in 1924 because of illness. The alliance between Congress and the Muslims and Sikhs, which had constituted a serious threat to British rule, was now a thing of the past; the Khilafat and Sikh agitations had petered out and, what was less fortunate for India, the Hindus and Muslims had once again turned against each other. This revival of communal antagonism had caused the Moplah rising as well as some terrible riots near the North-West Frontier in 1924; but these outbreaks served at any rate to bring home to thoughful men the danger of agitation. As Reading's Viceroyalty drew to its close, it seemed that Indian opinion was becoming more moderate; there was even a move among the right-wing Congress leaders to work with the Government.

To what extent this change was due to Reading himself rather than to circumstances over which he had no control is a matter of conjecture; just as it is hard to say how much the improvement in India's economy during his reign was due to his financial policy and how much to a series of good Monsoons. 'He leaves India better than he found it and if this be largely due to good seasons and dissensions among the Indians, he is entitled to the credit' Butler wrote of Reading shortly before he left. 'He has exercised the patience of his race and his training. He has made good speeches and been through a very difficult time.'[55] Yet Reading's departure was not much regretted, certainly not among the senior British officials. He was not the sort of person to inspire much affection in his associates; a little ruthless, a little calculating, a little egocentric for all his kindness and bonhomie. It was said in Delhi and Simla that his only policy was to stay out his time.

Stay out his time he did. 'The Readings won't go until they drop'[56] was Butler's firm belief; despite frequent rumours, born of wishful thinking, that the Viceroy was about to resign. There even seemed a possibility that Lady Reading would persuade her husband to ask for an extension. 'Her Ex don't want to leave, no, not she' Yvonne FitzRoy reported in 1924. 'She frankly admits ten years of it would not be too much for her. Ye gods and little fishes!' If the frail fifty-nine-year-old Vicereine could stand the pace, it was beginning to tell on the thirty-three-year-old Yvonne, who a few months later was complaining: 'I've been tied to Her Ex with shackles of steel and that dear lady is never at her easiest with her feet on a red carpet and the thunder of saluting guns in her ears. . she is always inclined to dispense more kicks than halfpence upon our labours.' [57] Yvonne's relationship with the Readings, whom she had grown to like and admire, ended sadly in a quarrel.

When the Readings left in April 1926, Lady Reading shared in the excellent Press which her husband – not without a certain amount of management on his part – was given. That her success had been if anything greater than his was the opinion of the then Secretary of State, Lord Birkenhead who, as F.E. Smith, had been the future Viceroy's no less brilliant colleague at the Bar. Immediately after his return to England, Reading was made a Marquess; one of the very few instances in the history of the British Peerage of someone rising higher than the rank of Earl who started life with no title at all. Apart from a few months as Foreign Secretary in 1931, he did not again hold office; but from the end of his Viceroyalty until his death in 1935 he remained closely in touch with Indian affairs.

During the years when Reading was in India, the concept of the Viceroyalty changed once again. Having originally been an autocrat and then at best an administrator and at worst a 'Great Ornamental', the Viceroy was now required to be a statesman. With the introduction into India of a parliamentary system – albeit a somewhat limited one – and the rapid spread of political ideas among the Indian masses, the Viceroy had in effect to act as the leader of the Government political party. Reading, however inadequate he may have seemed to those who expected him to be a Viceroy of the traditional pattern, was well suited to this new role. He was able to get across to the Indians, which Chelmsford had singularly failed to do; he had the power to win over public opinion. He could turn a Viceregal visit into a political triumph, as he did at Allahabad in 1923; so that even a notoriously undemonstrative English judge was seen 'skipping about like a schoolboy' at the Viceregal firework display, exclaiming: 'He has killed non-co-operation in Allahabad, he has killed it, I tell you!'[58] He was a born negotiator and an eloquent public speaker; though since he could not see clearly into the future and was too honest to hold out hopes which he knew might not be realised, his speeches were inclined to be vague on the subject of India's political advancement. The Indians became rather tired of phrases like 'India's feet are now on the road to freedom'. [59] They wanted to know what the next stage would be; and that, Reading would not tell them.

13

'The most christian and the most gentlemanly among them all'

A Hindu astrologer told John Lawrence in 1868 that a descendant of the former Secretary of State, Sir Charles Wood, would one day become Viceroy. That this prophesy should have been fulfilled more than half a century later when Sir Charles's grandson, Edward Wood, Lord Irwin, succeeded Reading, is perhaps less remarkable than that it should have been Irwin's grandfather who, in April 1880, told Ripon that he was about to be offered the Viceroyalty. For the names of Irwin and Ripon are linked in the minds of the Indians as the two Viceroys most sympathetic to their aspirations – at any rate up to the time of Mountbatten.

Irwin resembled Ripon in being a Yorkshireman of broad acres and high character who was deeply religious; but he differed from him in most other respects. Where Ripon was of unprepossessing appearance, Irwin was a splendid figure; tall, spare, graceful; his long, clean-shaven face with the high-domed forehead wore the thoughtful expression of a philosopher king. Where Ripon was inclined to be timid, Irwin was well endowed with aristocratic self-assurance for all his genuine humility and simplicity and his quiet manner. Where Ripon was a Radical, Irwin was a right-wing Conservative; perhaps the highest Tory ever to be Viceroy. Where Ripon was of only moderate ability, Irwin was brilliantly clever and possessed of a much broader vision. He had overcome the disability of having been born with no left hand and risen rapidly in politics, attaining Cabinet rank by the age of forty-one; he became Viceroy at forty-five. So while Irwin managed to appeal to Congress just as Ripon had appealed to the Indian progressives of an earlier generation, he was able to win the confidence and admiration of the Princes and other more traditionally-minded Indians, as well as of the British, in a way that Ripon failed to do. He was a Viceroy of the stamp of Mayo and Minto; and like those other two highly successful Viceroys, he was, despite his missing hand, an excellent horseman.

While considering himself qualified by birth to be a ruler, Irwin was so modest with regard to his personal ability that he had come near to refusing the Viceroyalty when it was first offered to him; he

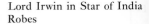

Lord Irwin in Star of India
Robes

told his wife 'that he did not think he was up to the job'.[1] He was also loth to be parted from his eighty-six-year-old father, Lord Halifax, to whom he was devoted. But the sprightly octogenarian Halifax, who is remembered for his collection of ghost stories and for his efforts to bring about a reconciliation between Canterbury and Rome – Irwin inherited his fervent Anglo-Catholicism – insisted that his son should accept the Viceroyalty, which seemed the crowning of all his hopes for him.

Irwin's reluctance to be Viceroy would also have stemmed from the fact that, like Lansdowne, he enjoyed rather too exalted a position

Lady Irwin

at home to be much attracted by Viceregal splendour. His wife Dorothy, who was good-looking, with large eyes and a touch of humour in her expression, faced the prospect of Viceregal life with no more enthusiasm than he did. The Readings were at Bombay when the Irwins arrived, Lady Reading very depressed at leaving; Dorothy Irwin found this hard to understand, unable to believe that when their own time came to leave, she and Irwin 'should not be skipping down the steps trying to hide our obvious delight'.[2] She had already shown her informality by carrying out running repairs to the Military Secretary's braces when they snapped in the launch.

There is a widely-held myth that the Irwins arrived at Bombay on Good Friday, and that Irwin insisted on going straight to church. In fact they arrived on Maundy Thursday. Nevertheless, it was immediately apparent to the Indians, and to Gandhi in particular, that the new Viceroy was a holy man as Ripon had been. Irwin and Dorothy seemed, to those who met them, so much simpler than the Readings; such was their natural dignity that they were able to maintain a Viceregal presence with a minimum of protocol.

Not that the Irwins were averse either to ceremonial or to grand entertainments. They were an excellent host and hostess and both looked magnificent in their finery; Irwin positively regal in Star of India robes, his long and shapely calves – over which, when he was riding, his boots fitted so perfectly – shown off to full advantage in knee breeches and silk stockings. But except when occasion demanded it, they avoided any sort of regal stiffness. Dorothy in particular was oppressed by the protocol of Delhi, when they first arrived there; though the temporary Viceregal Lodge, which still served as the Viceroy's Delhi residence pending the completion of Lutyens's palace, was in itself modest enough; with a portrait of Irwin's grandfather, the old Maharaja Wood, in the panelled dining room, to make them feel at home. She felt 'like a child caught doing something naughty'[3] when the Comptroller found her trying to rearrange the furniture in the drawing room; she objected to the custom whereby the Vicereine did not go to luncheon until fetched by an ADC. 'It also gets on my nerves' she wrote, soon after her arrival, 'to be called "Your Excellency", which I am sure is overdone by the ex-Reading Staff. One hardly ever calls the Queen and King "Your Majesty", it seems to me rather vulgar'.[4]

If the Irwins began by feeling that life in the Delhi Viceregal Lodge was oppressive, they were even more discouraged by their first sight of Viceregal Lodge at Simla, which reminded Irwin of a 'hydropathic establishment in a British watering place'.[5] The Simla life of fêtes and gymkhanas, dances and performances by the Amateur Dramatic Club seemed to Dorothy rather petty; she and Irwin were depressed by the monsoon, which brought weeping skies from the end of June to September. During their first Simla season, Irwin had a particularly unpleasant experience: the lady sitting next to him at dinner was, without warning, violently sick, which made the unfortunate Viceroy fear that he might be sick too. When the monsoon ended, the Irwins realised that Simla could be delightful; they loved exploring the Himalayas on hill ponies, staying at the Retreat at Mashobra or higher up in the camp at Naldera among the deodars.

If the Irwins' first impressions of India had something in common with Lansdowne's unenthusiastic view, they soon came to appreciate the glory of the Viceroyalty and the variety of their new life. 'All our Staff seems to be shaking down and to be a pretty happy family' Irwin wrote in his first letter home to his father.[6] A happy family party was what the Viceregal court seemed like to those fortunate enough to know it during the Irwin's reign. Irwin and Dorothy had a genius for making everyone around them happy; their houses were always full of laughter. When the laughter was particularly loud, the Viceroy himself would emerge from his study and hurry to where it was coming from, not wanting to miss any of the fun. Irwin's Staff not only liked him because he was so kind and informal and entered into the spirit of everything; but also because of his preternatural calm. No situation seemed critical or annoying enough to upset him; only once during his five years in India was he seen to lose his temper, and that was when he lost a shabby old Homburg hat to which he was much attached.

With his calm and his sweet nature went a strong belief in his own judgement; he was slow in coming to a decision, but once he had done so he seldom changed his mind and never recriminated. Those who worked with him were also much impressed by his administrative ability. His Private Secretary, George Cunningham – who was himself to achieve fame as an administrator, governing the North-West Frontier Province for many years – believed that 'he could with ease have taken over any of the six portfolios which the Civil Members of his Council administered'.[7]

But although Irwin had it in him to be an administrator almost of the calibre of Curzon, he did not make Curzon's mistake of trying to run all the departments of Government himself. In fact he left the running of several departments, notably Finance, entirely to the Members of Council in charge of them. He was well aware that the Viceroy was no longer primarily an administrator but a statesman; and as a statesman, he saw his task as being to speed the Indians along the road to self-government and to convince Indian politicians of the sincerity of British purpose. In performing this task he stood virtually alone; often going against the advice of his Council, influenced only by one eminent Civilian, Sir Malcolm Hailey, who during his reign was Governor first of the Punjab and then of the United Provinces. It was a task for which Irwin was well qualified. He was himself so obviously sincere; he had plenty of political experience; he was a good speaker, with a fine, deep voice; he had a remarkable talent for persuading people by quiet discussion, when he would usually spend more time listening patiently to the other point of view than putting forward his own.

Irwin's first opportunity to appeal to the country came in the summer of 1926, after antagonism between Hindus and Muslims had flared up once again, causing serious riots. In a speech which he

Lord Irwin with his two
pages, the son of the
Maharaja of Bharatpur and
his own youngest son
Richard Wood (now Lord
Holderness). Simla, August
1926

delivered at Simla to an audience that included the Congress leader
and President of the Legislative Assembly, Vithalbhai Patel, as well
as leading Muslims and moderates like Sir Tej Bahadur Sapru, he
made a passionate appeal for communal peace. 'I appeal in the name
of national life because communal tension is eating into it as a
canker. . I appeal in the name of religion because I can appeal to
nothing nobler.'⁸ The speech struck a note unheard in Viceregal
pronouncements since the days of Ripon; it also affirmed that the
Government, far from deliberately stirring up communal troubles as
was frequently alleged, was doing its utmost to check them.

If the Simla speech convinced India of Irwin's sincerity, the
speech he made in Calcutta the following December to a very
different audience, the hard-headed businessmen of the European
Association, showed that he was strongly in favour of giving the
Indians a greater measure of political responsibility; though he
reassured his audience by predicting that Parliament would not grant
full responsibility until the advance of education made a wider
electorate possible. 'An educated electorate' he declared, 'is the only
sure basis of democracy. Without it, politics are the possession of a
small class of the intelligentsia.'⁹

During that first Christmas in Calcutta, Irwin followed the
example of Dufferin and visited some of the worst of the city's slums.

In sharp contrast was the elegance of Belvedere, where the banqueting table used on State occasions in the vast ballroom was 114 feet long. On Christmas night the Irwins entertained sixty people to dinner and it was more like a jolly party in Yorkshire than a Viceregal banquet: 'Harry Stavordale leaping over chairs on all fours like a horse' and the Viceroy blowing his hunting horn.[10]

Irwin's second year as Viceroy, 1927, saw a rise in the political thermometer. A purely technical measure to stabilise the rupee was used by Congress as the pretext for an agitation against the Government throughout the length and breadth of the sub-continent. The opposition to this measure by the predominantly Hindu Congress Party caused a reaction in favour of the Government on the part of the Muslims, with a consequent increase in communal tension and more riots. The unrest inevitably gave rise to new demands for constitutional changes; particularly since there were now only two more years to go before the system of government introduced under the Montagu-Chelmsford Reforms was due for its statutory overhaul. Irwin, like Reading before him, was anxious for this revision to take place as soon as possible; and before the end of 1927 he had persuaded the Home Government to send out a Commission to enquire into the working of the system.

Before the appointment of the Commission was publicly announced, Irwin invited the leaders of all the Indian political parties to meet him at Viceregal Lodge in Delhi so that he could tell them about it privately. For the Viceroy to take the Indian political leaders into his confidence in this way was something quite without precedent; it was a move which touched the imagination of the Indian people. Among those invited was Gandhi, though he had not yet emerged from his self-imposed exile from politics. It was afterwards alleged that Irwin, at this first meeting with the Mahatma, simply handed him a document and dismissed him with a few abrupt words; but in fact he had a long conversation with him. For Gandhi, this interview was the beginning of what a contemporary observer speaks of as 'that attachement – no other word will do – for Lord Irwin which was to grow stronger with every personal contact and was not to be weakened'.[11] To Irwin, as he told his father, 'it was rather like talking to someone who had stepped off another planet'.[12]

The Simon Commission, as it was called, after its Chairman, the austere lawyer-politician, Sir John Simon, paid two visits to India, arriving for the first time in February 1928. It included a Press Lord and the future Labour Prime Minister, Clement Attlee, but not a single Indian; a blunder for which Irwin, as much as Birkenhead, was responsible. Experienced Indian politicians were summoned as witnesses before the Commission, but told that they were to have no major part in fashioning the new instrument of government; which

seemed, as Gandhi put it, an 'organised insult to a whole people'.[13]
There was a storm of protest throughout India and the Commission
was boycotted not only by the more extreme Congress leaders, but
also by moderates like Sapru as well as by many of the Muslims. The
boycott might not have been nearly so complete if Irwin had not been
laid low with fever when he visited Bombay at the end of 1927; which
prevented him from having personal discussions with the leaders of
the powerful political and business interests of that city. Had he been
able to meet them, as he had hoped, he might well have persuaded at
least some of them to co-operate with the Commission.

Irwin was now faced with a situation in which Congress was
united with other and more moderate groups in opposition to the
Government. Congress and its new allies held an 'All Party'
Conference in March 1928 and set up their own rival commission to
report on constitutional reforms; which had little effect other than
accentuating communal differences. And in the autumn of that year
the devious Patel began a campaign of obstruction in the Legislative

Lord and Lady Irwin at
the birthday party of the
young Maharaja of
Gwalior, Simla, 1927. The
little Maharaja and his
sister, named George and
Mary after the
King-Emperor and
Queen-Empress, in the
centre

Assembly of which he was President. Irwin somehow managed to prevent Patel from going too far; seeing him as often as he did at Viceregal Lodge, he even came to feel a sort of affection for him, maddening though he found him. Once, when Patel happened to complain of being constipated, the Viceroy made him a present of his own bottle of aperient medicine. Irwin and Dorothy also managed to be on friendly terms with the leader of the Congress opposition in the Assembly, Motilal Nehru. On one of his visits to Viceregal Lodge, the mischievous eyes of Dorothy lighted on the label inside his white 'Gandhi cap', which he had left in the hall; and she saw to her amusement that it had been made for him by a fashionable London hatter.

The chief bone of contention between Irwin and Patel was a Public Safety Bill which the Government saw fit to introduce in the autumn of 1928 to deal with a resurgence of terrorism caused mainly by communists. During that autumn and the months following, India was disturbed by many crimes of violence. Patel and the other Congress Members continued to oppose the Public Safety Bill even after they had experienced terrorism at first hand in April 1929, when two large bombs were thrown into the Government benches of the Legislative Assembly, exploding with shattering force, though by sheer good luck nobody was killed. Irwin took advantage of the atmosphere of horror and resentment caused by the outrage to pass the Bill by Ordinance; and at the same time as he did so, he addressed both Houses of the Legislature, alluding in no uncertain terms to those politicians who paid lip-service to the cause of law and order while doing their utmost to vilify the very people whose duty it was to ensure that order was maintained. 'To condemn a crime in one breath' he said, 'and in the next to seek excuse for it by laying blame on those against whom it is directed, is no true condemnation.'[14] He also put an end to Patel's obstructionism by announcing that if anything like it happened again, the Government would without delay amend the rules – that Patel accepted defeat and did not, as many expected him to do, resign from being President of the Assembly, is a tribute to Irwin's influence. There was the 'ring of authority and finality'[15] in the Viceroy's measured tones as he addressed the packed Chamber from his throne of scarlet and gold; he made it abundantly clear that as Viceroy, he intended to govern.

Having shown that, when it came to maintaining law and order, he could be as strong and decisive as any Viceroy of the past, Irwin redoubled his efforts in what he saw as his other role as an intermediary between the Indian people and the British Parliament. With the Simon Report not yet published and likely to be a dead letter as far as Indian opinion was concerned, he was able to take the initiative; particularly after the advent in June 1929 of a minority

Labour Government. Not only were the Labour Ministers more in sympathy with his views on Indian political advancement than the Conservatives had been; but being as they were inexperienced and unsure of themselves, they allowed him a freedom of action such as no Viceroy had enjoyed since the days when Lord George Hamilton gave Curzon his head.

In the same month that Labour came into power, Irwin went home on leave; overjoyed at the prospect of being reunited with his father, who had recently celebrated his ninetieth birthday. While he was in England, he made two momentous proposals to Ramsay MacDonald and his colleagues and obtained their assent to both of them. The first was that all sections of Indian opinion should be invited to a Round Table Conference with the British Government on the political future of India; which he hoped would redeem the blunder of excluding Indians from the Simon Commission. The second was that there should be a declaration that Britain intended, at an unspecified date in the future, to give India Dominion Status. This, he believed, would go a long way towards satisfying Indian aspirations, for Dominion Status had become a magic word in India; it was what almost every Indian politician wanted. It was implicit in the Declaration on the future of India made by the British Government in 1917; but the men in charge of India's destinies since then – in particular Reading and Birkenhead – had been averse to saying so.

The announcement of the Conference, which included the declaration on Dominion Status, was made by Irwin on the last day of October, shortly after his return to India. It provoked an indignant outburst from sections of the Conservative and Liberal Parties at home; but in India it was received with almost universal acclaim. In the words of a contemporary: 'Lord Irwin had accomplished a feat almost without precedent in the history of our dealings with India. At a stroke, he had entirely transformed the political situation, replacing ill-will and distrust by good-will, and the beginnings, at any rate, of a renewed confidence in British rule and its intentions.'[16] Unfortunately, by the end of the year, most of the Congress leaders had reverted to their attitude of distrust; though almost every other Indian politician was determined to co-operate with the Viceroy in making the forthcoming Conference a success.

It might be thought ironical that Irwin's step forward along the road to Indian self-government should have coincided with the completion of the palace at New Delhi; a palace which expresses so proudly, in blood-red and cream-coloured stone, the Imperial idea. And yet it could be seen as an auspicious moment, when everyone in India, apart from Congress, felt a renewed confidence in British rule. To Irwin, Indian aspirations were by no means incompatible with

Lady Irwin at Government House, Malabar Point, Bombay, at the end of 1927 when Lord Irwin was laid up with fever. On the Vicereine's left, in the centre of the front row, is Amanullah, the Amir of Afghanistan, who since his accession had assumed the title of King; he had arrived at Bombay on a visit to add to Lord Irwin's other worries. On Lady Irwin's right is Sir Leslie Wilson, Governor of Bombay 1923–28

Viceregal splendour; he and Dorothy had taken a keen interest in the building of the palace, which, having been delayed on account of the war, was still in its early stages when they first came to India. It therefore seemed almost like their own creation; and in a way it was; for of all the Viceroys and Vicereines associated with Lutyens in his great work, they were the ones he found the most helpful as well as the most sympathetic. Their patrician taste was entirely in accordance with his own; they had an instinctive feeling for classicism and the grand manner; their imagination was fired by his heroic concept. Unfortunately it was now too late to put right the damage done by Baker and officialdom to the grand approach; but the presence of a Viceregal couple like the Irwins during the final stages of the building meant that almost everything else was completed to

Lutyens's satisfaction. Dorothy herself collaborated with Lutyens in the decoration and furnishing, as well as in the planting of the vast Mogul garden; it entailed months of hard work on her part, in addition to all her other Viceregal duties.

There was still much that needed doing when, two days before Christmas, she and Irwin finally took up residence in the palace, which having been known during its building as Government House, was now, at the King-Emperor's behest, renamed Viceroy's House. They had arrived back at New Dehli that morning, having been away on tour; as their train was approaching the city, going along a high embankment at forty miles an hour, an attempt was made by terrorists to derail it with a bomb. Fortunately the explosion was mistimed, and not much harm was done; but had it occurred a few moments sooner the whole train might have gone over the side of the embankment. Irwin was completely unperturbed by this attempt on his life. 'I heard the noise and said to myself "That must be a bomb", and fully expected to hear something further happen' he afterwards wrote in a letter to his father. 'I then smelt all the smoke that came down the train..but as nothing happened I went on reading Challoner till someone came along and told me it had been a bomb and I went to see the damage.'[17]

A couple possessed of less courage and faith than the Irwins might have been put off their new home by this homecoming. But the outrage made no difference at all to their feelings for Viceroy's House. 'Admiration and affection for it steadily grew together' Irwin recalled, thirty years later. 'Every day that we lived there, we came to love it the more.'[18]

It was indeed a building of both power and beauty. Lutyens had succeeded triumphantly in his synthesis of Eastern and Western architecture; combining the strict proportion and grandeur of the European Classical tradition with the shapes, colours and water-effects of Mogul India. The long façades, crowned by the great dome rising from the centre with Imperial might, had a sculptured solidity, with boldly projecting wings, advancing and receding surfaces and colonnaded loggias. The capitals of the columns were of an order of Lutyens's own invention, incorporating stone bells; there being a legend that so long as the bells were silent, the dynasty would reign.

After a two-mile approach along King's Way, that splendid ceremonial avenue lined with canals and parks, the principal front was seen in its full glory from the entrance to the forecourt, where the wrought-iron screen was flanked by piers with sculptured elephants and stone sentry boxes sheltering mounted troopers of the Bodyguard. Immediately inside the portico was the circular Durbar Hall, rising into the dome, its walls lined with white marble, its floor of porphyry, and with columns of yellow jasper in the four apses. The thrones

Viceroy's House, New Delhi. The principal front and forecourt

faced the entrance from beneath their canopy of crimson velvet; this was the climax of the approach. From here, there were vistas along marble corridors leading, by way of other State apartments, to the Ballroom, which had walls of black looking-glass, and also to the State Dining Room, with its teak panelling, its portraits of Viceroys, its display of gold plate and its table for more than a hundred people. The Ballroom and the State Dining Room were separated by a great open loggia, behind which was a grand staircase open to the sky, so that its cornice framed an oblong of azure blue by day and of stars by night. On the ground floor below the State apartments ran a series of panelled rooms used on all but the grandest occasions. They overlooked the Mogul garden, which stretched away from the garden front, intersected by a criss-cross of waterways and fountains.

'In spite of its size, it was essentially a liveable-in house' Irwin afterwards recalled.[19] It also had the advantage of being close to the country; so that Irwin and his daughter Anne were able to go for early morning rides across the plain, accompanied by the Commander-in-Chief, Sir Philip Chetwode and his daughter Penelope – now Lady

Viceroy's House, New
Delhi. The Durbar Hall

Betjeman – with a single Indian ADC in attendance. Sometimes they
would have their breakfast among the fallen masonry of one of the
many tombs of forgotten dynasties with which the plain was strewn.

Irwin's imagination was fired not only by Viceroy's House and its
surroundings but by New Dehli as a whole. He watched the growth
of the Imperial city with as great an interest as he watched the growth
of the palace. His special concern, as was fitting in someone as
religious as he, was the building of an Anglican church worthy of the
new capital; for which he raised money in England to supplement
what had been raised in India. His other personal contribution to
New Delhi was the final version of the inscription on the base of the
Jaipur Column, a stately pillar standing before the main front of
Viceroy's House:

> In thought faith
> In word wisdom
> In deed courage
> In life service.
> —So may India be great.

The column was the gift of the Maharaja of Jaipur, whose youthful
successor was formally invested as Ruler of his State by Irwin in a
picturesque ceremony at Jaipur in 1931. As a romantic, Irwin was
attracted by the pageantry of the Chiefs, but as an aristocrat he was
by no means dazzled by their glitter. He was quick to realise which of
them were able and conscientious rulers – as the young Jaipur soon
showed himself to be – and which were, as he afterwards bluntly put
it, 'pretty hopeless'.[20] Among the latter was the cultured but sinister
Maharaja of Alwar; who when the Irwins were staying with him had
a goat tied up outside Dorothy's window, intending it to be killed by
a tame panther in the small hours so as to frighten her with its
screams; but the Vicereine foiled him by releasing the goat.

Irwin saw the future of the Princely States to lie in a Federation
with the rest of India. This was to be the principal subject discussed
at the forthcoming Round Table Conference, at which the Princes
would be represented, along with all other sections of Indian opinion.
Up to the end of 1929, there was still hope that the Conference would
be attended by Congress; and on the very day that Irwin took up
residence at Viceroy's House, his nerve entirely unshaken by that
morning's attempt on his life, he received Gandhi – now back in the
thick of politics – Motilal Nehru and Patel, together with Sapru and
the Muslim leader, Mohammed Ali Jinnah, in the hope of arriving at
some reasonable conditions under which Congress would agree to be
represented. But Gandhi was at his worst, 'petulant, impractical, full
of airy irrelevancies',[21] and insisted that Congress would have

nothing to do with the Conference unless India was granted Dominion Status immediately, which, of course, was impossible. So Irwin's great hope of having a Round Table Conference truly representative of Indian opinion was, for the present at any rate, doomed to disappointment.

Viceroy's House, New Delhi. The open staircase

From now on, it was a personal contest between Irwin and Gandhi; the one leading the forces of constitutional progress, the other at the head of those committed to sudden and total revolution. Irwin at the beginning of 1930 had on his side the All-India Liberal Federation as well as the Muslim League; he even had potential support from within the ranks of Congress itself. But Indian opinion at that time was highly volatile. Many of the leaders were 'poised on the razor edge of indecision'; so that the success or failure of the Conference depended very much on Irwin's handling of the situation during the months that preceded it.

It was for this reason that Irwin refrained from arresting Gandhi after he had started a new campaign of *Satyagraha* or civil disobedience in March and deliberately rendered himself liable to criminal prosecution by his now celebrated illicit manufacture of salt on the coast of Gujarat. Not for nothing did the Viceroy believe, as he put it, that in India 'all problems are ninety per cent psychological and ten per cent rational';[22] it was all too apparent to him that if Gandhi went to prison, people would boycott the Conference who would otherwise give it their support. So by allowing the Mahatma to remain at large despite his salt-manufacturing activities, Irwin won the first round of the contest. But the failure to arrest Gandhi at this juncture was denounced in certain quarters at home as weakness; notably by Winston Churchill, of whom Irwin afterwards wrote: 'I have no doubt at all that he has been more responsible than anybody else for India wishing to get rid of the British'.[23]

By the beginning of May, Irwin had decided that, Conference or no Conference, Gandhi would have to be arrested; for the civil disobedience movement was producing conditions close to anarchy. There were strikes, agrarian disturbances, a boycott of British goods, riots, robberies, murders; a mob took control of the city of Peshawar for several days; while in the opposite corner of India, at Chittagong in Bengal, a band of revolutionaries attacked and destroyed the armouries of the local police and volunteers. Faced with this new threat to law and order, Irwin showed himself as resolute as he had been in dealing with the earlier wave of unrest. He met force with force; not only were Gandhi and the two Nehrus sent to prison, but also thousands of their followers; the jails became quite full. Between April and December, the Viceroy issued no fewer than ten Ordinances, an unprecedented number, to deal with the multitudinous troubles of that year. He did not hesitate to muzzle the vernacular Press; and when necessary, he signed death warrants without losing a moment's sleep. In taking the stern measures he did, he could hardly be accused of over-reacting, since his calm and his courage were well known. Thus in normal circumstances he was not much worried by riots and regarded the use of force in quelling them as an admission of failure. Once, returning from a place where there was serious rioting, he scared the police by getting out of his car and mingling with the crowd, who cheered him and practically carried him shoulder-high to the station.

But even in the darkest days of 1930, amidst horrors like the burning of policemen alive by mobs, Irwin never lost his belief that force alone was not enough. He persevered in his efforts to reach an agreement with Congress; having at last accepted the fact that it was stronger than all the other Indian political parties put together. Up to now, he and his Government had tended to over-estimate the strength of the other parties, which, together with the Princes, were duly represented at the Round Table Conference when it opened in London in November. The eighty-odd delegates whom the King-Emperor addressed in person before the Conference got down to work included some of the most distinguished Indians of the day, ranging from Sapru to the Aga Khan. It was a truly historic occasion; yet the absence of Congress gave it an air of unreality.

Having failed with the other Congress leaders, Irwin decided to appeal to Gandhi himself. He prepared the way in a speech which he delivered to the Legislative Assembly in January 1931; a speech in which he spoke of Gandhi in terms such as had never before been used by a Viceroy of India when speaking of an opponent in jail for sedition. 'No one can fail to recognise the spiritual force which impels Mr. Gandhi to count no sacrifice too great in the cause, as he believes, of the India he loves.'[24] Irwin followed up this speech by releasing Gandhi and the rest of the Working Committee of Congress from prison, which caused yet another outcry, not only from the diehards at home, but from the Army in India and most of the officials outside the Council, to all of whom it seemed that the Viceroy had capitulated just as Congress was showing signs of being unable to continue the civil disobedience campaign for much longer.

Having been released from jail, Gandhi began by demanding an enquiry into what he called the 'excesses' of the police during the recent troubles. This was quite out of the question, as it would have destroyed the morale of a force which had behaved remarkably well in the most trying circumstances. Irwin refused Gandhi's demand categorically and appealed to him to forget the past and think of the future. Gandhi, who had been thrown very much on to his own resources by the death of Motilal Nehru on 6 February, accepted the Viceroy's rebuke and wrote to him on 14 February, asking for an interview. It was a strange letter for a released prisoner to write to the representative of the King-Emperor, beginning 'Dear Friend' and containing the remark: 'I would like to meet not so much the Viceroy as the man in you'.[25]

And so, on 17 February, 'the diminutive brown figure, with his bald head and toothless smile'[26] was escorted by two soldiers of the Bodyguard to the side entrance of Viceroy's House for what proved to be the first of an historic series of meetings with Irwin. Almost every servant in the house managed to find some urgent task near the door through which the Mahatma entered; and he, thinking they were ordinary people assembled there to meet him, greeted them as such, to the disgust of the ADCs and other members of the Staff. 'I remember Gandhi squatting on the floor and after a while a girl coming in with some filthy yellow stuff which he started eating without so much as by your leave' wrote a high official who was

Group at the Inauguration of New Delhi, February 1931. Lord and Lady Irwin are in the centre, Lady

Irwin with one dog beside her and another peeping out from under her arm. On Lord Irwin's right sits the former Viceroy, Lord Hardinge of Penshurst, and beyond him the Maharaja of Dholpur, from whose State came the red stone used in the building of Viceroy's House. On Lady Irwin's left sits the Governor of the Punjab, Sir Geoffrey de Montmorency, who was formerly Reading's Private Secretary. At the extreme right of the front row sits Sir Edwin Lutyens, whose wife, Lady Emily, a daughter of the former Viceroy, Lytton, sits at the opposite end of the row, next to the Metropolitan. The Indian sitting towards the right of the front row is the liberal politician V.S. Srinivasa Sastri, who was to play a part in Lord Irwin's negotiations with Gandhi a week or two later

present at one of these meetings, adding that he would have liked to have seen this happening to Curzon.[27] The disgust of the Staff was shared by many people in Britain, including, as might be expected, Churchill, who fulminated about 'the nauseating and humiliating spectacle of this one time Inner Temple lawyer, now seditious fakir, striding half-naked up the steps of the Viceroy's palace there to negotiate and parley on equal terms with the representative of the King-Emperor'.[28] He was certainly an unlikely guest in that palace which had, in the previous week, been filled with guests of a very different sort for the official inauguration of New Delhi.

Irwin listened to Gandhi's monologues with a patience such as no other Viceroy can have possessed in such abundance. As 'a Viceroy who was both willing and able to adjust to the Gandhian negotiating style',[29] he was uniquely qualified to come to an agreement with that 'strange little man'.[30] He also understood 'the springs that gave the Mahatma his astonishing power'.[31] Irwin's own religion made him see Gandhi as something much more than what he appeared to people like Churchill; it enabled the tall, brilliant, aristocratic Viceroy to talk to the 'half-naked fakir' on equal terms as one man of God to another, without in any way losing caste as his critics at home and in India feared he would. To the poetess and moderate Congress leader, Mrs. Sarojini Naidu, Irwin and Gandhi were the 'two Mahatmas'. To the liberal politician, V.S. Srinivasa Sastri, they were 'the two uncrucified Christs'.[32]

But while Irwin once went so far as to say to an official who asked him if Gandhi had been tiresome, 'Some people found Our Lord

very tiresome',[33] his respect for the Mahatma's spiritual power by no means blinded him to the fact that he needed handling with great circumspection. 'I must confess to having been much struck by his personality' he told his father, after his talks with Gandhi had begun, 'and although I am quite prepared to believe that he is what you may call a pretty astute electioneer, he left an absolutely clear impression on my mind that if he gave you any undertaking it would be scrupulously carried out.'[34]

In his negotiations with Gandhi, Irwin had the twofold object of getting him to the Round Table Conference and putting an end to civil disobedience. At first there was little progress. Then, on 3 March, the Viceroy was able to report: 'I had made up my mind on Sunday that we were bound to break. . but, very remarkably, things took a quite different turn and he was very much more reasonable'.[35] In the small hours of 5 March, Irwin and Gandhi finally came to an agreement. They celebrated the signing of it by drinking each other's health; Gandhi drank lime juice flavoured with a pinch of illegally-manufactured salt, Irwin drank tea.

'Taking tea with treason', Irwin's critics were to call it. But it was an agreement very much to Irwin's advantage. Gandhi agreed to go to the Round Table Conference and to take part in discussions on the scheme for an All India Federation which the delegates had already put forward. He also agreed to call off the civil disobedience campaign and the boycott of British goods. Irwin in return agreed to revoke some of the Ordinances which he had issued during the troubles of the previous year, and to release political prisoners. He did not revoke those Ordinances which dealt with terrorism; nor did he release prisoners who had committed or incited violence.

The agreement, which came to be known as the Irwin-Gandhi Pact, caused as much bad blood within the ranks of Congress as it did among the British diehards; that Gandhi should have been willing to go against his followers in this way was a sign of how much he liked and trusted Irwin. 'I succumbed' Gandhi afterwards said, 'not to Lord Irwin but to the honesty in him.'[36] But while he had in a sense emerged from his interviews with Irwin 'a conquered man', as Sastri had predicted he would,[37] he had at the same time gained personal prestige by appearing to negotiate with the Viceroy on equal terms. To people like Churchill, this boosting of the Mahatma's image was wholly to be deplored; yet it enabled him to get the agreement ratified by Congress at a time when feelings were running high over the execution of three terrorists convicted of murder. It is to Irwin's credit that he resisted all temptation to reprieve these three men, although to have done so would not only have facilitated his negotiations with Gandhi but would have won him a great deal of popular acclaim on the eve of his departure from India.

As it was, Irwin's Viceroyalty ended badly with a week of murder and arson in the ill-omened city of Cawnpore, caused by the local Congress Committee's protest against one of the executions, which sparked off the inevitable communal riots. At the same time as Cawnpore went up in flames, the Princes began to have second thoughts about the principle of Federation, to which Irwin was personally wedded; so that it seemed that the labours of the Round Table Conference would be to no avail. 'I am under no delusion as to the further difficulties that have to be surmounted, many of which may prove insurmountable' Irwin had written a few days after his pact with Gandhi was signed;[38] and if he himself had doubts as to the permanence of the settlement, the majority of officials and Indian loyalists felt that it would serve only to give Congress a breathing-space in which to prepare for another and more devastating assault.

In the event, Irwin's policy brought Gandhi to the Round Table and a few month's peace to India; which not only gave the constitutional experiment a chance but was good for the Indian economy. And apart from such short-term results, which may seem by all accounts short, it brought back a spirit of co-operation between the rulers and the ruled which had been destroyed by Curzon, restored by Minto and lost again in the unhappy aftermath of the war. Irwin was also proved right in believing, as he put it, that 'one of the most valuable results of the settlement we have reached will be that it brings the Congress people definitely to the point of having to apply their minds to practical facts instead of merely vociferating about the Rights of Man'.[39]

Having come to India in rather the same state of mind as Lansdowne, hoping that the five years of their reign would pass as quickly as possible, Irwin and Dorothy now felt sad at the prospect of leaving, for India had captivated their hearts. At the same time, Irwin had no wish to be Viceroy for any longer than his appointed term; when his successor thought of coming out to India by air, he did his best to discourage him; for as he told his father: 'I don't want him to run any risk of being dropped into the sea and my being told that I have to carry on for another six months'.[40]

Irwin's father was there to greet him when he arrived back at the family home in Yorkshire. It was a homecoming in no way marred by the adverse criticism to which he was subjected in certain quarters; for Irwin cared little about public opinion and was convinced that he had done right. To set the seal of Royal and Governmental approval on his Viceroyalty, he was given the Garter.

The fact that Irwin's policy had estranged him from some of his colleagues in the Conservative Party made no difference to his political career. As Lord Halifax, the name by which he is most generally remembered, he played a major role on the European stage as Foreign Secretary; he would have succeeded Chamberlain as Prime Minister in 1940 had he not, with a self-denying patriotism wholly characteristic of him, advanced the candidature of that vociferous critic of his Viceregal policy, Churchill. Instead, he and Dorothy did invaluable war service as Ambassador and Ambassadress in Washington. He lived until 1959, Dorothy until 1976; they were the last surviving couple to have been Viceroy and Vicereine in comparatively normal times.

By the time of his death, Halifax the Foreign Secretary, the Ambassador and the elder statesman had somewhat overshadowed Irwin the Viceroy; though in so far as he achieved greatness, it was as Viceroy rather than in his subsequent career. As a great Viceroy, a Viceroy who ranks with Canning, Mayo, Ripon and Minto, he was the last of an illustrious line; for while two of his successors were themselves great men, the circumstances in which they reigned were so unusual as to make it impossible to compare them with the Viceroys of earlier days. In his effort to get Congress to co-operate with Britain in the gradual political advancement of India, Irwin may have been trying to do the impossible; yet it is the measure of his success that a shrewd contemporary observer should have written of him: 'India's leaders. . came to regard him as, in a way, their leader as well as the representative of His Majesty's Government and the leader of the official forces in the country'.[41] If this is an exaggeration as far as the leaders of Congress were concerned, at any rate we have it on the authority of one of the greatest of their number, C.R. Rajagopalachari, that having dealt with many Viceroys, they were unanimous in regarding Irwin as 'the most Christian and the most gentlemanly representative of Great Britain among them all'.[42]

Lady Willingdon,
Freeman and Hopie

'We are getting a poor creature to succeed Lord Sydenham at Bombay'[1] Harcourt Butler wrote in 1913. This was official India's first impression of Lord Willingdon, who was to be a phenomenon of the Raj in its twilight years. Or rather, part of a phenomenon, of which Lady Willingdon constituted the other and major part; for it is hard to think of Willingdon except in conjunction with his pushful spouse. It was not Willingdon but the Willingdons who, starting with Bombay, went on to Madras and finally reigned over all India; a tenure of Government Houses unequalled in the history of the Raj, so that one is tempted to say of them, in the phraseology of modern advertising, not so much as Viceroy and Vicereine as a way of life.

That Willingdon did not strike people in 1913 as a particularly inspired choice for the Governorship of Bombay is understandable. He was typical of the minor, the very minor politicians who were appointed rather too frequently to Presidency Governorships as a reward for services to their Party. As Freeman Freeman-Thomas – the duplication was due to his having been christened Freeman and subsequently assumed it as a second surname – he sat for ten years as a Liberal MP, mostly as a back-bencher but for a short time as a Whip. At the end of the ten years he was raised to the Peerage and three years later he was sent to govern Bombay. Apart from politics, he was a Sussex country gentleman with a reputation as a cricketer; he had captained both the Eton and the Cambridge Elevens. He also had a name for being a beau and was known as 'The Eternal Head of Pop'. Slim and spare, he had a soldierly elegance though his soldiering had been limited to the Yeomanry; with his long, pointed chin and his slightly up-turned moustache, he might have been the caricature of a fashionable cavalry officer of the period. His expression was genial if a trifle smug; and there was also something a little wary in his heavily-lidded eyes, as though he were afraid of being caught out.

Limited though his qualifications may have been, Willingdon did have one strong point. He was a charming fellow. Everybody liked him; he quickly became as popular in India as he had been in

Parliament. The writings of his associates during the years when he was in Bombay and Madras are full of phrases such as 'Dear old Freeman' or 'Freeman was his delightful self'.[2] One has the impression that although people were aware of his shortcomings, he was such a good fellow as to be indispensable. Edwin Montagu, who appointed him to Madras, once wrote of him: 'What a pity he is at the same time such a good fellow and such a stupid fellow'.[3]

Opinion is divided as to whether Willingdon owed much of his success to his wife or whether she was an embarrassment to him. A large woman with large eyes and a determined face, she was a daughter of the first Earl Brassey and had inherited the drive and organising ability of her grandfather, Thomas Brassey, one of those mighty contractors of Victorian Britain who built harbours and bridges all over the world. Both the Willingdons had what a contemporary called 'the facility of invoking assistance';[4] but her talent for 'roping people in' far outrivalled his; she once admitted that 'she never met anyone for the first time without wondering how he or she would fit into her scheme'.[5] At Bombay she did wonders running hospitals for the troops from Mesopotamia; though there were many who found her rather more than they could stand.

She did, however, possess a certain rumbustious charm and was devoted to her husband whom she would refer to affectionately as 'My Freeman'. 'She is really a fascinating creature in a way, so vulgar and full of vitality' Mr. Malcolm Muggeridge observed, after meeting her twenty years later as Vicereine.[6] Harcourt Butler was quite captivated by her when he got to know her, as indeed he was by Willingdon, about whom he had at first written so disparagingly. He had them to stay with him in Burma when he was governing that Province and took them to a cave which had a raging torrent flowing through it and yet was surprisingly quiet. 'This symbolises the relentless energy of Nature and her infinite peace' Butler told them with some eloquence; to which Lady Willingdon's only comment was, 'A bit niffy, isn't it?' – for they were standing on a ledge of guano. As Butler afterwards remarked: 'One would not expect romance or exaltation from a daughter of old Brassey'.[7]

Having gone from Bombay to Madras, the Willingdons had hopes that the next step would be the Viceroyalty. And indeed, there was a possibility that Willingdon would be Chelmsford's successor; another candidate at that time was Butler, so that someone observed: 'I think Sir Harcourt would make a better Viceroy than Lady Willingdon'.[8] By the time the appointment of Reading was announced, the Willingdons had received 1,500 letters of congratulation. 'I think that the Ws feel much that they were not Viceroy' Butler wrote two years later, with a significant use of the plural, 'they'. 'I doubt if they would have done although they are good workers and

Lord and Lady Willingdon (standing left; and sitting right) with the 2nd Earl and Countess of Lytton. Lord Lytton, son of the Viceroy, was Governor of Bengal 1922–1927. Lady Lytton, the former Pamela Plowden, a great beauty, was an early flame of the young Winston Churchill

figureheads. She is too imperious.' By now, their time in Madras was drawing to a close and Willingdon was tired. 'He longs to get home' Butler observed. 'She dreads it'. It was hard for Lady Willingdon to have to go back into private life having been, as Butler put it, 'an unrivalled Queen for ten years'.[9]

In fairness to Lady Willingdon, it must be said that she not only loved being a queen; but that she and also Willingdon really loved India. They planned to return every year after their reign had ended.

It is probably true to say that they had made more close friends among the Indians than any other Lord Sahib and Lady Sahib sent out from home. Although their friends tended to be drawn from the Princely Order and the aristocracy rather than from the rising middle-class intelligentsia, their ability to get on well with Indians did much to bring Indians and British closer together in social life. With this object in view, they founded the Willingdon Sports Club at Bombay.

Having departed from India – their lights fled, their garlands dead – in 1924, the Willingdons obtained a new lease of Government House life two years later, when Willingdon was made Governor-General of Canada. Success followed them to that snow-girt Dominion, so different from their late kingdoms in Malabar and Coromandel; so that in 1931, when their reign in Canada came to an end, Willingdon was an obvious if unimaginative choice as the successor to Irwin, whose Viceroyalty providentially ended at the same time. And so their ambition – or at any rate Lady Willingdon's ambition – was realised; and the newly-promoted Earl and Countess of Willingdon returned in triumph as Viceroy and Vicereine to the India they loved. At sixty-four, Willingdon was older than any Viceroy before him; his moustache was now grey and he was a little frail; but he was still an exquisite figure in his grey frock coat and spats, the Star of India on his breast. Lady Willingdon, nine years younger than her husband, was as full of energy as ever.

To make the task of the ageing Viceroy easier, they planned to travel about India by air; which also showed how modern and 'air minded' they were. But it showed a remarkable lack of sensitivity that they should have thought of flying out from England to take possession of their Empire; for had they done so, they would have landed at Karachi and thereby hurt the feelings of all their old friends in Bombay, who naturally wished to be the first to welcome them back to India. They were dissuaded from this idea by Irwin; but later in their reign made Viceregal history by flying back to India after going home on leave. They also adhered to their plan of using an aircraft for their Viceregal tours, subjecting their entourage to many hours of bumpy flying which was misery for those of them who were bad air travellers.

While on the face of it, Willingdon's experience in Bombay and Madras as well as in Canada made him a likely candidate for the Viceroyalty, his past career was really more of a handicap than an advantage to him as the ruler of India in the difficult early nineteen-thirties. The fact that he had been a constitutional Governor-General of Canada and was no longer young meant that he was set in his ways as a social figurehead rather than a statesman. His Indian experience was of an India substantially different from that which he

Lord Willingdon. A
portrait by Sir Oswald
Birley

was now called upon to rule. Whereas the High Tory Irwin had come
to India with an open mind, the Liberal Willingdon came with a
mind conditioned by the ideas and prejudices of the most respectable
Indian liberal opinion of *circa* 1917. And having already been the
Governor of two Indian provinces meant that he had many Indian
cronies to influence him; friends who, being mostly Princes and

aristocrats, were if anything more opposed to Congress than the British.

Looking back, Irwin believed that much of the trouble and slowing down of constitutional progress after his time was due to Willingdon's liking for the Princes and dislike of the Congress leaders.[10] In particular, Willingdon disliked Gandhi, whom he regarded as 'a sort of Jekyll and Hyde'[11] and also as 'a little *bania*' who was 'the most astute and opportunist politician' he had ever met.[12] Sir Samuel Hoare, who became Secretary of State after the advent of the National Government in August 1931, attributed the incompatibility to the fact that Willingdon and Gandhi differed so much from each other. 'On the one hand, the accomplished man of the Western World, the engaging product of Eton, Cambridge and Westminster, in his beautifully cut grey suit and I Zingari tie, on the other, the toothless seer with his *khaddar* and spinning wheel.'[13] Yet Irwin was also an accomplished man of the Western World. It was not so much a question of background and dress as that Willingdon and Gandhi lacked the spiritual affinity which had existed between Gandhi and Irwin.

By the time Gandhi returned to India at the end of 1931 after attending the Round Table Conference, relations between the Government and Congress were once again at breaking-point. Each side accused the other of violating the Irwin-Gandhi Pact; Congress having stirred up trouble on the North-West Frontier and in the United Provinces, the Government having, since Irwin's departure, been rather too active in preparing to meet another Congress attack. Two new Ordinances for dealing with terrorism were introduced in December, which Gandhi referred to sarcastically as 'Christmas gifts from Lord Willingdon, our Christian Viceroy';[14] and before the Mahatma landed at Bombay, Jawaharlal Nehru had been arrested for inciting the peasants of the United Provinces to withhold their rent.

Gandhi, on his arrival, announced a return to civil disobedience on the pretext of the Government's measures; while at the same time asking for an interview with Willingdon; but the Viceroy refused to see him except on condition that certain matters, notably the Ordinances, were not discussed. Willingdon's refusal to see Gandhi unconditionally at this juncture caused a great outcry in India; and while he may have been justified in believing, as he did, that it would be dangerous to discuss the Government's security measures with him, 'true safety does not always lie in the avoidance of risks', as a contemporary put it.[15] One feels that Irwin, in similar circumstances, would have been willing to discuss anything with Gandhi in the hope of averting the conflict that was imminent. But Willingdon had no intention of negotiating with Gandhi on equal terms as Irwin had done; and in any case his Government had its own plans for dealing with the conflict. The new civil disobedience campaign started on 4 January and by 10 January Gandhi and most of the other Congress leaders had been arrested. In the same month, five more Ordinances were issued to revive the powers which had lapsed with the Irwin-Gandhi Pact. Congress was declared illegal; 34,000 political prisoners joined the Mahatma behind bars; and by the end of 1932 civil disobedience was effectively broken.

Because of the Government's handling of the 1932 civil disobedience campaign, a legend grew up that Willingdon was, in the words of Nehru, 'a hard and stern person'. But as Nehru goes on to point out, the policy was his Government's rather than his own.[16] As a Liberal, Willingdon was personally even more averse to repression than the High Tory Irwin had been; he complained to Hoare that he felt like a budding Mussolini.[17] He did not wish to use the big stick without showing the people some evidence of his desire 'to push them on towards responsibility for the management of their own affairs'[18] and proposed a scheme for increasing the number of Indians in his Council; which, however, was rejected by the Government at home. When speaking to a delegation of Congress sympathisers from England in the autumn of 1932, he became almost plaintive in his anxiety to justify Gandhi's arrest. 'I begged the fellow to co-operate with me and tried to make him understand that here was I, an elderly gentleman eager to give a few more years of service and anxious to help to get things straight in India. He simply would not respond.'[19]

Nevertheless, Willingdon was not sorry to have 'the little man', as he usually called him, safely under lock and key. He felt that this would stop the rot; and when, as a result of the Government's stern measures, civil disobedience came to an end and India entered into a period of tranquillity, it seemed as if he were right. In May 1933 Gandhi began one of his fasts and was consequently released from prison, since the Government had no wish to make a martyr of him; he was imprisoned again in August, but finally released later that month after starting another fast. From now on, Willingdon followed what he considered to be the best policy with regard to Gandhi, namely of making as little of him as possible. When Sir Mirza Ismail, the Maharaja of Mysore's *Dewan* or chief minister, expressed the view that Gandhi could serve as a genuine leader, he was reprimanded by the Viceroy at his next meeting with him. It was typical of Willingdon that the reprimand should have been administered in a friendly, man-to-man way: 'Look here, Mirza, what have you been doing?' and then, 'Don't do it again, my dear fellow'.[20]

In his dealings with the representatives of Princely India, like Mirza, Willingdon's chief concern was to persuade the Rulers to come into an All-India Federation such as had been mooted at the first session of the Round Table Conference; and which, after the Conference had met for the third and last time in 1932 without making any real progress, was adopted by the Home Government in its own scheme for Indian constitutional reform. This scheme, which became law with the passing of the Government of India Act in 1935, provided for reform in two phases. The first, scheduled for 1937, gave the provinces what amounted to self-government under responsible Ministers, except that the Governors were to retain emergency powers; the electorate was to be enlarged with safeguards for the various minorities. The first phase left the Central Government much as it was; but the second phase of reform set up a Federal Government at the centre consisting of representatives of the Princely States as well as of the provinces of British India. Since the Princes were in theory autonomous, Federation was not to come into being until a specified number of them agreed to join.

Although Willingdon's reign saw the passing of the Government of India Act, it was, compared with the Viceroyalty of Irwin, a period of constitutional stagnation. From 1934 onwards, Willingdon was very much under the influence of his Finance Member, Sir James Grigg – known as 'P.J.' – a masterful and obstructive Treasury official sent out from home. Grigg was to write of Willingdon that 'he invariably conveyed the impression that his visitor was the one person on earth he most wanted to see';[21] but one suspects that what 'P.J.' really liked about him was his acquiescence. During the latter part of his reign, Willingdon did less work than ever; his successor was to find little evidence of his reaction to the papers sent to him, not even the initial 'W' to indicate that he had read them.

But if Willingdon became increasingly inactive as a ruler, he did not in any way slacken the pace of his social duties. After watching the Viceroy and Vicereine greeting their guests at Viceregal Lodge during the Simla season of 1935, Mr. Malcolm Muggeridge observed: 'The great thing is, they enjoy it and their enjoyment is infectious'.[22] Mr. Muggeridge, who was then Assistant Editor of the Calcutta *Statesman*, describes Willington on this occasion as 'slight and frail, like a Max Beerbohm drawing, and studded with gleaming stars and orders. . he gave out no emanation of authority, but might have been, at a casual glance, a chairman of some board or other, or a City Alderman, or for that matter, what he really was – an amiable back-bench MP'.[23] He also seemed 'like the elderly beau of Restoration Comedy'; but his eyes were pale, 'as though life was draining out of him from the top downwards'.[24]

Speaking to Mr. Muggeridge at that party, Willingdon made the remarkable statement that he found India almost ridiculously easy to govern. Mr. Muggeridge, who subsequently met him several times, found him easy to talk to; 'he never really said anything about anything',[25] but he did appear to have some obsessions. One of them was Irwin. 'He thinks that Irwin was a bad Viceroy' Mr. Muggeridge confided to his diary. 'At the same time he has an uneasy feeling that he is, or is thought to be, a greater man than he.' Sitting next to Mr. Muggeridge after a Viceregal Lodge dinner, Willingdon, 'slightly tipsy', said: 'Halifax was very bad Viceroy, I'm quite a good one. Yet he'll be remembered and I'll be forgotten because he's managed to persuade people he's *good*'.[26]

Mr. Muggeridge also affords us a glimpse of Lady Willingdon, 'a large, zestful lady with a red sash', greeting her guests with 'a permanent unvarying smile which beamed upon one and all'; later, sitting on a sofa 'giving out waves of energy and enthusiasm'[27] and with a characteristic lack of discretion complaining to him – a young journalist whom she had never met before – of the Commander-in-Chief's stinginess in only giving three hundred rupees to her Jubilee Fund.[28] Lady Willingdon was as tireless at fund-raising and organising as her husband was lazy about ruling; the Viceroyalty was very much hers.

Though people admired Lady Willingdon's energy, there were many who could not stand her vulgarity and her autocratic ways. Once at a Viceregal dinner party, a senior official felt such a relief when the Vicereine rose to leave the dining room that he threw his napkin into the air and shouted 'Whoopee!' – for which he was punished by not being bidden to the Investiture to receive his CIE, which instead was delivered to him by a *chaprassi*. Lady Willingdon inevitably gave rise to stories, of which the best known, though it is probably apocryphal, is about the ADC who asked the Viceroy's permission to give up his post after only two months. Willingdon

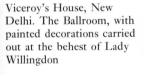

Viceroy's House, New Delhi. The Ballroom, with painted decorations carried out at the behest of Lady Willingdon

asked him why he wanted to go, and the young man blurted out: 'Well, Sir, quite frankly, it's Her Excellency'. To which Willingdon replied: 'I've had to put up with her for forty years, you've only had to put up with her for two months; you can damn well stay.'

Lady Willingdon's high-handedness extended to the barely-completed Viceroy's House at New Delhi, which she proceeded to alter with a total lack of feeling for what Lutyens had achieved. She removed the stone elephants from the forecourt screen and put them in the garden, where she planted unsuitable cypresses and cut down other trees that were just becoming established. She subjected many of the rooms to her favourite shade of mauve – causing the pun-loving Lutyens to refer to her as 'the mauvey *sujet*' – and embellished them with painted decorations described by a lady who saw them as 'wild duck falling into Dorothy Perkins roses'.[29] She covered the walls and ceilings of the ballroom with gaudy arabesques and Mogul motifs.

Lutyens was deeply distressed when he heard of how his masterpiece was suffering.[30] At his behest, Queen Mary wrote Lady Willingdon a sharp letter; but Lady Willingdon took no notice. In 1934, when the Willingdons came home on leave, Lutyens was able to tackle the offending Vicereine in person. 'I told her' he afterwards recalled, 'that if she possessed the Parthenon she would add bay windows to it. She said she did not like the Parthenon.'[31]

Spoilt though it may have seemed to Lutyens and his admirers, the Imperial palace at New Delhi looked magnificent enough to a visiting French Baron, who has left an account of a State Ball in the Willingdons' time. The open staircase seemed to him 'the most handsome staircase in the world'. There were two of the Bodyguard on each step; the gold costumes of the maharajas mingled with the shining lustre of saris, the red, blue and silver of uniforms, the glitter of diadems and the 'flaxen coiffures of the young Englishwomen'; while high overhead was the 'starlit splendour of the Indian night'. Ascending the stairs, he found himself advancing across the marble floor of the Durbar Hall to where, flanked by *chobdars* with maces, stood the Viceroy and Vicereine. Seen through the Baron's admiring eyes, the 'amiable back-bench MP' of Mr. Muggeridge's memory was transformed into 'a charming representative of the English aristocracy who looked his royal part to proud perfection'; while Lady Willingdon was 'his smiling vivacious wife, who with prodigious sleight of mind found something to say – infallibly the right and fitting thing – to every one of us'.[32]

An even more memorable festivity of the Willingdons' reign was the fancy dress ball which they gave at Belvedere during the Calcutta Christmas Week of 1935. The Viceroy and Vicereine appeared as Louis XVI and Marie Antoinette, with their Staff got up as courtiers of the *ancien régime*; all of them, needless to say, clad in mauve. For the sixty-nine-year-old Willingdon and his bulky, sixty-year-old consort to impersonate a King and Queen who were guillotined before they were forty can hardly have been very convincing; yet it was fitting that they should have appeared as this doomed Royal pair since their own days as King and Queen were numbered. For twenty years, on and off, in India and also in Canada, the Willingdons had stood side by side on red carpets, receiving guests; but after the following April they would do so no more. When he met her at Simla during the previous summer, Mr. Muggeridge realised how much Lady Willingdon dreaded the day when she would no longer be Vicereine; she told him that she wished she and Willingdon were staying on for another ten years. But Willingdon, elevated to a Marquessate on his retirement, had only another five years to live. Lady Willingdon was to survive until 1960; a prominent figure at charity balls and similar functions in London almost to the end.

Willingdon's fear that he would be forgotten and Irwin remembered as yet shows no sign of coming to pass; for in India today, the name of Willingdon is probably spoken more often than that of his illustrious predecessor. There is a Willingdon Hospital in Delhi and Mrs. Indira Gandhi lives – or lived until recently – in Willingdon Crescent. The Willingdon Sports Club at Bombay still flourishes and in the hall are photographs in coroneted silver frames of Lady Willingdon and her Freeman, redolent of an Imperial twilight that was only the day before yesterday but now seems infinitely remote.

'He's terribly pompous' Lady Willingdon said, when speaking to Mr. Muggeridge of her husband's successor, the Marquess of Linlithgow.[33] In fact the new Viceroy – known to his family and friends as Hopie, since he had started life with the courtesy title of Lord Hope – was not in the least pompous; but he gave that impression. Enormously tall, he suffered from the disability – caused by polio in his boyhood – of being unable to turn his head; which made him seen alarmingly stiff, particularly so as he was shy and often brusque with strangers. Those who knew him well, however, found him a delightful companion; modest to a fault, with a strong and often Rabelaisian sense of humour. His humour tended to show in his face, though at times it made him look supercilious; or rather, it gave him what might be called a debunking expression, an expression one tends to associate more with Americans than with British. There was something slightly American about the cast of his clean-shaven features: the beetling brow, the heavy jowl which on account of his disability made him appear at times to have not just a double but a triple chin, though he was by no means fat.

Since Linlithgow possessed no American blood, his transatlantic

air may perhaps be attributed to the fact that so many Americans are Scottish by descent; for as his Marquessate would imply, he was a Scot; he came from the opposite side of the Firth of Forth to where the Elgins came from. His family seat, Hopetoun, one of the most palatial country houses in Scotland, gives a false idea of his standing; for his ancestors were Scottish Earls of moderate means, like the Elgins and Mintos, rather than grandees; the Marquessate was conferred on his father who was the first Governor-General of Australia. His father overspent and died young, leaving him not very well off, so that he was obliged to go into business to make some money. He managed at the same time to play a part in politics and from 1926 to 1928 was Chairman of the Royal Commission on Agriculture in India, which took him to India on an extensive tour

Lord and Lady Willingdon leaving Croydon by air on their way back to India, July 1934 and caused him to be widely known among the Indians as 'Bull Sahib'. Having thus become one of the Conservative Party's acknowledged experts on Indian affairs, he was appointed Chairman of the Parliamentary Select Committee set up in 1931 to prepare the way for the Government of India Act of 1935. As such, he was well suited to be the Viceroy whose task it was to implement the Act.

Linlithgow had the reputation of being wise rather than clever; though Duff Cooper 'sometimes wondered whether his gigantic stature had anything to do with the impression of wisdom that he conveyed. . we believe that elephants are very wise'. [34] G.D. Birla, a prominent Indian industrialist and Congress supporter, who met Linlithgow in London shortly before he became Viceroy, summed him up as 'not brilliant but capable and sound; no imagination, matter-of-fact, at the same time straightforward, frank and well-intentioned'. [35]

As a Viceroy, Linlithgow was in complete contrast to Willingdon. He seemed, on first impression, another Irwin; for as well as being tall he was in the prime of life, only forty-eight when he assumed office. Like Irwin he was a good listener and a hard worker; the dust of the Willingdon regime was quickly swept away by his new broom. Again like Irwin, he was very much master in his own house, as the autocratic Finance Member, Sir James Grigg, soon discovered. 'The trouble with P.J.', Linlithgow drily observed, 'is that he thought he was Viceroy when Willingdon was here and he does not realise that now I am.' [36] If he had an _éminence grise_, it was his Private Secretary, Gilbert Laithwaite, a civil servant of outstanding ability from the India Office. He and Laithwaite were more like partners than master and secretary; though people exaggerated when they spoke, as they sometimes did, of the 'Linlaithwaite Administration'.

Not only was Linlithgow in the Irwin mould, but also his wife Doreen, who resembled Dorothy Irwin in being graceful, artistic and unassuming; while differing from her in appearance. She was as tall for a woman as her husband was for a man; together they made an imposing pair. Both the Linlithgows disliked having to be royal; which meant that the Viceregal entourage once again became a happy family party as in the Irwins' time. It was also a family party in the literal sense; for whereas the Willingdons only had one son, the Linlithgows had two sons and three daughters, all unmarried at the beginning of their reign and varying in age from twenty-four to sixteen. If the sound of the hunting horn had been heard not infrequently in the Viceregal residences during the Irwin regime, the sound most usually heard under the Linlithgows was a rousing chorus, for Linlithgow loved singing with his family and friends. When there were no official guests, he and his family would sing lustily to the music of _The Roast Beef of Old England_, which by a

'Freeman and Hopie'. The departing Lord Willingdon and the newly-arrived Lord Linlithgow at Government House, Malabar Point, Bombay

long-standing custom the Band always played as the company went in to dinner.

The idea that Linlithgow was another Irwin was current throughout India when he first arrived, particularly after he had made history by broadcasting to the Indian people, his talk being repeated in Hindustani. He was not a very good speaker, but he managed to give an impression of honesty and wisdom which went down well. 'You must get to their hearts' he had said, 'and this is what I mean to do.'[37] Unfortunately, for all his good intentions, he was to find getting to the hearts of the Indians extremely difficult. He had not the instinctive feeling for them which Irwin and Willingdon had. 'Freeman liked the Princes' Irwin afterwards wrote, 'Hopie had not much use for the Princes and did not really get on human terms with anybody'.[38] To say that Linlithgow did not get on human terms with anybody is certainly an exaggeration; but it expresses what many people, British as well as Indians, felt about him.

At times, Linlithgow behaved towards the Indians in a way that appeared thoughtless; though it was probably that he was less successful than other Viceroys in keeping the effects of extreme tiredness at bay. Soon after his arrival, he went to stay with the celebrated big game shot and writer, Jim Corbett, in a camp in the Himalayan jungle. There was naturally great excitement in the neighbourhood when it was heard that he was coming, for a Viceroy had never been in those parts before; an arch was put up with 'Well Come' written on it and a crowd of local dignitaries – one of them with a high fever – waited all day by the roadside in order to greet him. But when at last Linlithgow appeared, he drove past them as though they had not been there. Irwin, in similar circumstances, would have stopped his car, and so would Willingdon.

The Viceroy's ability to get on with the Indians was of paramount importance in his task of persuading them to accept the provisions of the 1935 Act, to which almost every community and party had its own particular objections. The first elections held under the Act at the beginning of 1937 resulted in Congress majorities in six out of the eleven Provincial Legislatures; but Congress refused to form Ministries in these provinces unless an assurance was given that the Governors' emergency powers would not be used. The Government would not yield on this point and in the resulting *impasse* Linlithgow maintained an Olympian silence, incurring much criticism for his refusal to see Gandhi or to hear of any sort of compromise. In the end, he triumphed; Congress climbed down and agreed to take office even though the Governors kept their emergency powers.

Having succeeded in getting Congress to take office, Linlithgow invited Gandhi to come and see him. This was the first of many such meetings; the good relations between Viceroy and Mahatma, which Irwin had established and Willingdon destroyed, were now restored and would endure for most of the new reign. Unlike Willingdon, Linlithgow did not underestimate Gandhi's importance as a political force and his hold over Congress. 'The more I see him' he wrote, 'the more I am convinced that he is the only man in that party who can deliver the goods.'[39]

The co-operation of Congress was necessary not only to make the first phase of constitutional reform work, but also to bring in the second, which was Federation. Congress objected to Federation for various reasons, notably because the representatives of the Princely States would constitute an undemocratic element in the Federal Government. There was a chance, however, that these objections

would be overcome once Federation came into being; particularly if it came into being while Gandhi was still alive. The Mahatma's age was therefore one of several reasons why Federation should be got off the ground as quickly as possible; another being that Congress was becoming increasingly active in the States; and the more trouble Congress gave the Princes, the less likely they would be to join a Federation in which Congress would of necessity play a big part. Linlithgow was fully aware of the need for haste, and he made many appeals to the Princes, the majority of whom were either opposed to Federation altogether or else would only join on their own terms. He also appointed three senior officials to go round the States and explain the Federation proposals to the Rulers with a view to getting them to join; but this was an impossible task for so small a number to accomplish.

As well as Congress and the Princes, Linlithgow had the Muslims to contend with. In the prevailing atmosphere of communal tension, it was inevitable that they should have had misgivings about a Federation in which the Hindus would be dominant. When Linlithgow first saw the Muslim League leader, Mohammed Ali

Investiture, New Delhi, 27 February 1937

Jinnah, in 1937, he seemed not wholly opposed to Federation; but during the next few months his attitude hardened and by the spring of 1938 he was already advocating a separate Pakistan. Linlithgow did not get on with Jinnah, but then very few people did; had he been one of those few, he might possibly have kept him to his original line. And while he can hardly be blamed for not liking the chilly and obstinate Muslim leader, he was perhaps guilty of an error of judgement in not foreseeing the hold Jinnah would eventually have over the Muslims; had he judged him better he might have done more with him.

Linlithgow spent a week in the great Muslim stronghold of Lahore in the autumn of 1937. The present writer, then aged seven, was there at the time with his parents; his memories of that visit, first-hand and from what his parents told him, serve to illustrate Linlithgow's virtues as well as his failings. At a Durbar for the Punjab Chiefs, held in the old palace or Fort of Akbar the Great, the Viceroy could not stop himself falling asleep. Another day, my father took his Indian officers to Government House for a select little tea party with the Viceroy – no small honour for them, though in fact they did not enjoy it; for not only did the Viceroy spend most of the time talking to my father about mutual friends in Scotland, rather than to the Indians; but he ate no tea, so that they, too, felt constrained to eat nothing, and resented being thus deprived of their curry puffs and iced cakes. For me, the most memorable event of that week was the presentation of new colours to an Indian regiment. The Viceroy, as he arrived, looked most impressive in his grey frock coat and top hat; and his smile seemed to me genial rather than supercilious. Later there was a dust storm, which caused the front part of the *shamiana* to collapse on top of him; the rest of us, in the less volatile main body of the tent, were treated to the spectacle of the Viceroy crawling out from under the fallen canvas. As his grey frock coat was dusted down, he said with a cheery laugh, 'That was an experience I've never had before!' which showed he had taken the mishap in good part. How good, I only discovered thirty years later, when I read Linlithgow's own account of that occasion, in a letter to the King-Emperor; which tactfully makes no mention of the collapse of the tent, but simply speaks of how 'a high wind and dust storm could not mar the very high level of the drill'.[40] Someone told me recently that as the tent was collapsing, an ADC, in the stress of the moment, came out with a four-letter word; to which the Viceroy responded by saying: 'Quite right to tell people to duck'.

Apart from that week in Lahore, my chief childhood memory of Linlithgow is of frequent photographs of him in the newspapers prodding cows. It was through his interest in improving Indian breeds of cattle – he started an All-India Cattle Show and kept two bulls at his own expense for the benefit of cultivators around New Delhi – that Linlithgow got the nearest he ever succeeded in getting to the Hindu heart, particularly to the heart of the Hindu *ryot*: one rural community greeted him with an arch bearing the words 'Welcome to our cow-protecting Viceroy'. Linlithgow felt an affinity with the cultivators of the soil, and arranged for a group of them to be present at his installation; he visited Indian villages and prided himself on keeping in touch with rural life.

Being very much a countryman, Linlithgow spent as much time as he could camping in the jungle with Corbett. He was a keen shot, though he preferred photographing tigers to shooting them; he was also devoted to fishing. When camping in the hills in the summer of 1937, he took up butterfly hunting, and put the detectives who shadowed him to good use by arming them with butterfly nets and killing-bottles. For the Linlithgows, as for so many other Viceroys and Vicereines, expeditions into the further hills were the one consolation for Simla, which they both found depressing.

It was always a happy moment for the Linlithgows and their family when October came and they returned from Simla to New Delhi. They loved Viceroy's House, which Doreen set about restoring to its pre-Willingdon glory. To help her rid the palace and garden of Lady Willingdon's 'vagarious vagaries', as he called them, Lutyens was invited out to India in the autumn of 1938. The stone elephants were returned to their proper places in the forecourt screen, the offending cypresses rooted up, the ducks and Dorothy Perkins roses painted out. The arabesques in the Ballroom, which certainly gave the room an air of richness, were allowed to stay.

In that last winter of peace, restored to its pristine state and with the garden now grown to maturity, Viceroy's House enjoyed a brief heyday before the war put an end for ever to State Balls and the other grander forms of Viceregal entertaining. Linlithgow may have lacked the social graces, but he and Doreen knew how to entertain and the two of them looked quite splendid on state occasions, he towering above the tallest troopers of the Bodyguard. A friend has left an account of one of their Investitures, for which more than four hundred people assembled in the Durbar Hall. 'A fanfare announced Their Excellencies, who processed in, led by the Staff in scarlet and gold uniforms, their trains carried by four little Indian Princes . . . Hopie looked magnificent in Privy Councillor's uniform over which he wore the mantle of the Star of India – pale blue velvet. Doreen in white with a diamond tiara and necklace'.[41]

With the outbreak of war, Federation was shelved. Earlier in 1939, the prospects of achieving it seemed more hopeful; nearly two-fifths of the Princely States had expressed their willingness to join. Linlithgow himself believed that if war had not supervened, it would

Viceroy's House in serene mood, as seen from the Mogul Garden

have come by 1941. Whether he could have got Federation off the ground before the war if he had tried harder is a matter of controversy. Assuming that the Princes could not have been persuaded any quicker than they were, it might have been possible for Linlithgow to have the 1935 Act amended by the Home Government so that Federation could have been brought in immediately, regardless of their wishes. It is true that a strong section of the Conservative Party, led by Churchill, would have fought tooth and nail against any suggestion of imposing Federation on the Princes; but Irwin who, as Lord Halifax, was himself a member of the Cabinet during those years, believed that if Linlithgow 'had really been willing to push the Federal idea and had not been inhibited by one Cause or another, either in approach to Princes or Congress', he 'would have been able to get the Cabinet and the Party to move more quickly'.[42]

Like Hardinge during the previous conflict, Linlithgow threw himself heart and soul into organising India's war-effort; a task in which he was to achieve a notable success. At the same time, he went rather too far in what he himself long-windedly called 'retaining even in times of stress such as these a sufficient degree of public appearance to indicate that we have not retired into our shell and sunk into the depths of depression'.[43] Although there were no more State Balls, Viceregal dinner parties and garden parties went on as usual; even the news of the fall of France could not prevent a garden party taking place at Viceregal Lodge in Simla, complete with ices, grey top hats and the Band. When the Linlithgows went into residence at Belvedere for the first Christmas of the war, a special train took the Bodyguard to Calcutta so that the Viceroy could drive on to the racecourse with his glittering escort of scarlet lancers. The *Statesman* wrote unkindly of Linlithgow's 'laboured continuance,

Lord and Lady Linlithgow entering the Mogul Garden to greet their guests (*right*)

Gilbert Laithwaite

apparently for reasons of prestige, of opulences that seemed unrelished'.[44]

In putting India onto a war footing, Linlithgow was faced with the problem of enlisting the support of Congress and the other communities in the fight against Nazi Germany. Gandhi, on the outbreak of hostilities, told the Viceroy that he contemplated the war 'with an English heart';[45] Nehru was no less sympathetic to the Allied cause. But Congress was soon demanding immediate and radical constitutional changes and a promise of complete independence after the war as the price of its co-operation. After talking to the leaders of all sections of opinion without arriving at a compromise, Linlithgow issued a statement that there would be no more major constitutional developments until the end of the war, when the Government would be willing to consult with the various communities over possible changes in the 1935 Act. The Viceroy's statement did not offer very much; and as might have been expected, it was condemned by Congress. Before the end of 1939, all the Congress Ministeries in the provinces had resigned.

However much Congress was to blame for this breakdown, one feels that it might have been averted had Linlithgow acted with a little more imagination, with a little more tact and finesse. For instance, a more imaginative Viceroy would have avoided giving offence, as Linlithgow did, over his declaration of war; which he issued without first asking the assent of the Legislative Assembly. To ask assent was not constitutionally necessary and there might have been an embarrassing situation if Congress had refused it; but out of deference to Congress susceptibilities, something ought to have been done as a matter of form. Clement Attlee's attack on Linlithgow in October, in which he criticised the Viceroy as being out of touch with realities and lacking 'imaginative insight'[46] was certainly ill-timed; but it was not wholly unfair. It was echoed in a very different quarter, by a young Civilian in the United Provinces, who expressed himself 'revolted by Lord Linlithgow's heavy-footed dealing with the Congress Ministries'.[47] And the former Conservative Secretary of State, Sir Samuel Hoare, observed in November after hearing the opinion of Sir Muhammad Zafrulla Khan, a very sensible Muslim leader who was Law Member of the Viceroy's Council: 'Hopie has been too Olympian and remote'.[48]

After the fall of France, Linlithgow and the Secretary of State, Leo Amery, worked on a new statement which they hoped might break the deadlock. Both of them wished to announce that the British Government would aim at giving India Dominion Status within a year of the ending of hostilities; but Churchill, who despite his other commitments as a wartime leader was henceforth to make repeated incursions into Indian affairs, watered this down, so that the rejection of the document by Congress became a foregone conclusion. It contained nothing of any significance except for an announcement that the Viceroy's Council would be expanded to admit more Indians.

Relations between the Government and Congress took a turn for the worse in the autumn of 1940 when Gandhi ordered his disciples to engage in *Satyagraha* or civil disobedience one by one, which led to a number of arrests; the Government naturally taking a serious view of attempts by some of his followers to interfere with the recruitment of Indians into the armed forces. Nehru was arrested in October, not in connection with Gandhi's campaign but for making seditious speeches; he was sentenced to four years' imprisonment, which Linlithgow considered unduly severe, while being unwilling to overrule the Judiciary in this matter.

Linlithgow's term of office was due to end in the spring of 1941, but Churchill persuaded him to stay on for another year and then for another year and a half after that. Though he was becoming increasingly tired, his sense of duty made it impossible for him to refuse. During 1941, he was mainly concerned with the war, which was moving closer to India. Within India itself, that year was relatively quiet, so that Linlithgow, on the advice of the Indians in his Council – who were now in the majority – agreed to release Nehru and the other Congress prisoners. He himself was not particularly in favour of this; but he realised that it would be a blow to the prestige of his newly-appointed Indian colleagues if he were to disregard their advice. The release of the prisoners entailed a lengthy tussle with Churchill, who eventually told Amery that he gave in; adding *sotto voce* some remark like 'when you lose India don't blame me'.[49] Churchill's policy with regard to India made his Government appear dishonest; for while he saw the necessity of paying lip-service to Indian aspirations, he hoped that, by delaying tactics, he could prolong the Raj indefinitely.

A couple of months later, it seemed that Churchill had departed completely from his accustomed standpoint; for he adopted a radical scheme for Indian constitutional reform thought out by his left-wing colleague, Sir Stafford Cripps, who had long been committed to the cause of Indian nationalism. Linlithgow, who had not been consulted, regarded the scheme as dangerous and amateurish and nearly resigned; but in fact Churchill's real purpose was to show Roosevelt and American public opinion that Britain had done all she could to solve the Indian problem; and he was relieved when Cripps, having come to India in the spring of 1942, failed to persuade either Nehru or Jinnah to accept his offer.

Linlithgow, who felt it was hardly the time for major constitutional innovations when the armies of Japan were advancing towards India's eastern frontier, was also in a way relieved; yet at the same time Cripps's failure saddened him, in that it showed all too plainly that self-government was incompatible with the unity of India. The Muslim League had gone beyond the point of no return in its determination to have a separate Pakistan. This was a state of affairs for which Linlithgow was himself to some extent responsible, through his failure to exercise a moderating influence on the League before it was too late. Much as he disliked Jinnah, he had been reluctant to do anything which might have caused the break-up of what was, after all, the only political organisation of any consequence in India outside Congress. Moreover, he felt it important to remain on good terms with the Muslims, who were not only doing their best to make the constitution work in the provinces where they had a majority, but had provided more than half the troops in the Indian Army.

After Cripps had retired from the scene, Linlithgow was far too concerned with the present to think much about India's political future. While the Japanese continued to advance, Gandhi attacked the British with his 'Quit India' campaign and in August Congress came out in open rebellion. Linlithgow and his Council acted quickly; and on the morning after the 'Quit India' rebellion was proclaimed, all the Congress leaders were arrested. Gandhi was detained in the luxury of the Aga Khan's palace at Poona; the other leaders were sent to a fortress. In making these arrests, Linlithgow was greatly helped by the fact that his Council, which gave him unanimous support, had recently been enlarged once again; so that it now consisted almost entirely of Indians, including several Hindus; one of the latter being Dr. B.R. Ambedkar, leader of the Untouchables now known euphemistically as the 'Scheduled Castes'.

While the Congress leaders settled down to their imprisonment,

The last Christmas. Fun and games after farewell dinner

their followers began a campaign of violence and sabotage all over the country. For a time, Bengal was cut off from the rest of India; but with the help of the troops the situation was quickly got under control. The crisis had a sequel early in the following year when Gandhi, in his palace-prison, began to fast for three weeks. Linlithgow and his Council decided to do as Willingdon's Government had done, and release him when his life was in danger; but the Cabinet at home felt that this would be too much like surrender. After he had fasted for ten days, the Mahatma seemed on the point of death; the Government prepared to face the repercussions. Then, suddenly, his condition began to improve and by the time he entered the final week of his fast he was out of danger. Many believed it to be a miracle; others were convinced that he had been surreptitiously fed by his attendants.

Despite the satisfactory conclusion to Gandhi's fast, Linlithgow's Viceroyalty ended sombrely on account of a severe famine in Bengal. This was one of the provinces where there was still a constitutional Government; but the Ministry was weak and the Governor, who was a sick man, unable to cope; so that the arrangements for famine relief had broken down and people were dying of starvation in the streets of Calcutta. Linlithgow was widely criticised for not going to Bengal to see things for himself. Even Doreen begged him to go; but he had a reason for not going in that he did not wish to be accused of interfering in the affairs of a self-governing province; having brought in the constitution, he tended to be over-meticulous in observing it. He was also by now utterly exhausted; when his successor arrived he told him that he had never been so glad to welcome anybody.

The departure of the Linlithgows in the autumn of 1943 seemed like the passing of an institution, for their reign had been longer than that of any other Viceroy and Vicereine. 'Lord Linlithgow has made mistakes, but India will remember him with kindness' one newspaper wrote; which summed up what most people thought about him. Even Gandhi, while reproaching him in his farewell letter, was to remember Linlithgow with kindness; he afterwards told an English friend of Congress that of all the Viceroys he had known, he much preferred Linlithgow to work with.

On his return home, Linlithgow was given the Garter; an exceptional honour since he already had the Thistle. Though only fifty-six when he ceased to be Viceroy, he did not play any further part in public life and died at the comparatively early age of sixty-four. Doreen Linlithgow lived on until 1965.

Willingdon has been called an Imperial handyman; but the description could be better applied to Linlithgow, who during the course of a long and extremely difficult reign tackled the problems as they arose with wisdom and often with success. If the overall

Lord Linlithgow with his
grandaughter

picture of his reign is one of lost opportunity – the opportunity of a united Federal India developing in partnership with Britain
– this was due primarily to the war. A more brilliant statesman than
Linlithgow might conceivably have got Federation off the ground
while there was still time; but in the dark years when the Germans
and Japanese were approaching and Congress threatening to rebel,
such brilliance might not have been worth so much as Linlithgow's
courage and his monumental patience.

Wavell and Mountbatten

At times during the latter part of Linlithgow's long reign, he was spoken of as likely to be the last Viceroy. In a manner of speaking he was; for his two successors, Wavell and Mountbatten, reigned in abnormal times and were sent to India not so much as Viceroys as on special missions – Wavell to keep India's war effort going, Mountbatten to wind up the Raj. The two of them also differed from their predecessors in that Wavell was the only great soldier to become Viceroy – though Kitchener had been considered for the post and, at a later period, Haig – just as Mountbatten was the only Viceroy who was a great sailor, or for that matter a sailor of any description. Mountbatten was also alone among the Viceroys in being Royal.

As war heroes, Wavell and Mountbatten were the only two Viceroys – with the exception of John Lawrence – who were household names at the time of their appointment. Both had the quality of greatness and the special qualities necessary for a successful commander in war – energy, courage, leadership, the ability to think clearly, to make quick decisions, to inspire loyalty and affection in others and to get them to give of their best. Wavell and Mountbatten were also alike in being imaginative, in thinking for themselves and in possessing a strong streak of unconventionality.

In most other respects, the squat, rugged, dog-like Wavell, who showed every sign of his sixty-odd years, and the tall, glamorous, boyish Mountbatten were strikingly different. They differed in background – Wavell coming from an honourable if unspectacular line of soldiers and Mayors of Winchester, Mountbatten descended from half the Royal Houses of Europe – as well as in character. Wavell was silent, detached, modest and unassuming, totally lacking in the social graces; Mountbatten was a flamboyant extrovert who did not suffer from any undue modesty, could charm anybody and never feared to speak his mind. Wavell's interests, outside the profession of arms, were artistic and intellectual; he was fond of history, he loved poetry and was a poet himself; he compiled an anthology of his favourite verse entitled *Other Men's Flowers*. Mountbatten's tastes were less highbrow; he was a keen polo-player and had written a popular textbook on that game under the pseudonym of 'Marco'; he was also a film fan. When he was in New Delhi as Supreme Allied Commander at the beginning of Wavell's Viceroyalty, he had a private film show almost every night and was surprised to find that Wavell did not have one too – 'so much easier and quicker than reading a novel' he said; to which Wavell replied: 'But I seldom read novels'.[1]

Just as Mountbatten was stationed in New Delhi during the earlier part of Wavell's reign, so was Wavell there under Linlithgow as Commander-in-Chief; which makes him the only Viceroy to have been a Member of Council before his appointment to the Vice-royalty; that he had thereby acquired experience of Indian govern-ment was certainly taken into account by Churchill in choosing him as Linlithgow's successor. His experience of Indian government had, however, convinced him that he 'had no inclination or capacity for that sort of work';[2] he was not at all at home with politics or politicians. But when, during a protracted visit to England for consultations in the summer of 1943 he was summoned unexpectedly to Downing Street and offered the Viceroyalty, he felt bound to accept; for, as he wrote in his journal: 'One goes where one is told in time of war without making conditions or asking questions'.[3] He had reason to believe that the appointment, though it carried a peerage with it and was ostensibly a very great honour, was in actual fact a polite way of removing him from his military command; for Churchill, who had never liked him, blamed him unfairly for the failure of the operations in the Arakan province of Burma a few months earlier.

Before giving Churchill a definite answer, he asked leave to consult his wife; and thought, rather touchingly, of how 'she would obviously make an excellent Vicereine'.[4] Wavell and Lady Wavell – a large, humorous, motherly woman of Irish descent whose name was Eugenie but who was called Queenie by her husband – adored one another; although according to Wavell's somewhat unlikely friend, the aesthete and social butterfly 'Chips' Channon, he 'rarely listened to what she said'.[5] As Vicereine, she came well up to her husband's high expectations, except that, being rather vague, she was inclined to be unpunctual. 'D'you realise you're keeping half a sub-continent waiting?' Wavell once bellowed at her as she came late aboard the Viceregal Dakota in which they were about to take off for Calcutta. Her response to her husband's occasional outbursts was to exclaim in a manner at once plaintive and admonitory: 'Archie!'

Wavell made great use of his Dakota during the course of his Viceroyalty. He liked to see things for himself and would go at short notice to wherever he felt his presence was needed, just as he had done as an army commander, accompanied only by such Staff as his aircraft would hold. It was a change from Linlithgow's old-style Viceregal progresses 'in the long white Viceregal train with a retinue running into hundreds'.[6] In his very first week as Viceroy, Wavell made good Linlithgow's omission by flying to Calcutta to see the horrors of the Bengal famine at first hand. He went round the Calcutta streets by day to see how the destitutes were being fed and by night to see how they were sleeping; he interviewed Ministers, officials and non-officials in order that steps might be taken as quickly as possible to clear up the administrative mess. He was back in Bengal a few weeks later, in December 1943; not to spend Christmas at Belvedere, which was now a convalescent home; but to make a more extensive tour of the famine areas. He also walked five miles underground in a coal mine; for the shortage of coal was one of the problems he had to face, along with the shortage of food. These shortages were to occupy his mind a great deal; he ordered the Army to distribute supplies and he asked the Home Government for imports of grain. When this request was turned down, he sent a 'spirited riposte', backed by Mountbatten and the new Commander-in-Chief, Sir Claude Auchinleck, warning the Cabinet that there would be a large-scale disaster in India if imports were refused. Wavell eventually had his way, but only after a protracted struggle. It seemed to him, during his first year as Viceroy, that the Cabinet was taking every opportunity to thwart and snub him. 'His Majesty's Government must really give up trying to treat the Government of

In the abnormal circumstances of his reign, Wavell occasionally found time for some of the traditional Viceregal ceremonial. Here, he and Lady Wavell are seen receiving a Tibetan mission in the Durbar Hall of Viceroy's House in March 1946

India as a naughty and tiresome child whose bottom they can smack whenever they feel like it' he told Amery in the summer of 1944.[7]

'Be it ever so humble, there's no place like home' Wavell wrote in his journal on returning to Viceroy's House after his second visit to Bengal. Lutyens's palace kept much of its Viceregal splendour, though the Wavells endeavoured to make things as simple as possible, in accordance with the times. Owing to the constant flow of important visitors to wartime New Delhi, there were still the luncheon and dinner parties of fifty or a hundred; but although the new Viceroy and Vicereine were unable to cut down on the number of guests, they reduced the number of courses.

Curtailed though they were, the Viceroy's social duties constituted a daunting task for Wavell, with his proverbial inability to remember faces and his total lack of small talk. In addition, he suffered a little from deafness and had a glass eye, having lost an eye in the Great War; it was off-putting, to say the least, for his neighbour at luncheon or dinner to be subjected to his baleful one-eyed stare during one of his notorious silences. Mr. Philip Mason, who saw much of him at this time, maintains that his silences 'were of two kinds: professional and social'.[8] The former were deliberate; he would remain silent at interviews and conferences, often wandering about the room or engaged in some extraneous occupation, apparently not listening to what was being said; while in fact taking in every point. His social silences were a sign of his humility; he just could not imagine that anything he could think of saying would be of interest to whoever he was with; particularly so if he was in feminine company. To overcome this difficulty, he hit on the expedient of asking the lady next to him what she would choose to be in another life if she had to be an animal. If his companion was brave enough to start him on a topic that interested him, like poetry or biography, he could be quite talkative and often very amusing; for he had a great sense of humour. On car journeys, however, he preferred to be left alone with his thoughts; a cultured young ADC, who once tried to entertain him on a long drive by reciting a poem, was rewarded with an angry grunt.

Those who knew him well did not find Wavell's gruffness alarming; and they came to love him for what Channon called his 'gruff gentleness'.[9] When he smiled, his smile was delightful; he had a charm all of his own. His relations with his Staff were extremely good, particularly with his Private Secretary, Evan Jenkins, a Civilian as distinguished as those other Civilians who served the Viceroys from Curzon to Irwin in the same capacity. 'Jenks' acted as the Viceroy's mentor, giving him advice tempered with a dry wit. 'Not long enough or dull enough for a Viceroy' was his comment on the draft of one of Wavell's early speeches.[10]

Wavell's personality unfortunately did not get through to the

Indian politicians in the same way as it got through to his British associates. They recognised his integrity and his sense of purpose; but in other respects he remained an enigma to them. Because he was a soldier and had been responsible for putting down the Congress rebellion of 1942, they assumed that he was unsympathetic to Indian aspirations; whereas his views on India were progressive – as Churchill only discovered after appointing him. And apart from his own inclinations, he felt that Britain, having promised India self-government, could not in honour disregard her pledges, as Churchill seemed to have no compunction in doing. He was realist enough to know that the point had been reached where the British would either have to come to terms with Congress and the Muslim League, or else hold down India by force. Even if the latter course were feasible, he knew that it would not be tolerated by British or world opinion.

He was therefore convinced that the Indians would have to be given their independence at an early date after the war; though with this conviction went an almost Curzonian pessimism regarding their ability to govern themselves. It seemed to him that the Indian leaders had no real sense of nationhood; that only a few saw beyond their personal and sectarian interests. Yet for all his pessimism, Wavell continued to hope that a way could be found of giving India independence without partition. When addressing the Legislative Assembly for the first time early in 1944, he emphasised that India was a 'natural unit'. In the same speech, he appealed to Congress to renounce non-co-operation and the 'Quit India' movement and declared his intention of not releasing the leaders detained in 1942 until there was evidence that such a change of heart had taken place.[11]

In May of that year, Wavell's Government decided to release Gandhi even though he showed no change of heart; for the reason that his health was failing and it was deemed inexpedient that he should die in captivity – Wavell speculated as to whether, if that were to happen, he would himself be seen by future generations in the role of Pontius Pilate. Two months later, the Mahatma was still alive and Churchill sent 'a peevish telegram' to ask why he hadn't died yet.[12] At the same time, Gandhi demanded an interview with Wavell, who refused to see him so long as he remained obdurate; his refusal being backed unanimously by his almost wholly Indian Council. In this, Wavell took much the same line as Willingdon had taken in 1932; and indeed, his opinion of Gandhi was not so very different from Willingdon's. He would speak of him as 'malignant' and 'malevolent', as 'obstinate, domineering and double-tongued'; he once summed him up as fifteen per cent saint, fifteen per cent charlatan and seventy per cent extremely astute politician.[13] In judging him, Wavell could not forget that Gandhi had been responsible for the Quit India rebellion which had disrupted his communications with the Eastern Front when, as Commander-in-Chief, he was defending India against the Japanese.

If Gandhi did not see the Viceroy during the summer of 1944, he had talks with Jinnah; in which he went so far as to agree to the principle of a separate Pakistan while conceding far less territory than the Muslim leader was prepared to accept. The talks ended in a deadlock which Wavell decided could only be broken by a political move by the British. He proposed calling a conference of party leaders with a view to setting up an Interim Government at the Centre representing the major political groups; which would have the task of deciding on a constitution for India's independence. This plan was turned down by Amery, who put forward some remarkably unrealistic counter-proposals of his own; Wavell continued to press for something better and the Home Government continued to drag its feet. Now that victory was in sight, Churchill was no longer as anxious to placate American opinion as he had been at the time of the Cripps offer. With so much happening in Europe, he had lost interest in India; he was bored with Wavell's pesterings. In kicking Wavell upstairs to the Viceroyalty, he had fondly imagined that the Soldier-Viceroy would do little else but keep India quiet until the war was over; he now found he had got more than he had bargained for.

In the autumn of 1944 Wavell appealed directly to Churchill, who agreed that he should fly home to discuss his proposals with the Cabinet. But the Home Government put off these discussions and only on Wavell's insistence consented to see him at the end of March 1945. He was then kept hanging about London for over two months before the Government came to a decision – though he had the consolation of being able to go to a few Shakespeare plays – and complained in his journal that the Cabinet Ministers treated him 'as an Untouchable in the presence of Brahmins'. In the end, Churchill gave him more or less what he wanted; for the reason, as he afterwards admitted to him, that he was sure it would fail.

Wavell's proposals were received without much enthusiasm by his colleagues in Council, who nevertheless supported him in carrying them out. As a preliminary to the conference of leaders, Nehru and the other members of the Congress Working Committee were released from detention. Wavell also saw Gandhi, whom he had never met before; he found him in a reasonably helpful mood.

The conference took place in late June and early July at Simla, where Wavell only went for short visits and not for the whole summer as previous Viceroys had done. Though Gandhi and Nehru were both in Simla at the time, they preferred to stay on the sidelines rather than attend the conference itself. At the conference, therefore, Jinnah was the lion; the only personage of his standing on the

Congress side was C.R. Rajagopalachari. Surveying the delegates, Wavell concluded that most of them were 'poor stuff' and wrote gloomily in his journal: 'If we can build a self-governing India on this sort of material, we shall have emulated the legendary rope-trick'.[14] The conference failed, on account of Jinnah's intransigence; Wavell magnanimously took the blame for its failure, since it was his idea in the first place. In fact the Simla Conference, though it failed, has been described as in some ways 'the greatest achievement of Wavell's Viceroyalty'.[15] That it took place at all was a triumph, particularly as he managed to get it going in an atmosphere of goodwill. 'So my efforts to bring better understanding between the parties have failed and have shown how wide is the gulf' Wavell wrote sadly after the final session. To cheer him, there was a letter from Ahmed Jan, who had been his *munshi* when he was in India forty years earlier as a subaltern; condemning all politicians and adjuring him 'to use the big stick to both Congress and League'.[16]

The failure of the Simla Conference was followed in quick succession by the Labour landslide in Britain and the ending of the war with Japan a year sooner than expected. 'Now for the horrors of peace' Wavell commented drily when Japan surrendered. He had hoped to get his Interim Government going while he still had the war as an excuse for overruling his Ministers if they ran into difficulties; but thanks to the atom bomb and Churchill's delaying tactics this was not to be. Now that the war was over, the Indian politicians were less inclined than ever to be kept waiting for their independence; and while the Simla Conference had served to convince the more reasonable of them that Wavell was sincere and meant business, the Congress extremists were spoiling for a fight. During the autumn of 1945 and the following winter, Nehru and his colleagues took the opportunity afforded by the trial of some of the officers of the so-called Indian National Army – a quisling force recruited by the Japanese from among Indian prisoners of war – to arouse popular feeling against the Government. By November, Wavell believed that Congress was all set for another Quit India rebellion.

That first cold weather of peace was a worrying time for Wavell; there were threatened strikes and the threat of famine in the South; there were riots in Calcutta and Delhi and mutinies in some of the ships of the Royal Indian Navy. India was in the throes of elections, the results of which showed an ominous increase in the strength of the Muslim League. In the midst of his troubles, Wavell lost the services of the invaluable 'Jenks', who left him to become Governor of the Punjab; fortunately his new Private Secretary, George Abell, was a Civilian of Jenkin's calibre. On top of everything else came the shock of the death in a motor accident of the Wavells' son-in-law, the husband of their third and youngest daughter. This was not the only anxiety the Wavells suffered on account of their children during the course of their reign; in 1944 their son, Archie John, was severely wounded in Burma, losing a hand.

During the early months of 1946, the danger of a Congress rising grew less, at any rate for the time being. Counsels of moderation prevailed in the Congress leadership; Nehru was cured of his sympathy for the Indian National Army by a visit to Malaya, where he had his first meeting with Mountbatten; who told him that these men 'were not politically conscious heroes fighting for their country but cowards and traitors who betrayed their loyal friends'.[17] Meanwhile the Labour Government was planning to send out three Cabinet Ministers to India to negotiate a settlement directly with the Indian political leaders. Although he had doubts as to the wisdom of this plan, Wavell found it a change for the better to be serving under a Government even more in a hurry than he was to solve the Indian problem. It was clear to him, however, from the talks he had with Attlee and his colleagues when he went to London for consultations soon after they came into power, that their hurry had more to do with placating opinion in the Labour Party and in America than with the good of India. Wavell also had misgivings about Cripps, who was deeply committed to the Congress point of view and wielded far more power than the new Secretary of State, Lord Pethick-Lawrence. It seemed all too likely that under his influence the Cabinet would favour a solution acceptable to Congress but not to the Muslim League.

The Cabinet Mission, which arrived in New Delhi at the end of March, consisted of Cripps, Pethick-Lawrence and A.V. Alexander. Wavell did not entirely trust Cripps, his fellow-Wykehamist; but he liked Alexander, whom he described as 'the very best type of British Labour'. The aged pacifist and one-time champion of the militant suffragettes, Pethick-Lawrence, who looked for all the world like Gandhi in a suit, Wavell found amiable enough; though vain, obstinate and long-winded. Wavell was associated with the 'three Magi', as he called them, in the negotiations, which dragged on until the end of June. In their seemingly impossible task of getting Congress, which wanted a united India, and the Muslim League, which insisted on a separate Pakistan, to agree to a constitutional settlement, the Ministers started with the disadvantage of having brought no real plan with them. Eventually, on Wavell's recommendation, they offered Jinnah the choice between a small but completely independent Pakistan and a larger Pakistan enjoying autonomy within an Indian union. Both Jinnah and Congress accepted the second proposal as a basis for negotiations, and they sent delegates to a conference held at Simla in May to discuss it. This second Simla Conference fared no better than the first; and so Wavell

Wavell with the Cabinet
Mission, Viceroy's House,
New Delhi, 1946. Sir
Stafford Cripps and Lord
Pethick-Lawrence sit at the
table on the Viceroy's
right; A.V. Alexander sits
on his left

and the three Ministers went back down to the heat of New Delhi to
continue the discussions. By the end of June it seemed that some sort
of agreement had been reached; but then Gandhi threw a final
spanner into the works.

Throughout the negotiations, Cripps maintained unofficial con-
tacts with Congress, which naturally aroused the suspicions of
Jinnah and the League. Wavell felt he had been put in an impossible
position by this double-dealing and came near to resigning. Cripps
did not even bother to say goodbye to him when he left, so little was
the love lost between them by that stage. It was a relief to Wavell to
see the last of the Cabinet Mission; even Alexander had begun to get
on the unmusical Viceroy's nerves with his habit of playing the piano
after dinner until the small hours, singing his way solo through a
repertoire that consisted of music-hall ditties such as *Lady of Laguna*
and *My Old Dutch*, interspersed with revivalist hymns. Exhausted
and dispirited though he was by those weeks of windy argument,
Wavell's sense of humour did not desert him. Shortly before the
Mission departed, he picked up *Alice Through the Looking Glass* and
wrote a parody entitled 'Jabber-Weeks, from Phlawrence through
the Indian Ink':

Beware the Gandhiji, my son,
The satyagraha, the bogy fast,
Beware the Djinnarit, and shun
The frustrious scheduled caste.[18]

For all its frustrations, the Cabinet Mission had at least produced the plan for an Indian union which Jinnah had accepted and to which Congress had come near enough to agreeing for there to be hope that it might yet be acceptable to both sides. While the Mission was still in New Delhi, Wavell had produced what he called his Breakdown Plan, to be employed if the Mission's plan was not accepted; according to which the British would withdraw immediately from the southern part of the country, where there was not much communal problem; but remain in the North for a further though strictly limited period – the date he fixed for the final evacuation being March 1948. This early deadline was necessary not only to spur on the Indians to settling their differences, but because the administrative machine of the Raj was running down and could not last much longer – no British had been recruited into the Civil Service since 1939. Whether or not the Breakdown Plan would have worked – Wavell himself nicknamed it Operation Madhouse – it might have served as a lever to induce Congress to accept the plan which the Muslim League had agreed with the Mission, which was in fact Wavell's chief reason for proposing it. The question of getting Congress to agree became academic after the end of July, when Jinnah went back on his earlier acceptance of the Mission's plan.

After the Mission had left, Wavell set to work to form an Interim Government. At first, neither Congress nor the League would agree to join it except on terms unacceptable to the Viceroy. Then Wavell compromised with Congress with the result that, at the beginning of September, a Government took office which included Nehru, Rajagopalachari and Vallabhbhai Patel – a brother of Irwin's old sparring partner. Of his Congress Ministers, Patel – a practical realist like the Viceroy himself – was the one Wavell most respected and got on with best; he regarded him as more of a leader than the others. Nehru he found likeable enough, but doctrinaire and lacking in balance. From now on, some of the Congress leaders came to luncheon and dinner at Viceroy's House, having hitherto refused to accept Viceregal hospitality. Out of deference to them, the menu on those occasions was exclusively vegetarian.

Shortly before the Interim Government took office, the Muslim League had announced a departure from constitutional methods and held what they called a Direct Action Day. The day passed off without any serious disturbances except in Calcutta, where it caused a three-day holocaust in which some 20,000 people were either killed or seriously injured – what came to be known as the Great Calcutta Killing, the start of a new and horrible chapter of communal violence. Having flown to Calcutta to see its horrors for himself, Wavell became more than ever determined to get the League into his Government; and after another six weeks of complicated negotiations, he appeared to have worked the miracle. The League nominated five Ministers and Congress agreed to stay with them in a coalition; Jinnah himself preferred not to be of their number, but they included one of his principal lieutenants, Liaquat Ali Khan, for whom Wavell had a high regard. On the face of it, the establishment of a Government drawn from both Congress and the Muslim League marked a great step forward; but the situation was not as hopeful as it seemed. Against a background of recurring communal violence, the coalition which Wavell had cobbled together with such difficulty was constantly in danger of falling apart. 'It is all very wearing' he wrote at the end of October. 'For almost the first time in my life I am really beginning to feel the strain badly – not sleeping properly and letting these wretched people worry me. However, some courage and a sense of humour usually returns with the morning ride and carries me through the day.'[19]

In December Wavell went to London once again and tried to persuade the British Government to adopt the Breakdown Plan. In particular he insisted that a definite date for the ending of the Raj should be announced forthwith. By the time he left it seemed that Attlee and his colleagues were going to give him what he wanted; but he had not been back in India long before they changed their mind. 'So ends 1946, the most gruelling year I have ever had, and I think in some ways the most unhappy' Wavell wrote on New Year's Eve; and he did not look forward to 1947 with much confidence.[20] January saw the Muslim League more determined than ever in its rejection of the Mission's plan; and then, at the beginning of February, a letter came from Attlee dismissing the Viceroy at a month's notice. 'Not very courteously done' was Wavell's comment;[21] and indeed it was the way in which he was dismissed rather than the actual dismissal that was to be deplored. The time had come when a Viceroy of exceptional vigour and with remarkable powers of persuasion was needed to get the Indian leaders to agree; Wavell was becoming stale and his health was suffering through overwork; and as he was notoriously inarticulate, persuasion was not one of his strong points. There were other less creditable, though understandable reasons why Attlee and his colleagues might have wished to get rid of him; there was the mutual antipathy of Wavell and Cripps; and it also seems that Wavell antagonised the Labour Ministers by speaking to them roughly when he was in London in December 1946.

Since Wavell had been given to understand by Churchill that he had not been appointed for the customary five years but would probably be replaced soon after the war came to an end, the Government did not need to wait for an excuse to remove him; in fact, a few months before his dismissal, he had actually asked when he would be expected to go. Attlee offered Mountbatten the

Viceroyalty in December, when Wavell was actually in London; but instead of informing him of this, he preferred to keep him in the dark and gave him the impression that he agreed to the Breakdown Plan. Then, after Wavell had returned to India, he wrote him a curt letter of dismissal, giving him only a month in which to wind up the affairs of his Viceroyalty. He did, however, make some small acknowledgement of Wavell's services and offered to recommend him for an Earldom, which in the event Wavell did not live long to enjoy, for he died three years later. The Wavell peerage was itself short-lived; for the Viceroy's only son, Archie John, was killed in action in Kenya in 1953, while as yet unmarried. Lady Wavell is still alive at the time of writing; the last surviving Vicereine, she has, like several Vicereines before her, lived into her nineties.

Gandhi and Lord Pethick-Lawrence

An episode early in Wavell's Viceroyalty illustrates the difference between his approach and Mountbatten's. Wavell wanted to meet Gandhi, but was refused permission to do so by Amery. Mountbatten, when he heard about this, was astonished that the Viceroy should have asked permission; and told him: 'If you had seen Gandhi and then telegraphed a report of your meeting they could hardly have sacked you'.[22]

As Viceroy, Mountbatten did not have to fall back on such tactics; since he made it a condition for accepting the post that he should be given plenary powers. 'How could I possibly negotiate with the Cabinet breathing down my neck?' he demanded of Attlee and Cripps, when they told him that what he asked for was quite without precedent. 'But you are asking to be above the Secretary of State!' Cripps exclaimed, to which Mountbatten replied laconically: 'Exactly'. Mountbatten doubted if he would get his way over this, but in the end he did. Soon after his arrival in India, Nehru asked him 'Have you by some miracle got plenipotentiary powers?' 'Suppose I

The soldier and the sailor meet: Wavell with Mountbatten at Viceroy's House before his departure

have' said Mountbatten, 'what difference would it make?' 'Why then' replied Nehru, 'you will succeed where all others have failed.'[23]

Another of Mountbatten's conditions for accepting the Viceroyalty was that there should be a deadline for the handing over of power. This was just what Wavell had been urging without success; and indeed, the date for which Mountbatten and the Cabinet now settled, June 1948, was the date Wavell had advocated in the previous December. Mountbatten always maintained that he had been in complete agreement with Wavell's policy, at any rate up to June 1946, which was the last time the two of them met in India before Mountbatten arrived as Viceroy-designate. He also showed his confidence in Wavell's judgement by taking over his entire Staff; Abell continued as Private Secretary. To the existing Staff, however, he added a team brought out with him from England, including Churchill's wartime military adviser, Lord Ismay; he also brought out a Press Attaché, a functionary hitherto unknown at Viceroy's House.

In dictating his terms, Mountbatten rather hoped that the Government would not agree to them, which would have enabled him to refuse the Viceroyalty with a clear conscience. His ambitions were centred entirely on his naval career; he hoped to become First Sea Lord to vindicate the memory of his father, who had been driven from that post by the anti-German hysteria of 1914 on account of his German Royal birth; though he was a naturalised British subject and had served with loyalty and distinction in the British Navy for almost half a century. But although to be First Sea Lord was Mountbatten's chief object in life, he wished to be successful in everything he undertook; and in seeking success he was, as Mr. Kenneth Rose puts it, 'untrammelled by diffidence'. In this respect, he resembled Curzon; and like Curzon he scorned what Mr. Rose calls 'that amateurishness which is the passport to every Establishment heart'.[24]

There are a number of similarities between Mountbatten and Curzon, the Viceroy who ended the Raj and the Viceroy who, more than any of the others, sought to perpetuate it. They both could at times be rash; in Mountbatten's case.'this was a reflection alike of his courage and of his incurable optimism'.[25] They both had a streak of vanity and they both could be ruthless. Both brought a superhuman energy to their task; Mountbatten was more fortunate in this respect than Curzon in enjoying excellent health and in knowing that he would only have to keep up the tremendous pressure of work for just over a year at the longest. Both looked absurdly young; though whereas Curzon was thirty-nine when he became Viceroy, Mountbatten was forty-six. They were also alike in being both married to rich and glamorous wives.

Edwina Mountbatten had not only inherited the fortune of her maternal grandfather, the financier Sir Ernest Cassel, but also the estates of the Victorian Prime Minister Palmerston, to whom her father's family was connected; she owned Broadlands, Palmerston's elegant Hampshire seat – situated, incidentally, not far from Winchester, where Wavell had his roots. The fact that, with all her wealth, she was known to be of socialistic views, inevitably made her suspect in the eyes of British-Indian diehards; just as she was suspect in similar circles at home. Mountbatten, too, had a reputation for being more than a bit of a radical. This reputation was naturally exaggerated on account of his having been made Viceroy by the Labour Government; whereas his personal politics had little or nothing to do with his appointment and it actually seems that he was considered as a possible successor to Linlithgow by the staunchly Conservative Amery.

Such hostility as the political reputation of the new Viceroy and Vicereine might have aroused among stalwarts of the Raj was offset by Mountbatten's Royal blood – he was, after all, a great-grandson of Queen Victoria and a second cousin of the King-Emperor. And whatever their politics, the Mountbattens were Viceregal to the manner born. At his swearing-in ceremony – the last great function to be held in the Durbar Hall of Viceroy's House while the Raj was still in being – they looked superb as they sat side by side on their thrones of crimson and gold; he in light blue Star of India robes with his dark blue Garter ribbon and a galaxy of orders and decorations across his chest; she in a dress of ivory brocade with the blue and white ribbon of the Crown of India and a number of other decorations and war medals acquired through her work for the St. John Ambulance Brigade. As well as being the last occasion of its kind, it was the first and only one to be filmed; the Durbar Hall had never before known the whirr of the ciné-camera and the flash of the flash-bulb. It was likewise unprecedented for the Viceregal thrones to be flanked by the leaders of the new India; Nehru was there and so was Liaquat Ali Khan. Yet another unusual feature of the ceremony was that Mountbatten followed the example of Lytton and made a speech; in which he began by referring to the Government's resolve to transfer power by June 1948; adding that since many administrative questions had to be settled before power could be transferred, this in effect meant that a solution had to be reached 'within the next few months'.

While he did not commit himself to a more exact time-limit in his speech, he had already made up his mind that six months was the maximum time available for reaching a solution. Having arrived in India towards the end of March he therefore had until the end of September – the months when New Delhi is at its hottest – in which

Lord and Lady
Mountbatten on the
Viceregal thrones in the
Durbar Hall of Viceroy's
House

to produce a plan acceptable to the major parties. The Home
Government had stipulated that he should if possible preserve
India's unity; and to this end the Cabinet Mission's plan was to be
given first consideration.

Mountbatten hoped to talk the Indian leaders into agreement by
meeting them individually; a method to which he was particularly
well suited with his charm, his diplomacy and his personal touch.
With the more important leaders, he was in no hurry to get down to
business; but devoted the earlier meetings simply to getting to know
them. He lost no time in making the acquaintance of Gandhi and
Jinnah; Nehru he had already met in Malaya a year earlier. He had

his first meeting with Gandhi a week after his swearing-in; he saw him again the next day and on the day after that there was the astonishing spectacle of Viceroy and Mahatma having breakfast *à deux* on the terrace overlooking the Mogul Garden. Mountbatten was sensible enough not to treat Gandhi as a negotiator, but simply as 'a friendly if baffling personality to be cultivated, listened to and kept sweet'.[26]

Jinnah, as might be expected, proved tougher going. 'My God, he was cold' Mountbatten said after meeting him for the first time;[27] and having originally planned for him and his sister to come to dinner that evening, he had them put off to the evening of the following day; feeling that once in twenty-four hours was the most of Jinnah that he could take. Far from being won over by the confident and outgoing Mountbatten charm, the Muslim leader was, if anything, repelled by it: 'I drove the old gentleman quite mad' Mountbatten wrote after one of his meetings with him, not without a certain schoolboyish pride. It was simply that the two of them were temperamentally incompatible; but it gave Mountbatten a sense of failure; for he recognised that Jinnah was, as he put it, 'the man who held the key to the whole situation'.[28] Being as he was over-sensitive to criticism and to praise, his attitude towards the Muslim leader inevitably came to be influenced a little by the knowledge that Jinnah did not like him; just as the fact that Nehru regarded him with feelings akin to hero-worship could not but prejudice him a little in the Congress leader's favour.

When they met for the first time in Malaya, Mountbatten and Nehru had taken an instant liking to one another; now, an

Gandhi breakfasting with Mountbatten at Viceroy's House, April 1947

affectionate friendship grew up between them in which Edwina Mountbatten also had a part. Unlike Wavell, both the Mountbattens were able to get through to Nehru, who was basically shy and a little unsure of himself. He was also inclined to be lonely, though he was constantly surrounded by people; and as a widower, he craved feminine sympathy which the Vicereine was able to provide. Edwina Mountbatten was a tremendous help to her husband in his relations with the Indian leaders; she loved India and the Indians as much as he did and was able without the slightest effort to break down the barriers of race, caste and creed. As well as adding her charm to his in dealing with the leaders themselves, she made friends with their wives, daughters and sisters. At the same time as she helped her husband in this way, she became deeply involved in social work, particularly to do with the welfare of Indian women. And she had been Vicereine for little more than a month when she started that other work for which she is now chiefly remembered, of bringing relief to victims of communal violence; going off by herself on an adventurous tour of riot-stricken areas in the Punjab.

Mountbatten's talks with the leaders convinced him that there was virtually no hope of a solution which would keep India intact – he might have been more hopeful had he known that Jinnah was in the last stages of tuberculosis. With the communal situation fast deteriorating so that there was a very real danger of civil war, he deemed it 'impossible to exaggerate the need for speed'.[29] Accordingly, at the end of April, a draft plan was produced enabling provinces to secede on the decision of their Legislatures. Having been approved in principle by Nehru, it was taken to London by Ismay for the approval of the Cabinet; the Cabinet returned the draft to India with some amendments which did not appear to be of much consequence. After inviting the political leaders to meet him a week later in order that he might secure their acceptance of the amended draft, Mountbatten had what he called 'an absolute hunch' that he should first of all show it to Nehru, who turned it down. Mountbatten was thankful for his hunch. 'We would have looked complete fools with the Government at home' he said ruefully, 'having led them up the garden to believe that Nehru would accept the Plan.'[30] As it was, Nehru's rejection could be kept quiet and an excuse found for postponing the meeting of leaders while the Plan was revised yet again. This time, the Reforms Commissioner, V.P. Menon* – a remarkable man who acted as a link between successive Viceroys and the political leaders – hit upon a solution; which was to hand over power as soon as possible to two Dominions. Dominion Status had been India's constitutional destiny ever since Irwin's

*not to be confused with Nehru's close friend, Krishna Menon

declaration of 1929; but more recently Congress had resolved that India should become an independent sovereign republic. Partition was therefore seen as the setting up of two separate republics, or of a republic and a Dominion, with all the complications and potential dangers which that implied. But if India and Pakistan were both Dominions, they would not be so widely separated; for in those days the British Commonwealth was a closer association than what it is now.

The Plan, revised in accordance with Menon's simple yet none the less brilliant suggestion, was taken to London by Mountbatten himself; he arrived back with it, duly approved, on the last day of May. Two days later, the leaders met in his study at Viceroy's House. Nehru accepted the Plan on behalf of Congress; Jinnah, autocrat though he was, argued that he could not give a definite answer without consulting his followers. Mountbatten gave him till midnight in which to do so; he returned at the appointed hour to say that he needed more time. To this the Viceroy replied firmly that he would tell the meeting next morning that the Muslim leader had given him the necessary assurances. He insisted that Jinnah should on no account contradict this statement, but should nod his head in acquiescence – he clearly felt it would be asking too much of him to expect him to say 'Yes'. At next day's meeting, Jinnah duly nodded; and in answer to a subsequent question of Mountbatten's a 'Yes' was actually forthcoming – though the Plan only gave him the small 'moth-eaten' Pakistan, as he himself had called it, which Wavell and the Cabinet Mission had offered him in the previous year.

Mountbatten had triumphed; though there were still innumerable problems and it was all too likely that one side or both might yet have second thoughts. He announced his success to the newspaper correspondents of India and the world at a Press Conference – the first time a Press Conference had ever been held by a Viceroy – at which he also disclosed, as if by accident, that the date of the transfer of power would be 15 August. There was every reason for choosing so early a date; not only was it extremely unlikely that the Interim Government would be able to carry on for much longer, but with every day that passed the chances of the settlement being wrecked by some fearful communal outbreak or other crisis were ever greater. Nevertheless, ten weeks afforded precious little time for winding up the Raj and bringing the two new Dominions into being. For Mountbatten, as for his Staff and officials, it meant ten weeks of frenzied activity. As a reminder of how little time there was, he devised his celebrated tear-off calendar; which had printed under each day's date in large figures the number of days left to prepare for the transfer of power.

One of the chief problems still to be solved was that of the future of

4 AUGUST 1947

11

DAYS LEFT TO PREPARE

FOR

TRANSFER OF POWER

Eleven days left to prepare for the transfer of power

the Princely States. With the transfer of power, the paramountcy of the British Crown would automatically lapse and the Rulers would become independent sovereigns; but the chances of the States being able to survive for long before being swallowed up by one of the new Dominions were pretty slender; whatever might have been held to the contrary by some of the Princes themselves and by certain romantics on the British side. Mountbatten did his best to ensure that if the Princes agreed to join one or other Dominion they would be treated generously. This involved him in a battle with Nehru, who had much more to do with the matter than Jinnah; since the vast majority of States were geographically part of the new India rather than of Pakistan. Eventually, through the good offices of Patel, who was put in charge of the newly-established States Department, it was agreed that the Princes who joined India would be allowed to keep most of the powers which they had enjoyed under the Raj. By 15 August, thanks largely to Mountbatten's persuasion, there were only three States that had not yet come into line; though these included the two most important of all, Hyderabad and Kashmir.

Persuading the Princes was a task for which the polo-playing Royal Viceroy was uniquely qualified; many of the more important Ruling Chiefs were old friends of his; most of the others liked and trusted him on account of his Royal connections. He was able to tell them how his own family had fared perfectly well after their Grand Duchy of Hesse had become part of the German Empire in 1871. He might have known that democratic politicans are less inclined than Emperors to keep their word; yet he can hardly be held responsible for the subsequent treatment of the Princes by Nehru and his daughter Indira. Given the climate of the times, he did the most he could for them; one doubts whether any other Viceroy would have done as much. The more usual British attitude towards the Princes was that by failing to agree to Federation before the war they had made their bed and must lie on it. Among the few high officials who thought otherwise was Sir Conrad Corfield, the last head of the Political Department which under the old dispensation looked after the States. When winding up his Department, this staunch friend of the Princes made a bonfire of files containing incriminating material on their private lives, past and present. Nehru claimed that these papers belonged to the Government about to take over and complained to Mountbatten; whose reaction was typical. 'I will not stop you burning papers' he told Corfield, 'but don't do it so obviously.'[31]

In agreeing to come into the new India, the Princes were encouraged by the thought that Mountbatten would almost certainly be staying on as a constitutional Governor-General for some months after the transfer of power. The original idea was that he should be Governor-General of Pakistan as well as of India and in that capacity supervise the putting into effect of Partition; but whereas the Congress leaders were anxious to have him as their first Governor-General, the Governor-Generalship of Pakistan was eventually earmarked by Jinnah for himself. Mountbatten wondered whether, in that case, he would be wise to stay on in India; but Ismay, whom he sent home to sound out opinion, reported that not only the Cabinet but also Churchill and other leading members of the Conservative Opposition – including the former Irwin, now Halifax – all felt strongly that he should stay.

The Mountbattens' last official duty as Viceroy and Vicereine was to fly to Karachi to convey greetings to the new Dominion of Pakistan on 14 August, the eve of Independence. Mountbatten and Jinnah drove together in state, ignoring the threat of a bomb which in the event never materialised. Late in the evening of that same day the Indian Constituent Assembly met in New Delhi and on the stroke of midnight took over as the Legislative Assembly of an independent India; this particular hour having been chosen because the astrologers, who through an oversight had only been consulted at the last minute, had pronounced 15 August inauspicious. At the moment when the Raj ended and he ceased to be Viceroy, Mountbatten, back from Karachi, sat waiting in his study for Nehru and the Congress elder statesman Rajendra Prasad, who were about to call on him with the formal invitation to become Governor-General. Next morning, in the Durbar Hall of what was henceforth known as Government House – the name by which Lutyens's palace had been known up to the time of its completion – Mountbatten was sworn-in as Governor-General in a ceremony remarkably similar to that of the previous March. There followed a day of celebrations with drives in the State carriage through tumultous crowds shouting 'Mountbatten Ki Jai' and even 'Pandit Mountbatten' as well as the more usual 'Jai Hind'. At home, the Prime Minister acknowledged Mountbatten's achievement by recommending him for an Earldom; which, since he had no son, was destined to pass by special remainder to his elder daughter.

Mountbatten's settlement left much to be desired, as subsequent events were, all too tragically, to prove; yet one doubts very much if Wavell, or any other Viceroy, could at that late hour have done better. To be set against the horrors of Partition is the fact that India and Pakistan both stayed in the Commonwealth; and, more important, the atmosphere of mutual goodwill in which Britain handed over power to the people of her Indian Empire. The ties of friendship which are the most enduring legacy of the Raj might well have been broken for ever by the manner of its ending; instead, the tradition of Canning, Mayo and Ripon, which Minto and Irwin had revived, was maintained up to the very end by Mountbatten.

The months when Mountbatten was Governor-General of an independent India constitute a remarkable epilogue to the history of the Viceroys. They were months of continual crisis; relations between India and Pakistan were at breaking-point even before the cheers of Independence Day had died away. In the now-divided Punjab, the communities were fighting and massacring each other with a ferocity worse than anything that even the gloomiest prophets of doom had foretold. The migration of refugees southwards across the boundary line between the two new Dominions grew into an overwhelming flood; Edwina Mountbatten redoubled her efforts to bring some relief to their sufferings; but it was a task beyond human endeavour. By the beginning of September, with rioting in Delhi and half a million refugees advancing on the capital, which was perilously close to the fighting, the situation was getting out of control. And so it was that, only three weeks after Mountbatten had handed over his powers with such good grace to the new India and become a constitutional figurehead, the new India begged him to take charge again. Since it would have been politically more than he was worth for Nehru himself to go cap in hand to the former British Viceroy, the initiative was taken by the admirable V.P. Menon; who telephoned Mountbatten at Simla, where he was resting after the exertions of the past few months, and asked him to return immediately to Delhi; knowing that this was what Nehru and also Patel wanted.

With the power once again in his hands, Mountbatten lost no time in getting things straightened out; bypassing the political Ministers and dealing directly with Heads of Departments. To one of the latter who lamented that there were no trains, or aircraft, or whatever it was he was asked to provide, Mountbatten said, 'You jolly well go and get some and you mustn't eat or drink or sleep till you do so'. [32] Government House became rather like the operations room of his wartime headquarters; a Military Emergency Staff was set up under one of the ablest of his divisional commanders in the Burma campaign, Major-General 'Pete' Rees; to whom the Mountbatten's younger daughter Pamela acted as personal assistant. Since a shortage of food was one of the prime causes of the emergency, Edwina Mountbatten put Government House on to austerity rations. When, towards the middle of September, Lord Listowel, who had been the last Secretary of State, came to stay accompanied by that pillar of the Linlithgow regime, Sir Gilbert Laithwaite, they dined with Viceregal ceremony on Spam and potato.

From the autumn of 1947 until the end of Mountbatten's reign, India and Pakistan were on the brink of war over Kashmir; where a predominantly Muslim population was ruled by a Hindu Maharaja. Having hesitated for some months between the two Dominions, the Maharaja hurriedly threw in his lot with India at the end of October, after his country had been invaded by tribesmen from the North-West Frontier. India then flew in troops to his aid, which Pakistan saw as part of a plot to annex a predominantly Muslim State. Mountbatten was alleged to have aided and abetted this plot and to have been actually in command of the military operation; but while it is true that he was in effect acting as India's war minister, the idea that he played a tactical role is disproved by the fact that when the fighting was at its height, he was in London attending the marriage of his nephew to the future Queen Elizabeth II. And far from plotting to bring Kashmir into the Indian fold, the evidence shows that, on the contrary, Mountbatten tried to persuade the Maharaja to follow the wishes of his Muslim subjects.

When the Mountbattens returned from England at the end of November, having not been at all happy about being away from India at such a time, the situation seemed a little less tense. And then, early in the New Year, came the murder of Gandhi. As Mountbatten arrived on the scene, somebody said to him: 'It was a Muslim who did it'. Mountbatten instantly replied: 'You fool, don't you know it was a Hindu?' [33] When he said this, he had no idea as to whether it was true or not; but he felt that by saying it he might have prevented a riot; and that if the assassin turned out to have been a Muslim, his falsehood would be overlooked in the general holocaust. Fortunately for India, Mountbatten's wishful thinking proved correct. Next day, the Mahatma's long association with Viceroys, which had begun auspiciously with his praise of Curzon and more recently fluctuated between bouts of imprisonment and breakfast at Viceroy's House, ended with the last Viceroy and Vicereine, their two daughters and their son-in-law, sitting on the dusty ground beside his funeral pyre.

A month after Gandhi's death, the country seemed to have calmed down sufficiently for the Mountbattens to go on tour. They visited Burma, where Mountbatten handed back the throne of King Thibaw which had been taken to Calcutta in the time of Dufferin. They went to Kapurthala in the Punjab, where the old beau of a Maharaja referred to them absent-mindedly in his speech as 'Lord and Lady Willingdon'. They went to Cochin in the far South where another ancient Maharaja asked Mountbatten if he had ever met Stalin. When they returned to New Delhi, a crisis was boiling up over Hyderabad. Here the situation was the opposite to what it was in Kashmir; a predominantly Hindu population was ruled by a Muslim, the Nizam, who clung to his independence despite increasing pressure on him to join India, which completely surrounded his kingdom. Mountbatten had tried to persuade him to come to terms with India while the going was still good, rather than risking a war in which his troops would be no match for the Indian Army. The Nizam remained obdurate; but Mountbatten, as he told Patel, continued to hope for a peaceful settlement with him for the sake of India's good name. He was therefore dismayed, when he returned from Burma, to find that in his absence a plan had been prepared for a military invasion of the Nizam's dominions; which 'to add insult to injury' had been named 'Operation Polo' – though not with any deliberate intention of foisting its authorship on to the polo-playing Governor-General. [34] 'Operation Polo' was not, however, implemented until after Mountbatten had left India; when, as he and almost everybody else had foreseen, it proved a walk-over.

Mountbatten's time as Governor-General ended on 21 June 1948, when he handed over to Rajagopalachari, who was to be his successor. On the day before they left, he and Edwina went to receive a farewell address from the Delhi Municipality. They were mobbed and cheered as they drove through the streets of the old city; and, as a demonstration of love and gratitude, a crowd estimated at half a million had gathered on the open space by the Jumna where

Gandhi's pyre had been. In his speech at the State banquet that evening, Nehru turned to Edwina and said: 'Wherever you have gone you have brought solace, hope and encouragement. Is it surprising therefore that the people of India should love you?' Next day, as the Mountbattens drove out of the forecourt of Government House in the State carriage on their way to the airport, the colonnades of Lutyens's palace were thronged with people eager to catch a final glimpse of them. All in all, it was a worthy send-off for the last Viceroy and Vicereine.

Lord and Lady Mountbatten driving away from the palace at New Delhi on their way to the airport, 21 June 1948

Select bibliography

BENCE-JONES, MARK: *Palaces of the Raj*, London 1973.

BIRKENHEAD, EARL OF: *Halifax*, London 1965.

BLUNT, WILFRED SCAWEN: *India under Ripon, a Private Diary*, London 1909.

BROWN, JUDITH M.: *Gandhi and Civil Disobedience*, Cambridge 1977.

BUCHAN, JOHN: *Lord Minto*, London 1924.

BUCK, EDWARD J.: *Simla, Past and Present*, Bombay 1925.

BURNE, SIR OWEN: *Memories*, London 1907.

BUTLER, IRIS: *The Eldest Brother*, London 1973.

—: *The Viceroy's Wife*, London 1969.

CAMPBELL-JOHNSON, ALAN: *Mission with Mountbatten*, New York 1953.

COATMAN, JOHN: *India, The Road to Self-Government*, London 1941.

COATMAN, JOHN: *Years of Destiny*, London 1932.

COTTON, SIR HENRY: *Indian and Home Memories*, London 1911.

CURZON OF KEDLESTON, MARQUESS: *British Government in India*, 2 vols, London 1925.

DILKS, DAVID: *Curzon in India*, 2 vols, London 1969–70.

DUFFERIN AND AVA, MARCHIONESS OF: *Our Viceregal Life in India*, London 1890.

DURAND, SIR MORTIMER: *Alfred Lyall*, London 1913.

ELGIN, JAMES, 8TH EARL OF: *Letters and Journals* (ed Theodore Walrond), London 1872.

GILBERT, MARTIN: *Servant of India*, London 1966.

GLENDEVON, JOHN: *The Viceroy at Bay*, London 1971.

GOPAL, S.: *British Policy in India 1858–1905*, Cambridge 1965.

GOPAL S.: *The Viceroyalty of Lord Irwin*, Oxford 1957.

GOPAL, S.: *The Viceroyalty of Lord Ripon*, London 1953.

HALIFAX, EARL OF: *Fulness of Days*, London 1957.

HARDINGE OF PENSHURST, LORD: *My Indian Years*, London 1948.

HARE, AUGUSTUS: *The Story of Two Noble Lives*, 3 vols, London 1893.

HODSON, H.V.: *The Great Divide*, London 1969.

HUNTER, W.W.: *Life of the Earl of Mayo*, London 1875.

HUSSEY, CHRISTOPHER: *Life of Sir Edwin Lutyens*, London 1950.

IRVING, ROBERT GRANT: *Indian Summer, Lutyens, Baker and Imperial Delhi*, New Haven and London 1981.

LUTYENS, MARY: *Edwin Lutyens*, London 1980.

LUTYENS, MARY: *The Lyttons in India*, London 1979.

LYALL, SIR ALFRED: *Life of the Marquis of Dufferin and Ava*, London 1905.

LYTTON, ROBERT, FIRST EARL OF: *Letters* (ed Lady Betty Balfour), London 1906.

MACLAGEN, MICHAEL: *Clemency Canning*, London 1962.

MALLET, BERNARD: *Thomas George, Earl of Northbrook*, London 1908.

MENZIES, MRS. STUART: *Lord William Beresford VC*, London 1917.

MERSEY, VISCOUNT: *The Viceroys and Governors-General of India*, London 1949.

MINTO, MARY, COUNTESS OF: *India, Minto and Morley*, London 1934.

MONTAGU, EDWIN: *An Indian Diary*, London 1930.

MOORE, R.J.: *The Crisis of Indian Unity*, Oxford 1974.

MORISON, J.L.: *Eighth Earl of Elgin*, London 1928.

NEWTON, LORD: *Lord Lansdowne*, London 1929.

NICOLSON, HAROLD: *Helen's Tower*, London 1937.

READING, 2ND MARQUESS OF: *Rufus Isaacs, 1st Marquess of Reading*, 2 vols, London 1943–5.

REED, SIR STANLEY: *The India I Knew*, London ND (1952).

RIVETT-CARNAC, J.H.: *Many Memories*, Edinburgh and London 1910.

ROBERTS, FIELD-MARSHAL LORD:*Forty-One Years in India*, 2 vols, London 1897.

RONALDSHAY, EARL OF: *Life of Lord Curzon*, 3 vols, London 1928.

ROSE, KENNETH: *Superior Person*, London 1969.

SMITH, R. BOSWORTH: *Life of Lord Lawrence*, 2 vols, London 1883.

SURTEES, VIRGINIA: *Charlotte Canning*, London 1975.

TEMPLE, SIR RICHARD: *Men and Events of my Time in India*, London 1882.

TEMPLEWOOD, VISCOUNT: *Nine Troubled Years*, London 1954.

Wavell: The Viceroy's Journal (ed Penderel Moon), London 1973.

WOLF, LUCIEN: *Life of Lord Ripon*, London 1921.

WOODRUFF, PHILIP (PHILIP MASON): *The Men Who Ruled India*. Vol I, 'The Founders', London 1953; vol II, 'The Guardians', London 1954.

Source references

Note. Documents prefixed with IO are in the India Office Library.

1 The Office and the Men Before it

1. Quoted Marquess Curzon of Kedleston, *British Government in India*, 2 vols, London 1925, II
2. Ibid, II
3. Quoted Iris Butler, *The Eldest Brother*, London 1973
4. Sir Alexander Cardew, *The White Mutiny*, London 1929
5. Victor Jacquemont, *Letters from India 1829–1832* (trs Catherine Alison Phillips), London 1936
6. Quoted Curzon, op. cit. II
7. Ibid, II
8. IOR NEG 4377, Journal of Lewin Bentham Bowring
9. Quoted Curzon, op. cit. II

2 Clemency Canning

1. Augustus Hare, *The Story of Two Noble Lives*, 3 vols, London 1893, I
2. Quoted Virginia Surtees, *Charlotte Canning*, London 1975
3. Quoted Curzon, op. cit. II
4. Sir Mortimer Durand, *Alfred Lyall*, London 1913
5. Quoted Michael Maclagan, *Clemency Canning*, London 1962
6. Quoted Hare, op. cit. II
7. Ibid. II
8. Ibid. II
9. Quoted Maclagan, op. cit.
10. Quoted Hare, op. cit. II
11. Ibid. I
12. Ibid. II
13. Ibid. II
14. Quoted Maclagan, op. cit.
15. Quoted Hare op. cit. II
16. Quoted Christopher Hibbert, *The Great Mutiny*, London 1978
17. Quoted Maclagan, op. cit.

18. Ibid.
19. Ibid.
20. Ibid.
21. Ibid.
22. Ibid.
23. Quoted Hare, op. cit. II
24. Quoted Maclagan, op. cit.
25. Quoted Hare, op. cit. II
26. Quoted Curzon, op. cit. II
27. Curzon, op. cit. II
28. Quoted Ibid. II
29. *Letters of Queen Victoria* (ed. Benson and Esher), 3 vols, London 1907 III
30. Quoted Maclagan, op. cit.
31. Ibid.
32. Ibid.
33. Ibid.
34. Ibid.
35. Quoted Surtees, op. cit.
36. Quoted S. Gopal, *British Policy in India 1858–1905*, Cambridge 1965
37. Quoted Hare, op. cit. II
38. Bowring Journal
39. Quoted Hare, op. cit. III
40. Quoted Maclagan, op. cit.
41. Quoted Gopal, op. cit.
42. IO MSS Eur F 127, Strachey Collection, Richard Strachey to his wife, 9 September 1862
43. Quoted Gopal, op. cit.
44. Hon John Stanley, quoted Surtees, op. cit.
45. IO MSS Eur D 661
46. Hare, op. cit. III
47. Quoted Surtees, op. cit.
48. IO MSS Eur D 661

3 Elgin and Plain John Lawrence

1. Sir Richard Temple, *Men and Events of My Time in India*, London 1882
2. Strachey Collection, Richard Strachey to his wife, 18 March 1962
3. Quoted S. Gopal, *British Policy in India 1858–1905*, Cambridge 1965
4. Strachey Collection, Richard Strachey to his wife, 16 June 1862
5. Quoted J.L. Morison, *Eighth Earl of Elgin*, London 1928
6. Ibid.
7. IO MSS Eur F 78, Wood Collection, Elgin to Wood

8. *Letters and Journals of James, 8th Earl of Elgin* (ed. Theodore Walrond), London 1872. To Sir Charles Wood, 17 June 1862
9. Quoted Maclagan, *Clemency Canning*, London 1962
10. *Elgin Letters and Journals.* To Sir Charles Wood, 21 May 1863
11. Ibid. 9 May 1862
12. Ibid. 2 May 1863
13. Ibid.
14. Quoted Gopal, op. cit.
15. Temple, op. cit.
16. R. Bosworth Smith, *Life of Lord Lawrence*, London 1883, II
17. John Beames, *Memoirs of a Bengal Civilian*, London 1961
18. Philip Woodruff (Philip Mason), *The Men Who Ruled India*, vol. I 'The Founders', London 1953
19. Bosworth Smith, op. cit. II
20. Ibid.
21. Quoted Curzon, *British Government in India*, 2 vols, London 1925, II
22. Bosworth Smith, op. cit. II
23. IO MSS Eur D 661
24. Quoted *Complete Peerage*
25. Gopal, op. cit.
26. Ibid.
27. Bosworth Smith, op. cit. II
28. Ibid.
29. Quoted Maclagan, op. cit.
30. Quoted Gopal, op. cit.
31. Temple, op. cit.
32. Wood Collection, Lawrence to Wood
33. Temple, op. cit.
34. Quoted Bosworth Smith, op. cit. II
35. Temple, op. cit.
36. Bosworth Smith, op. cit. II

4 Mayo

1. W.W. Hunter, *Life of the Earl of Mayo*, London 1875
2. Temple, *Men and Events of my Time in India*, London 1882
3. Mayo Papers, Mayo to Duke of Argyll, 18 January 1869
4. Hunter, op. cit.
5. J.H. Rivett-Carnac, *Many Memories*, Edinburgh and London 1910
6. Sir Owen Burne, *Memories*, London 1907
7. Rivett-Carnac, op. cit.
8. Strachey Collection, John to Richard Strachey, 19 April 1872
9. Quoted S. Gopal, *British Policy in India 1858–1905*, Cambridge 1965
10. Mayo Papers, Mayo to Sir Henry Marion Durand, 29 April 1870

11. Ibid. to Duke of Argyll, 18 January 1869
12. Rivett-Carnac, op. cit.
13. Quoted Hunter, op. cit.
14. Quoted Burne, op. cit.
15. Quoted Temple, op. cit.
16. Rivett-Carnac, op. cit.
17. Mayo Papers, Mayo to Argyll, 19 April 1869
18. Ibid. 17 May 1869
19. Ibid. to Lord Napier, 20 November 1870
20. Temple, op. cit.
21. Strachey Collection, Richard Strachey to his wife, 2 April 1870
22. Quoted Gopal, op. cit.
23. Quoted Burne, op. cit.
24. Quoted Gopal, op. cit.
25. Burne, op. cit.
26. Rivett-Carnac, op. cit.
27. Mayo Papers, Mayo to Argyll, 17 May 1869
28. Quoted Gopal, op. cit.
29. Mayo Papers, Mayo to Argyll, 24 January 1872
30. Quoted Hunter, op. cit.
31. Ibid.
32. Burne, op. cit.
33. Hunter, op. cit.
34. Curzon, *British Government in India*, 2 vols, London 1925, II

5. Quoted Bernard Mallet, *Thomas George, Earl of Northbrook*, London

1. Sir Charles Dilke, quoted Roy Jenkins, *Sir Charles Dilke*, London 1958
2. Strachey Collection, John to Richard Strachey, 10 June 1872
3. Quoted Sir Mortimer Durand, *Alfred Lyall*, London 1913
4. Philip Woodruff (Philip Mason), *The Men Who Ruled India*, vol. II, 'The Guardians'
5. Quoted Bernard Mallet, *Thomas George, Earl of Northbrook*, London 1908
6. Ibid.
7. Strachey Collection, John to Richard Strachey, 24 April 1874
8. Mallet, op. cit.
9. Durand, op. cit.
10. Quoted Mallet, op. cit.
11. Ibid.
12. Ibid.
13. *Edward Lear's Indian Journal* (ed. R. Murphy), London 1953
14. IO MSS Eur C 144, Northbrook Collection, Northbrook to Argyll, 17 May 1872

15. Quoted Mallet, op. cit.
16. Quoted Woodruff, op. cit. II
17. Ibid.
18. Northbrook Collection, Northbrook to Sir George Clerk, 27 February 1874
19. Ibid. to Salisbury, 31 March 1876
20. Mallet, op. cit.

6 The Horse that Bolted

1. Disraeli to Lady Bradford, 20 January 1876, in *Letters of Disraeli to Lady Bradford and Lady Chesterfield* (ed. Marquis of Zetland), 2 vols, London 1929, II
2. I owe this analogy to Dr S. Gopal who writes of him as 'a runaway horse' (op. cit.)
3. W.H. Mallock, *Memoirs of Life and Literature*, London 1920
4. Quoted Mary Lutyens, *The Lyttons in India*, London 1979
5. Ibid.
6. Lytton to Queen Victoria, 14 April 1876, in *Letters of Robert, First Earl of Lytton* (ed. Lady Betty Balfour), London 1906
7. Strachey Collection, John to Richard Strachey, 22 April 1876
8. Ibid.
9. Quoted S. Gopal, *British Policy in India 1858–1905*, Cambridge 1965
10. IO MSS Eur E 218, Lytton Collection, Lytton to Salisbury, 14 April 1876
11. Ibid. 25 April 1876
12. *Letters of Robert, Earl of Lytton*
13. Lytton to John Morley, 30 April 1876, in ibid.
14. Lytton to Lady Holland, 23 July 1876, in ibid.
15. Lytton to Lady Salisbury, 1876, in ibid.
16. Sir Henry Cotton, *Indian and Home Memories*, London 1911
17. Ibid.
18. Lutyens, op. cit.
19. Lytton to FitzJames Stephen, 29 May 1876, in *Letters of Robert, Earl of Lytton*
20. Strachey Collection, Richard Strachey to his wife, 4 January 1878
21. Lytton to M. Villers, 1877, in *Letters of Robert, Earl of Lytton*
22. Lytton to Lady Holland, 29 November 1879, in ibid.
23. IO MSS Eur F 132, Lyall Collection, Alfred to James Lyall, 15 October 1877
24. Quoted Cotton, op. cit.
25. *Letters of Robert, Earl of Lytton*
26. Lytton to Salisbury, 11 May 1876, in ibid.
27. Ibid.

28. Lytton to Disraeli, 30 April 1876, in ibid.
29. Lytton to Salisbury, 11 May 1876, in ibid.
30. Durand, op. cit.
31. Field-Marshal Lord Roberts, *Forty-One Years in India*, 2 vols, London 1897, II
32. Burne, op. cit.
33. Ibid.
34. Quoted Lutyens, op. cit.
35. Ibid.
36. Lytton to his wife, August 1877, in *Letters of Robert, Earl of Lytton*
37. Quoted Philip Woodruff (Philip Mason), *The Men Who Ruled India*, vol. II 'The Guardians'
38. *Letters of Robert, Earl of Lytton*
39. Quoted Gopal, op. cit.
40. Quoted Lutyens, op. cit.
41. Ibid.
42. Quoted Gopal, op. cit.
43. Ibid.
44. Quoted Cotton, op. cit.
45. Lytton to John Morely, 30 January 1879, in *Letters of Robert, Earl of Lytton*
46. Strachey Collection, John to Richard Strachey, 8 September 1879
47. Quoted John Morley, *Life of Gladstone*, 3 vols, London 1903, II
48. Lytton to Queen Victoria, 4 May 1880, in *Letters of Robert, Earl of Lytton*
49. Quoted Lucien Wolf, *Life of Lord Ripon*, London 1921
50. Quoted ibid.
51. Quoted ibid.
52. Lytton Collection, Lytton to Cranbrook, 11 May 1880
53. Quoted Lutyens, op. cit.
54. Quoted Mallock, op. cit.
55. Quoted Curzon, *British Government in India*, 2 vols, London 1925, II

7 Ripon

1. Wilfred Scawen Blunt, *India under Ripon, a Private Diary*, London 1909
2. Quoted S. Gopal, *British Policy in India 1858–1905*, Cambridge 1965
3. Quoted Wolf, *Life of Lord Ripon*, London 1921
4. Ripon Diary 1878–80 (ed. John P. Rossi) in *Recusant History* (Journal of Catholic Record Society) October 1974
5. Quoted Wolf, op. cit.
6. Hon. Mrs. Maxwell Scott, *Henry Schomberg Kerr, Sailor and Jesuit*, London 1901

7. Quoted Wolf, op. cit.
8. Strachey Collection, John to Richard Strachey, 8 June 1880
9. Mrs. Stuart Menzies, *Lord William Beresford VC*, London 1917
10. Ibid.
11. Strachey Collection, John to Richard Strachey, 15 June 1880
12. Quoted Wolf, op. cit.
13. Ibid.
14. Ibid.
15. Quoted Wolf, op. cit.
16. Strachey Collection, John to Richard Strachey, 15 June 1880
17. Curzon, *British Government in India*, 2 vols, London 1925, II
18. Ripon to W.E. Forster, May 1881
19. Quoted Wolf, op. cit.
20. Sir Henry Cotton, *Indian and Home Memories*, London 1911
21. Quoted Gopal, op. cit.
22. Quoted Wolf, op. cit.
23. Ibid.
24. Ibid.
25. Ibid.
26. IO MSS Eur D 727, Durand Collection, Durand to Duchess of Northumberland, 19 February 1882
27. Quoted Cotton, op. cit.
28. Wolf, op. cit.
29. Lyall Collection, Alfred to James Lyall, 27 May 1883
30. Quoted Wolf, op. cit.
31. Sir Mortimer Durand, *Alfred Lyall*, London 1913
32. S. Gopal, *The Viceroyalty of Lord Ripon*, London 1953
33. Lyall Collection, Alfred to James Lyall, 28 December 1883
34. Cotton, op. cit.
35. Quoted Durand, op. cit.
36. Sir Auckland Colvin, quoted Wolf, op. cit.
37. Blunt, op. cit.
38. Queen Victoria to Sir Henry Ponsonby, 20 May 1892, in Arthur Ponsonby, *Henry Ponsonby, His Life from his Letters*, London 1943

8 Kipling's Viceroy

1. Harold Nicolson, *Helen's Tower*, London 1937
2. Ibid.
3. Ibid.
4. IO MSS Eur C 125–6, Hamilton Collection, Lord George Hamilton to Curzon, 3 January 1901
5. Quoted S. Gopal, *British Policy in India 1858–1905*, Cambridge 1965
6. Curzon, *British Government in India*, 2 vols, London 1925, II

7. Quoted Gopal, op. cit.
8. Sir Alfred Lyall, *The Life of the Marquis of Dufferin and Ava*, London 1905
9. Durand Collection, 1887
10. Ibid. Durand to Sir H. Norman, 20 June 1885
11. Ibid. to H.L. St. Barbe, 2 June 1885
12. Quoted Lyall, op. cit.
13. Durand Collection, Durand to Col. Ridgeway, 5 January 1885
14. Quoted Sir Mortimer Durand, *Alfred Lyall*, London 1913
15. Durand, quoted Lyall, op. cit.
16. IO MSS Eur F 130, Dufferin and Ava Collection, Dufferin to Durand
17. Ibid. Dufferin to Viscount Cross, 17 January 1888
18. Lyall, op. cit.
19. Dufferin and Ava Collection, Dufferin to Earl of Kimberley, 15 December 1884
20. Nicolson, op. cit.
21. Quoted Curzon, *British Government in India*, 2 vols, London 1925, II
22. Quoted P. Woodruff (Philip Mason), *The Men Who Ruled India*, vol. II 'The Guardians'
23. Quoted Gopal, op. cit.
24. Ibid.
25. Ibid.
26. Quoted Lyall, op. cit.
27. Quoted Nicolson, op. cit.
28. Durand Collection, Durand to Col. Ridgeway, 31 May 1885
29. Nicolson, op. cit.
30. Durand Collection, Durand to Col. Ridgeway, 31 May 1885
31. Marchioness of Dufferin and Ava, *Our Viceregal Life in India*, London 1890
32. Quoted Nicolson, op. cit.
33. Dufferin and Ava, op. cit.
34. Quoted Gopal, op. cit.
35. Quoted Nicolson, op. cit.
36. Gopal, op. cit.
37. Quoted Lyall, op. cit.
38. Dufferin and Ava, op. cit.
39. Ibid.
40. Ibid.
41. Quoted Lyall, op. cit.
42. Edward J. Buck, *Simla, Past and Present*, Bombay 1925
43. Quoted Lyall, op. cit.
44. Dufferin and Ava, op. cit.
45. Ibid.
46. Quoted Lyall, op. cit.
47. Dufferin and Ava, op. cit.

48. Lyall Collection, Alfred to James Lyall, 8 October 1885
49. Dufferin and Ava, op. cit.
50. Ibid.
51. Lord Birkenhead, *Rudyard Kipling*, London 1978
52. Nicolson, op. cit.
53. Quoted Lyall, op. cit.
54. Dufferin and Ava Collection, Dufferin to Granville, 6 June 1887
55. Ibid. to Viscount Cross, 3 December 1888
56. Quoted Gopal, op. cit.
57. Dufferin and Ava, op. cit.
58. Quoted Lord Newton, *Lord Lansdowne*, London 1929
59. Nicolson, op. cit.

9 *Imperial Siesta*

1. Aberigh Mackay, quoted P. Woodruff, *The Men Who Ruled India*, vol. II 'The Guardians'
2. S. Gopal, *British Policy in India 1858–1905*, Cambridge 1965
3. Ibid.
4. Lord Ernest Hamilton, quoted Newton, *Lord Lansdowne*, London 1929
5. Durand Collection, Durand to Sir Alfred Lyall, 14 February 1890
6. Quoted Gopal, *British Policy in India 1858–1905*, Cambridge 1965
7. Mary, Countess of Minto, *India, Minto and Morley*, London 1934
8. Quoted Newton, op. cit.
9. Ibid.
10. Ibid.
11. Ibid.
12. Ibid.
13. Ibid.
14. Ibid.
15. Ibid.
16. Ibid.
17. Ibid.
18. Ibid.
19. Ibid.
20. Ibid.
21. Ibid.
22. Ibid.
23. Diary of Lady Beatrix Petty-Fitzmaurice, in family possession
24. Viscount Mersey, *The Viceroys and Governors-General of India*, London 1949
25. Curzon, *British Government in India*, 2 vols, London 1925, II
26. Diary of Lady Elisabeth Bruce, privately printed

27. Quoted Gopal, op. cit.
28. Ibid.
29. Lord George Hamilton, quoted ibid.
30. Quoted ibid.
31. Ibid.
32. Lady Elisabeth Bruce, diary
33. Ibid.
34. Ibid.
35. Ibid.

10 Curzon

1. David Dilks, *Curzon in India*, 2 vols, London 1969–70, I
2. Cecil Spring-Rice, quoted Kenneth Rose, *Superior Person*, London 1969
3. Viscount D'Abernon, *Portraits and Appreciations*, London n.d.
4. Harold Nicolson, *Some People*, London 1927
5. Curzon, 'Charma Virumque Cano', 1891, quoted Rose, op. cit.
6. Dilks, op. cit. I
7. Rose, op. cit.
8. Kenneth Rose, 'The Supremo with a touch of Ruritania', in *Sunday Telegraph*, 2 September 1979
9. Rose, *Superior Person*
10. Quoted Dilks, op. cit.
11. Quoted Earl of Ronaldshay, *Life of Lord Curzon*, 3 vols, London 1928, II
12. Sir Harcourt Butler, quoted P. Woodruff, *The Men Who Ruled India*, vol. II
13. Quoted Dilks, op. cit. I
14. Quoted Ronaldshay, op. cit. II
15. Quoted Dilks, op. cit. I
16. Ibid.
17. Ibid.
18. Ibid.
19. Quoted Ronaldshay, op. cit. II
20. Woodruff, op. cit. II
21. Quoted Ronaldshay, op. cit. II
22. Curzon, op. cit. I
23. Ibid.
24. Sir Malcolm Darling, *Apprenticeship to Power*, London 1966
25. Buck, op. cit.
26. Quoted Dilks, op. cit. I
27. Quoted Ronaldshay, op. cit. II
28. Sir Bampfylde Fuller, *Some Personal Experiences*, London 1930

29. Curzon, op. cit. II
30. Quoted Ronaldshay, op. cit. II
31. Quoted ibid.
32. Quoted Dilks, op. cit. I
33. Quoted Gopal, *British Policy in India 1858–1905*, Cambridge 1965
34. Quoted ibid.
35. Quoted Ronaldshay, op. cit. II
36. Quoted Dilks, op. cit. I
37. Quoted Rose, op. cit.
38. Quoted Ronaldshay, op. cit. II
39. Quoted Gopal, *British Policy in India*
40. Quoted Ronaldshay, op. cit. II
41. Curzon, op. cit. II
42. Quoted Ronaldshay, op. cit. II
43. Quoted Max Egremont, *Balfour*, London 1980
44. Quoted Sir Evan Maconochie, *Life in the Indian Civil Service*, London 1926
45. Quoted Gopal, op. cit.
46. Quoted Dilks, op. cit. I
47. Quoted Gopal, op. cit.
48. Woodruff, op. cit. II
49. Quoted Gopal, op. cit.
50. Quoted Rose, op. cit.
51. Quoted Ronaldshay, op. cit. III
52. Ibid.
53. Quoted Gopal, op. cit.
54. Ronaldshay, op. cit. II
55. Told by this lady to the present writer
56. Quoted Rose, op. cit.
57. Quoted Gopal, op. cit.
58. Ibid.
59. Earl of Midleton (St. John Brodrick), *Records and Reactions*, New York 1939

11 *The Gentleman who Jumped Hedges*

1. Mersey, *The Viceroys and Governors-General of India*, London 1949
2. Quoted John Buchan, *Lord Minto*, London 1924
3. Minto, op. cit.
4. Ibid.
5. J.H. Rivett-Carnac, *Many Memories*, Edinburgh and London 1910
6. Minto, op. cit.
7. IO MSS Eur F 116, Butler Collection, Sir Harcourt Butler to his mother, 2 November 1924

8. Quoted Martin Gilbert, *Servant of India*, London 1966
9. Minto, quoted ibid.
10. Quoted Minto, op. cit.
11. Ibid.
12. Ibid.
13. Minto, op. cit.
14. Quoted Gilbert, op. cit.
15. Quoted Minto, op. cit.
16. Quoted P. Woodruff, *The Men Who Ruled India*, vol. II
17. Quoted Minto, op. cit.
18. Buchan, op. cit.
19. Quoted Minto, op. cit.
20. Ibid.
21. Ibid.
22. Ibid.
23. Butler Collection, Butler to his mother, 24 November 1910
24. Quoted Minto, op. cit.
25. Quoted Gilbert, op. cit.

12 Delhi, Dyarchy and Disobedience

1. Lord Hardinge of Penshurst, *My Indian Years*, London 1948
2. Butler Collection
3. Ibid.
4. Christopher Hussey, *Life of Sir Edwin Lutyens*, London 1950
5. Quoted Mary Lutyens, *Edwin Lutyens*, London 1980
6. Ibid.
7. Hussey, op. cit.
8. Hardinge, op. cit.
9. Ibid.
10. Butler Collection
11. Hardinge, op. cit.
12. Butler Collection
13. Ibid. Butler to his mother, 25 November 1913
14. Quoted Mary Lutyens, *Edwin Lutyens*
15. Butler Collection, Butler to his mother, 17 January 1913
16. Ibid. 24 September 1915
17. Ibid. 23 April 1916
18. Ibid. 15 August 1916
19. Edwin Montagu, *An Indian Diary*, London 1930
20. IO MSS E 238, Reading Collections (Viceregal Collection), Reading to Edwin Montagu, 12 May 1921
21. Buck, op. cit.
22. Butler Collection

23. Montagu, op. cit.
24. IO MSS Eur E 264, Chelmsford Collection, Chelmsford to Austen Chamberlain, 16 June 1916
25. Ibid. 6 October 1916
26. Montagu, op. cit.
27. Ibid.
28. Ibid.
29. Sir Stanley Reed, *The India I Knew*, London n.d. (1952)
30. Montagu, op. cit.
31. Ibid.
32. Ibid.
33. Chelmsford Collection, Chelmsford to Montagu, April 1919
34. Ibid. 11 June 1919
35. Ibid. 24 December 1919
36. Butler Collection, Butler to his mother, December 1920
37. Ibid. 21 March 1920
38. Reading Collections (Viceregal Collection), Montagu to Reading, 20 April 1921
39. Montagu, op. cit.
40. Butler Collection, Butler to his mother, 2 December 1920
41. Ibid. 13 January 1921
42. Ibid. 25 January 1921
43. Ibid. 5 May 1921
44. MSS Eur E 312, FitzRoy Collection
45. Told by Lord Mountbatten to the present writer
46. Butler Collection, Butler to his mother, 3 February 1923
47. FitzRoy Collection
48. Butler Collection, Butler to his mother, 12 April 1922
49. Ibid. December 1924
50. FitzRoy Collection
51. Butler Collection
52. Reading Collections (Private Collection), Reading to Lady Reading, 30 September 1923
53. FitzRoy Collection
54. E.M. Forster, *The Hill of Devi*, London 1953
55. Butler Collection, Butler to his mother, January 1926
56. Ibid. 26 August 1923
57. FitzRoy Collection
58. Ibid.
59. Quoted Earl of Lytton, *Pundits and Elephants*, London 1942

13 *'The Most Christian and the Most Gentlemanly Among Them All'*

1. Quoted Earl of Birkenhead, *Halifax*, London 1965

2. Ibid.
3. Ibid.
4. Ibid.
5. Earl of Halifax, *Fulness of Days*, London 1957
6. IO MSS Eur C 152, Halifax Collection, Irwin to his father, 12 April 1926
7. Quoted Birkenhead, *Halifax*
8. Ibid.
9. Ibid.
10. Ibid.
11. J. Coatman, *Years of Destiny*, London 1932
12. Halifax Collection, Irwin to his father
13. Quoted Judith M. Brown, *Gandhi and Civil Disobedience*, Cambridge 1977
14. Quoted Coatman, op. cit.
15. Coatman, op. cit.
16. Ibid.
17. Halifax Collection, Irwin to his father
18. Halifax, op. cit.
19. Ibid.
20. IO MSS Eur E 240, Templewood Collection, Halifax to Templewood, 1953
21. Coatman, op. cit.
22. Quoted R.J. Moore, *The Crisis of Indian Unity*, Oxford 1974
23. Templewood Collection, Halifax to Templewood, 31 July 1953
24. Quoted Birkenhead, *Halifax*
25. Ibid.
26. Birkenhead, *Halifax*
27. Quoted ibid.
28. Ibid.
29. Brown, op. cit.
30. Halifax Collection, Irwin to King-Emperor
31. Viscount Templewood, *Nine Troubled Years*, London 1954
32. Quoted Brown, op. cit.
33. Quoted Birkenhead, *Halifax*
34. Halifax Collection, Irwin to his father, 23 February 1931
35. Ibid. 3 March 1931
36. Quoted S. Gopal, *The Viceroyalty of Lord Irwin*, Oxford 1957
37. Quoted Birkenhead, *Halifax*
38. Halifax Collection, Irwin to his father, 10 March 1931
39. Ibid.
40. Ibid.
41. Coatman, op. cit.
42. Quoted Birkenhead, *Halifax*

14 Lady Willingdon, Freeman and Hopie

1. Butler Collection, Butler to his mother, 9 January 1913
2. Reading Collection (Viceregal Collection), Reading to Montagu, 1921
3. Chelmsford Collection, Montagu to Chelmsford, 4 March 1919
4. Sir Thomas Strangman, *Indian Courts and Characters*, London 1931
5. Ibid.
6. Malcolm Muggeridge, *Like it was*, London 1981
7. Butler Collection, Butler to his mother
8. Ibid. 15 December 1920
9. Ibid. 15 April 1923
10. Templewood Collection, Halifax to Templewood, 13 July 1953
11. Quoted J.M. Brown, *Gandhi and Civil Disobedience*, Cambridge 1977
12. Quoted Birkenhead, *Halifax*, London 1965
13. Templewood, op. cit.
14. Quoted ibid.
15. J. Coatman, *Years of Destiny*, London 1932
16. Jawaharlal Nehru, *An Autobiography*, London 1936
17. Brown, op. cit.
18. Quoted ibid.
19. Quoted *Condition of India*, Report of the Delegation sent to India by The India League in 1932
20. Sir Mirza Ismail, *My Public Life*, London 1954
21. Quoted Mersey, *The Viceroys and Governors-General of India*, London 1949
22. Muggeridge, op. cit.
23. Malcolm Muggeridge, *Chronicles of Wasted Time*, vol. II, 'The Infernal Grove', London 1973
24. Muggeridge, *Like it was*
25. Muggeridge, 'Infernal Grove'
26. Muggeridge, *Like it was*
27. Muggeridge, 'Infernal Grove'
28. Muggeridge, *Like it was*
29. Doreen, Lady Brabourne, to the present writer
30. Mary Lutyens, *Edwin Lutyens*
31. Quoted Catalogue of Lutyens Exhibition 18 November 1981–31 January 1982, Arts Council of Great Britain
32. Baron Jean Pellenc, *Diamonds and Dust*, London 1936
33. Muggeridge, *Like it was*
34. Duff Cooper, *Old Men Forget*, London 1953
35. Quoted John Glendevon, *The Viceroy at Bay*, London 1971
36. Ibid.
37. Ibid.
38. Templewood Collection, Halifax to Templewood, 13 July 1953
39. Quoted Glendevon, op. cit.

40. Ibid.
41. Ibid.
42. Templewood Collection, Halifax to Templewood, 13 July 1953
43. Quoted Philip Mason, *A Shaft of Sunlight*, London 1978
44. Quoted P. Woodruff, *The Men Who Ruled India*, vol. II 'The Guardians'
45. Quoted Glendevon, op. cit.
46. Quoted Glendevon, op. cit.
47. Quoted Woodruff, op. cit. II
48. Templewood, op. cit.
49. Quoted Glendevon, op. cit.

15 Wavell and Mountbatten

1. *Wavell: The Viceroy's Journal* (ed. Penderel Moon), London 1973
2. Ibid.
3. Ibid.
4. Ibid.
5. *Chips: The Diaries of Sir Henry Channon* (ed. Robert Rhodes James), London 1967
6. H.V. Hodson, *The Great Divide*, London 1969
7. *Viceroy's Journal*
8. Philip Mason, *A Shaft of Sunlight*, London 1978
9. *Channon Diaries*
10. *Viceroy's Journal*
11. Ibid.
12. Ibid.
13. Ibid.
14. Ibid.
15. Penderel Moon, in *Viceroy's Journal*
16. *Viceroy's Journal*
17. Hodson, op. cit.
18. *Viceroy's Journal*
19. Ibid.
20. Ibid.
21. Ibid.
22. Hodson, op. cit.
23. Ibid.
24. Kenneth Rose, 'The Supremo with a touch of Ruritania', in *Sunday Telegraph*, 2 September 1979
25. Hodson, op. cit.
26. Ibid.
27. Alan Campbell-Johnson, *Mission with Mountbatten*, New York 1953
28. Quoted Hodson, op. cit.

29. Ibid.
30. Campbell-Johnson, op. cit.
31. Hodson, op. cit.
32. Recounted by Lord Mountbatten in conversation with the present writer
33. Campbell-Johnson, op. cit.
34. Hodson, op. cit.
35. Ibid.

Index

Italic figures indicate illustrations